Adam,

Thanks for your introduction to Codebreaker & the support throughout.

All the best.

TTG, you're it!

Ben

# [ PRAISE ]

*The Ideas Guy* is a captivating and empowering guide for educators, dreamers, and innovators alike. It blends vision with actionable strategies to inspire creativity and ignite the pursuit of transformative ideas. Through compelling examples of trailblazers, the book highlights how the power of individual vision can reshape education and inspire global movements. Packed with thought-provoking insights and relatable narratives, this book not only champions innovation but also demonstrates how education can be a cornerstone of change. By exploring the intersection of digital tools, strategy, and authentic teaching, it equips educators with the mindset to dream bigger and drive impactful change. *The Ideas Guy* is a compelling call to action for anyone ready to challenge the status quo, ignite change, and make a meaningful impact.

*Paddy McGrath*
*Head of Education, Texthelp Group, International Speaker*

*The Ideas Guy* is a bold and inspiring guide for innovators, educators, and entrepreneurs who refuse to settle for the status quo. The book is centred on the principles of IDEAS—Innovation, Digital, Education, Authenticity, and Strategy—and it challenges readers to embrace creativity, courage, and collaboration to effect meaningful change. Ben Whitaker offers practical insights on transforming ideas into reality with a conversational tone. *The Ideas Guy* is both a motivational read and a very practical toolkit. Whether you're an entrepreneur, educator, or anyone with an idea or vision, this book will inspire you to harness your potential and follow some well proven steps forwards.

*Al Kingsley*
*Group CEO, NetSupport*

Your competition will wish you'd never found this book. *The Ideas Guy* pries open the greatest minds of our time and displays their inner workings. If you're ready to learn how transformative ideas really happen, you need this on your desk. Now.

*Dan Fitzpatrick*
*Bestselling Author of The AI Classroom*

This book shows how Ben Whitaker thinks differently than most. It is a manifesto for thinking differently and everyone—in education, business, or anywhere—should read it!

*Steven Hope*
*CEO of C-Learning, Co-host of the Edufuturists Podcast*

*The Ideas Guy* is the kind of book that fills you with energy and makes you want to dive straight into something new. Reading it feels like sitting down for a proper chat with Ben—thoughtful, inspiring, and full of ideas you can actually use. Ben doesn't just tell you about innovators; he brings their stories to life in a way that makes you feel part of the journey. Before you know it, you're not just reading about other people's ideas—you're thinking about how to spark your own and light the fuse on your own *psychic dynamite*. Whether you're toying with an idea or you're already working on something big, this book has something for you. It's not just a book you read; it's one you carry with you.

*Matthew Wemyss*
*International School Leader, Author of the AI in Education Handbook Series*
*Edufuturist A.I. Pioneer 2024*

*The Ideas Guy* doesn't disappoint. Compelling narrative around visible people helps to demystify the thought of us and them and gives a new take on changing the narrative around self-belief but on a far deeper level. A must read!

*Mike Walker*
*Co-founder @StopPress*

Ben Whitaker's latest work is nothing short of profound. He has an extraordinary ability to take real-world examples of innovation and impact and distill them into lessons that are not only practical but also profoundly empowering. Reading this book was an uplifting experience. It instilled a belief that I could do more, achieve more, and create a bigger impact in my own work. It offers not just ideas but also actionable steps, making even the most ambitious goals seem achievable. This book is not just a read; it's an experience—one that inspires, empowers, and drives change.

*Philippa Wraithmell*
*EdRuption Founder, Author of The Digital Ecosystem*

*The Ideas Guy: Unleash Your Inner Genius*


First edition 2025



Code BREAKER
www.codebreakeredu.com

# The Ideas Guy

# THE !DEAS GUY

[ UNLEASH **YOUR** INNER GENIUS ]

Ben Whitaker

CODE BREAKER INC.

The only reason I write this book is because I want to make my family proud. Martha, your sass and passion make me smile. Niamh, your drive and understated power warm my heart. Amanda, your unconditional love fuels my fire. To be famous in my own home…

# [ TABLE OF CONTENTS ]

# [ FOREWORD ]

WRITTEN BY
STEFAN POWELL
EXECUTIVE COACH & AWARD-WINNING ARTIST

In a world that seems to move faster now than ever before, the significance of ideas cannot be overstated. Ideas are the seeds from which innovation, progress, and change emerge. *The Ideas Guy* intricately unravels the lives of extraordinary individuals whose flawed yet captivating journeys illuminate how ideas can shape destinies and tackle urgent issues, paving the way for a thriving planet.

The chapters explore characters who are not merely figures of inspiration but are also marked by their imperfections. This serves as a reminder that the tapestry of humanity is woven with threads of experience, vulnerability, and untapped potential. The authenticity of these stories resonates deeply, revealing that greatness often emerges from the chaos of life.

Ben's approach to business, education, and this book sets him apart, urging us to challenge conventional wisdom while fostering a profound appreciation for human relationships. Whilst the world is increasingly connected through screens and algorithms, he emphasises the importance of nurturing genuine connections and creativity. He advocates for using AI and digital tools as enablers that facilitate more meaningful engagements.

With a heart as big as his dreams, formed by his remarkable journey, it has been an honour to work with and coach him. Witnessing his evolution into the leader I always believed he could be—and the leader he had yet to discover within himself—has been truly inspiring.

In a world that often celebrates perfection, this book reminds us of the beauty found in our flaws. It encourages readers to reflect, grow, and unleash their potential, revealing that the power of ideas lies within each of us, waiting to be uncovered amid the messiness of life. I was beyond proud, and subsequently, more than willing to be asked to write this foreword to an incredible book. I know it will help you unleash your inner genius.

# [ INTRODUCTION ]

This book, *The Ideas Guy*, is for the dreamers, the doers, the innovators. It's for those who wake up with a mind buzzing with possibilities, those who fall asleep with a heart full of dreams. It's for the creative souls who sketch ideas on napkins and the pragmatic ones who jot down plans in notebooks. Even for those with a Kanban board or a Gantt chart.

It's for the bold entrepreneurs starting from a garage, the visionary leaders in boardrooms, and the inspired teachers in classrooms. It's for anyone who has ever looked at the world and thought, 'What if?'.

It's for the curious and the courageous, those not afraid to question, to imagine, to innovate. It's for those who believe in the power of an idea, in the magic of a dream, in the beauty of a design.

It's for those who have lost their mojo, given up the ghost or fear the 'inevitable.' If you have no energy or feel like hope has gone, it's a call back to arms.

So if you've got a spark inside you, a passion, a vision - this book is for you. If you're ready to dive deep into the realm of **I**nnovation, **D**igital, **E**ducation, **A**uthenticity, and **S**trategy, to explore new ideas, to discover new perspectives - then, welcome.

*The Ideas Guy* is your guide, your companion, your catalyst on this journey of ideation and creation. This book is for you, the Ideas Guy - not just a "guy", but a human, regardless of gender, age, or background, who's ready to birth new realities, to shape new futures, to be an architect of change.

On this journey, it's not about where you start, but where your IDEAS can take you.

# [ OUR DINNER TABLE GUESTS ]

STEVE JOBS
INGVAR KAMPRAD
ELON MUSK
ANNE WOJICKI
SIR TIM BERNERS-LEE
DANIEL EK
SAM ALTMAN
REID HOFFMAN
MARIA MONTESSORI
SIR KEN ROBINSON
SAL KHAN
SUGATA MITRA
YVON CHOUINARD
BRENÉ BROWN
MAYA ANGELOU
PHIL KNIGHT
HOWARD SCHULTZ
JEFF BEZOS
REED HASTINGS
VIJAY GOVINDARAJAN
SERGEI BRIN AND LARRY PAGE
SHERYL SANDBERG
JOE ROGAN
OPRAH WINFREY

# [ CHAPTER 0 ]

# WHO IS THE IDEAS GUY?

"Guy." Picture it. A silhouette forms in your mind, defined, sharp.

"Ideas." Sparks fly, stars burst, creativity unfurls, the silhouette fills with light and colour.

But wait.

Hold that image. Now, let it blur. Let it dissolve. Let it reshape. It's not about being a "guy." It's not about gender or age or occupation. It's not about who you're supposed to be. It's about who you are.

Breathe life back into that silhouette. See it now as a beacon, not bound by preconceptions. It's filled with dreams, with ideas, with courage. It's every person who has dared to dream, to innovate, to learn. It's the educator, the entrepreneur, the inventor, the disruptor. It's the restless spirit who looks at the world and thinks, "I can make this better."

That's the Ideas Guy.

And the Ideas Guy? He's you. It's me. It's her. He's him. It's them. It's an all-encompassing, all-embracing term that knows no boundaries.

The Ideas Guy is the one who sees what could be, not just what is. The one who acts, not just dreams. The one who shapes, not just follows.

That's who the Ideas Guy is. That's who we all can be.

More importantly, the Ideas Guy is a collective. In the universe of the Ideas Guy, the notion of a singular, solitary figure fades into obscurity. Instead, the focus illuminates a dynamic, multi-faceted collective – a team bound by the threads of shared vision and mutual respect. The Ideas Guy is no longer a lone individual, but a potent embodiment of a collaborative effort.

This team, this collective, emerges as a vibrant mosaic. Each piece, distinct in its characteristics, adds unique value to the whole. It's a rich tapestry of ideas, perspectives, and experiences that swirl together, creating a landscape fertile for Innovation and growth. In this diversity, the team finds its strength and momentum.

There is wisdom in crowds.

Within this collaborative entity, ideas are the lifeblood. Every voice counts, every perspective matters. Meetings transform into idea incubators, crackling with the electricity of collective brainstorming. Ideas, once tiny sparks, are fanned into roaring fires, sculpted and refined by the combined effort of the team.

But the spirit of collaboration extends far beyond the generation of ideas. It infuses every aspect of the journey, from distributing tasks based on individual strengths, to providing support during challenges, celebrating collective victories, and extracting lessons from shared failures.

In our digitised, hyper-connected world, the power of collaboration is magnified. Geographical constraints are rendered irrelevant as teams can connect, ideate, and create across miles and time zones. In the realm of the Ideas Guy, this is the essence of teamwork.

Together, this team is a force to be reckoned with. They thrive in the fertile soil of diversity, embracing a vast spectrum of perspectives and backgrounds. Their collective strength lies in their ability to bridge gaps, dismantle barriers, and channel the power of unity.

As the team comes together, it is not just the individual brilliance that shines; it's the symphony of collaboration that orchestrates greatness. Each member brings their unique instrument to the ensemble, and together they create a harmonious melody that resonates far beyond the boundaries of their collaboration.

Collaboration is more than just a means to an end; it's an ethos that infuses every decision, action, and interaction. The team thrives in an environment of openness and trust, where ideas are nurtured and challenges are embraced as stepping stones to growth.

As they embark on their journey of Innovation, the team is not immune to setbacks or obstacles. But they navigate through them, drawing strength from the collective spirit that fuels their progress. In times of doubt or uncertainty, they find solace in knowing they are not alone. The team becomes a support system, bolstering each other's confidence and pushing one another to reach new heights.

The Ideas Guy collective is not bound by conventional hierarchies or rigid structures. Instead, it champions a flat and agile approach, where leadership is fluid and ideas can flourish without unnecessary bureaucracy. This flexibility allows the team to adapt quickly to changing circumstances and seize opportunities with agility.

Through their shared experiences, the team members develop a deep sense of camaraderie. They celebrate each other's victories and take pride in the collective impact they create. Their bond transcends geographical distances and time zones, united by a common purpose that drives them forward.

Beyond the boundaries of their collaboration, the team of Ideas Guys inspires others to embrace collaboration as a driving force for progress. They serve as beacons of possibility, showing the world what can be achieved when diverse minds come together and unite in pursuit of a shared vision.

The collective spirit takes precedence over individual glory. It's not about competing for recognition; it's about elevating ideas, embracing differences, and fostering an environment where creativity knows no bounds.

As the team continues to thrive, its impact reverberates far beyond its own achievements. The ripple effect of their collaborative efforts extends to communities, industries, and the world at large. The Ideas Guy collective becomes a catalyst for positive change, igniting a chain reaction of Innovation and progress.

The Ideas Guy is not a solitary figure, but a collective force of dreamers, disruptors and doers. United by a shared vision and bound by a commitment to collaboration, they wield the power of IDEAS to transform lives and shape the future.

In this ensemble, every note counts, and every voice matters. It's a celebration of diversity, a journey of discovery, and a testament to the transformative power of IDEAS. As the collective continues to evolve and grow, their impact will endure, leaving an indelible mark on the world.

# [ WHAT'S IT GOING TO TAKE TO BE THE IDEAS GUY? ]

Courage. Not the blinding, brazen courage of superheroes in comic books, but the quiet, steady courage that wakes you up in the morning and whispers, "You can do this."

Anais Nin, a real iconoclast, famously said, "Life shrinks or expands in proportion to one's courage." Ideas Guys want big lives. And as Marianne Williamson wrote (but most brilliantly portrayed in one of the greatest films of all time, Coach Carter):

> *"Our deepest fear is not that we are inadequate. Our deepest fear is that we are powerful beyond measure. It is our light, not our darkness that most frightens us. We ask ourselves, 'Who am I to be brilliant, gorgeous, talented, fabulous?' Actually, who are you not to be? You are a child of God. Your playing small does not serve the world. There is nothing enlightened about shrinking so that other people won't feel insecure around you. We are all meant to shine, as children do. We were born to make manifest the glory of God that is within us. It's not just in some of us; it's in everyone. And as we let our own light shine, we unconsciously give other people permission to do the same. As we are liberated from our own fear, our presence automatically liberates others."*

It's going to take curiosity. The insatiable thirst to know, to understand, to explore. The kind of curiosity that looks at a closed door and doesn't just walk away but turns the knob. I love how the writer, C. J. Cherryh puts it: "Ignorance killed the cat; curiosity was framed!" The great Samuel Johnson reminds us: "Curiosity is, in great and generous minds, the first passion and the last."

It's going to take humility. The ability to acknowledge when you're wrong, to learn from others, to celebrate their success as much as your own. Humility isn't about thinking less of yourself, it's about thinking of yourself less. Einstein, possibly the greatest thinker of the 19th and 20th centuries, acknowledged, "A true genius admits that he/she knows nothing."

And it's going to take vision. Not just the ability to see what's right in front of you, but to gaze beyond, to imagine what's not yet there, and have the audacity to believe it can be real. The remarkable Helen Keller, who was both blind and deaf, yet changed the world, could comment with some authority: "The most pathetic person in the world is someone who has sight but no vision."

It will take patience. The capacity to allow ideas to simmer, to mature, to unfold in their own time. Because the best ideas, like the finest wines, often need time to develop their full flavour. Aristotle shows us that "Patience is bitter, but its fruit is sweet." The wine is worth the press.

And yes, it will take action. Because ideas, no matter how brilliant, how revolutionary, how world-changing, are only as good as the actions that follow them. Ideas are the spark, action is the fire. Perhaps, most fittingly, Mohandas Gandhi, a man who had ideas that sparked a revolution, but who did most of his talking by his doing, said:

> *"Your beliefs become your thoughts,*
> *Your thoughts become your words,*
> *Your words become your actions,*
> *Your actions become your habits,*
> *Your habits become your values,*
> *Your values become your destiny."*

That's what it's going to take to be the Ideas Guy, to fulfil your destiny. But don't let that overwhelm you. Because you've got it in you. We've all got it in us. It's not about being born with these qualities, it's about nurturing them, cultivating them, celebrating them.

Let's talk about the "Guy" in Ideas Guy. Picture it, contemplate it, let it roll off your tongue. Guy. It's about humanity, about being a person navigating the world. It's about being a dreamer, a doer, a thinker. It's about having a heart that beats to the rhythm of ideas.

Guy is an everyman term, a word that knows no boundaries. It does not discriminate between male or female, young or old, experienced or novice. It is inclusive, embracing all those who dare to dream, to innovate, to learn. It is a call to action, a call to embrace the spirit of IDEAS.

Guy is you. Guy is me. Guy is all of us, striving, pushing, imagining. Guy is the collective spirit of human creativity, human courage, human curiosity. It's not about the gender you were assigned at birth, nor one you choose in life, it's about the actions you take, the ideas you nurture, the impact you have.

So, Ideas Guy? It's not a label. It's a declaration. It's an invitation. An invitation to step beyond limitations, to dream big, to be bold. An invitation to be part of something bigger, something profound, something transformative.

That's why we use Guy. Because in this journey, in this exploration of IDEAS, we are all the Ideas Guy. It's a title not given, but earned. Earned through action.

## [ WHO IS THE IDEAS GUY NOT? ]

Paint the picture, hold it up to the light. Examine it, scrutinise it. The Ideas Guy? They're not the one hugging the shadows of the past, ensnared by the rusty chains of "this is the way it has always been." No. They don't cower from change, they invite it in. They don't recoil from the unknown, they reach out, they welcome it.

The Ideas Guy isn't the one gripping knowledge with a vice-like grip, locking it away like a miserly dragon hoarding gold. No. She knows the true worth of knowledge lies in its ability to circulate, to enlighten, to empower. She wants knowledge to fly, not to be caged. Knowledge is power but only when it is released.

The Ideas Guy isn't the one who steps on others to reach the peak. He doesn't believe in a world where victory for one means loss for another. His vision of success isn't a pie, cut into slices, with only so many to go around. He envisions an ever-expanding circle, where success breeds success, where we lift as we rise.

The Ideas Guy isn't the spectator, the bystander, the one waiting for others to light the fire. She doesn't shrug off responsibility, she doesn't point and say, "That's not my job." She steps forward. She ignites. She takes the mantle. She dances with action.

And the Ideas Guy? He's not the one haunted by the spectre of failure. She knows that failure isn't success's nemesis, it's its companion. They see in failure not a full stop, but a comma, a pause that allows for growth, for strength, for wisdom.

So, that's who the Ideas Guy is not.

But if you see yourself mirrored in these descriptions, don't lose heart. Change is not a myth, it's a promise. Growth is not a rumour, it's a fact. Becoming the Ideas Guy? It's not an illusion, it's a possibility. And it starts here, with one step.

Now, let's get to know these five companions we'll be journeying with. Five guiding lights. Five fingers on the hand that will lift us up. Five principles that form the backbone of the Ideas Guy. They are IDEAS: **I**nnovation, **D**igital, **E**ducation, **A**uthenticity, and **S**trategy.

**INNOVATION.** It's the fresh wind that scatters the leaves of the status quo, letting us see new paths, new possibilities. It's not content with what is, it yearns for what could be. It's the trailblazer, the maverick.

**DIGITAL.** It's the thread that binds us in this 21st century and beyond, the invisible current that pulses through our lives, transforming, connecting, enabling. It's not just about technology, it's about how we use that technology to create, to communicate, to change.

**EDUCATION.** It's the lamp that lights our way, the nourishment that fuels our growth. It's not just about knowledge, it's about understanding, it's about wisdom. It's not just about learning, it's about unlearning and relearning.

**AUTHENTICITY**. It's the mirror that reflects our true selves, the compass that points to our north. It's about being real, being genuine, being brave enough to show the world who we truly are.

**STRATEGY**. It's the map we chart our journey on, the rudder that steers our ship. It's about planning, about foresight, about making choices today that will shape our tomorrow. Not just reacting.

That's IDEAS. It's not an acronym, it's a philosophy. It's not just a word, it's a world. A world where we can all be the Ideas Guy.

So, let's unveil the canvas on which we're going to paint our 'IDEAS.' Imagine a book, a journey, a conversation. A conversation not just with words, but with lives, with stories. Each chapter will be an encounter with an IDEAS Guy, a beacon who embodies one of our guiding principles.

Men and women, young and old, from all walks of life. Each one, a unique tapestry of experiences, triumphs, challenges. Each one, a testament to the power of IDEAS. Each one, a guide on our journey.

Our book, our journey, will unfold in five sections. Each section, a deep dive into one part of IDEAS. Each chapter, a step on our path to becoming the Ideas Guy. The point? We look at guests at a dinner party. People from all walks of life sat around, kindling fires and chugging their customary beverage. Each chapter focuses on an Ideas Guy who embodies one of our guiding principles. We unpick *their* stories to learn for *our* stories.

It's important to mention here that not every note these Ideas Guys play is good. Who knows what good really means anyway? But, some of the people we will look at over the course of this book may have questionable methods and motives. Some have amassed inordinate amounts of wealth (perhaps at the detriment of others), haven't always considered the global or ethical impact of their actions or have run roughshod in the pursuit of success. Including them isn't endorsement of every facet of their character or conduct. There are lessons to learn from all of them. Could we have chosen others? Of course. Will they also have skeletons in the closet or gaping holes in their conscience? Also likely.

Learning from does not imply endorsement of. And that, folks, is the reason we don't put people on immovable pedestals and blindly accept their lore and lure.

Let's dive into the lessons we will learn from these imperfect Ideas Guys.

First, we'll explore Innovation, meeting those who dared to defy convention, to challenge the status quo, to think different. Then, we'll dig into the world of Digital, learning from those who have harnessed the power of technology to transform, to connect, to inspire.

We'll then turn the pages to Education, immersing ourselves in the stories of those who understand the power of knowledge, the beauty of wisdom, the necessity of learning and unlearning.

Then comes Authenticity. Here, we will encounter those who have had the courage to be genuine, to be true, to be themselves in a world that often demands conformity.

Finally, we'll navigate the realm of Strategy, guided by those who have understood the art of planning, the science of decision-making, the wisdom of foresight.

That's our book. That's our journey. It's not just about reading, it's about reflecting. It's not just about understanding, it's about internalising. It's about becoming.

## [ PSYCHIC DYNAMITE ]

Winston Churchill said,

> *"Every prophet has to come from civilisation, but every prophet has to go into the wilderness. He must have a strong impression of a complex society and all that it has to give, and then he must serve periods of isolation and meditation. This is the process by which psychic dynamite is made."*

Psychic dynamite. Let's pause there for a moment. What an arresting phrase, what a vivid image. It isn't just an intriguing, almost poetic concept.

To truly understand this concept, we must first examine its two key components: the psychic and the dynamite.

The word "psychic" pertains to the mind, to consciousness. It's where thoughts take root, where curiosity unfurls, where Innovation begins. It's the fertile ground where ideas are conceived and nurtured.

Now, "dynamite". Ah, dynamite - a powerful, transformative substance. Once lit, it causes a rapid, forceful explosion capable of altering physical landscapes. It has the power to destroy, yes, but also to create anew, to pave the way for progress. It breaks down barriers, removes obstructions, creates paths where there were none.

And so, when Churchill speaks of "psychic dynamite," he's drawing our attention to the explosive power of ideas born in the realm of the mind. An idea, he suggests, is no ordinary thought. No, an idea is a force of change, an agent of disruption, a beacon of Innovation. It has the power to transform the landscapes of our societies, our cultures, even our own personal lives. And like a stick of dynamite, once ignited, an idea can lead to a forceful, explosive chain of events.

Now, why does it matter? It matters because ideas are the engines of progress. They are the seeds from which great forests of Innovation grow. They are the starting points for every invention, every discovery, every advancement that has shaped the course of human history.

Every transformative movement, every revolutionary product, every groundbreaking discovery, began as an idea in someone's mind. The Ideas Guy, the one who harnesses the psychic dynamite, has the potential to effect profound change.

But it's not just about the big ideas that alter the course of history. Even small ideas can have a ripple effect, creating waves of change that extend far beyond their point of origin. Every day, we interact with the world around us, and each of those interactions is shaped by ideas. From the technology we use, to the social norms we adhere to, to the personal beliefs we hold - all are products of ideas.

So, every time we dare to imagine, every time we ask "What if?" we engage with our inner psychic dynamite. We tap into the explosive, transformative power of ideas. And in doing so, we participate in the grand human endeavour of growth and progress. That is the essence, the heart, the soul of psychic dynamite. It's the spark that lights the fuse, and its potential is limited only by the bounds of our imagination.

Now, you may be wondering, what on earth does that mean? And that is where we embark on a journey of exploration, of imagination, of...ideas.

Ideas, you see, are not just mere thoughts. They're not simple notions or whims that casually float into our minds and then drift away. No, ideas - true, powerful, world-changing ideas - are a bit like fire. They spark into existence, catch light, and then... oh, then they can rage, blaze, illuminate the darkest corners of the world with their brilliance. They have the power to warm us, guide us, even scare us a little. And just like a piece of dynamite, once ignited, an idea can lead to a powerful, earth-shaking explosion.

But let's step back for a moment, away from the fire and the dynamite, and talk about the Ideas Guy. You know the one. The person in the room who always seems to have a new perspective, a different way of looking at things. The one who's never content with the status quo, who's always pushing, always questioning, always imagining what could be. The one whose mind is a fertile ground for the seeds of Innovation, where ideas sprout, grow, and flourish with wild abandon.

The Ideas Guy is like a gardener of the mind. She plants seeds of thought, nurtures them with curiosity and courage, and then watches as they bloom into ideas that are vibrant, unique, and profoundly impactful. But the thing about gardeners is, they don't just work in isolation. They engage with the earth, with the elements, with the very fabric of life itself. And that's exactly what the Ideas Guy does. She's not just an individual, but a part of a greater whole, a cog in the machinery of progress.

The Ideas Guy is not just about having ideas. It's about recognising their power, their potential. It's about understanding that ideas are indeed like psychic dynamite - they have the ability to explode boundaries, shatter conventions, reshape the landscapes of our minds and our societies.

But here's the thing about dynamite. It's a tool. It can be used to cause harm, to destroy. But it can also be used to clear a path, to create a way forward. And so it is with ideas. They're tools, powerful ones, and in the hands of the Ideas Guy, they become instruments of progress, catalysts for change, vehicles for reinvention.

The Ideas Guy understands this. She knows that her ideas, once ignited, have the potential to create ripples of change that can spread far beyond her immediate surroundings. She knows that her ideas can touch lives, can influence minds, can alter the course of history.

But it's not just about coming up with ideas. It's about being brave enough to share them, to stand up and say, "Here's what I think, here's what I imagine, here's what I believe could be possible." It's about being willing to take risks, to challenge the status quo, to push boundaries and break barriers. It's about daring to be different, to think differently, to dream differently.

When we dare to ignite the spark of an idea and let it explode into a brilliant, blazing fire of change. When we dare to be psychic dynamite.

Remember, the world is full of problems waiting to be solved, questions waiting to be answered, opportunities waiting to be seized. And they're all waiting for the Ideas Guy. For you. So go ahead, light that fuse. Ignite your ideas. Unleash your psychic dynamite.

# [ PART I ]

# INNOVATION - BIRTHING NEW REALITIES

WE CANNOT SOLVE OUR PROBLEMS WITH THE SAME THINKING WE USED WHEN WE CREATED THEM.
ALBERT EINSTEIN

Let's venture into the realm of Innovation. Feel it pulsing, vibrating, humming with energy. It's the heartbeat of the new, the spark that lights the torch of progress. It's the place where "what is" bows before "what could be." It's the playground of the Ideas Guy.

It matters because it is the lifeblood of evolution, the currency of progress, the propeller of advancement. It's the audacious belief that we can improve, that we can be better, that we can transcend the constraints of the past, the limitations of the present.

Innovation is about birthing new realities, creating not just new products, new services, but new ways of thinking, new ways of being. It's about challenging the status quo, not to disrupt, but to elevate. It's about refusing to accept "good enough" and striving for "even better."

In this section, we'll meet the pioneers, the trailblazers, the visionaries who have dared to dream big, to think different, to birth new realities. We'll learn from their triumphs, their challenges, their journeys. We'll understand that Innovation isn't a flash of genius, but a process, a mindset, a commitment.

Let's dance with the possible, flirt with the unimaginable, embrace the novel. Let's birth new realities. It's as if we're standing at the edge of a vast, unexplored wilderness, teeming with possibilities, ripe with potential. This is a landscape of the maybe, of the not yet, of the could be. It thrives on questions yet unanswered and problems yet unsolved. It invites us to step into the unknown, to challenge the familiar, and to befriend the unconventional.

Innovation is the forge where the future is shaped, the canvas where new realities are painted. It's the alchemist that turns "what if" into "what is." It embraces the extravagant, the bold, the brave. It calls us to step out of our comfort zones, to abandon the safe harbour of the known, and set sail into uncharted waters.

Within this space, the accepted rules of yesterday bow to the bold ideas of today. It's not a realm of disruption for the sake of disruption, but rather, a realm where improvement, enhancement, and betterment reign. It's a place where "good enough" is the starting line and "even better" is the horizon we chase. The Ideas Guy is a positive disruptor, poking bears, prodding conformity.

As we traverse this section, we'll rub shoulders with the mavericks, the visionaries, the pioneers. We'll listen to their stories, their triumphs, their challenges. Through their eyes, we'll see that Innovation is not a singular moment of genius, but rather a process, a journey. It's a journey of curiosity, courage, and conviction.

Immerse yourself in its pulsating energy, its relentless optimism, its unwavering belief in the potential for better. Innovation is not a destination, but a sojourn to birth new realities, to shape new futures, to become the Ideas Guy.

Innovation is calling.

In all its shimmering grandeur, it is not a fancy mask for destruction, nor is it a licence for reckless disruption. It is not about tearing down for the sake of novelty, nor about disrespecting the wisdom of what came before.

Innovation is not about quick fixes or short-term gains. It isn't a buzzword to throw around or a magic wand to wave and suddenly solve all problems. It's not about being different for the sake of being different or new for the sake of being new. It does not imply a constant need for change simply for change's sake. But it does push against the "we've always done it this way" BS.

Innovation isn't the exclusive realm of the tech-savvy or the genetically gifted. It's not the divine birthright of a select few, nor the privileged playground of geniuses. It does not discriminate based on age, gender, background, or Education.

And crucially, Innovation isn't a destination. It's not a peak to conquer, a box to check, a goalpost to reach. It's a path, a process, a mindset. It's a commitment to continuous improvement, to never settling, to always striving for "even better."

It's a myriad of things, a throng of possibilities, but it also knows its boundaries. It understands its essence, its spirit, its purpose. And understanding what Innovation is not, is just as important as understanding what Innovation is. For in this understanding, we find clarity. We find direction. We find a deeper appreciation for its power and potential.

Within the kaleidoscope of Innovation, we can identify certain patterns, certain models that guide the creation of the new.

**1. THE DISRUPTIVE INNOVATION MODEL:** Coined by Clayton Christensen, it describes how simple, convenient, and affordable solutions can upset established market leaders. Think of how streaming services transformed the film and television industry.

**2. THE BLUE OCEAN STRATEGY:** Introduced by W. Chan Kim and Renée Mauborgne, it's a model that encourages organisations to create uncontested market space (or "blue oceans") rather than competing in an existing industry.

**3. OPEN INNOVATION MODEL:** Popularised by Henry Chesbrough, this model advocates using external as well as internal ideas and paths to market, creating a more fluid collaboration between an organisation and its environment.

**4. THE LEAN STARTUP:** This model, as proposed by Eric Ries, suggests that startups can innovate faster and more effectively by adopting a "build-measure-learn" approach, and by using agile development principles.

**5. THE NETWORK EFFECTS MODEL:** This model, named by Bob Metcalfe, posits that a product or service gains additional value as more people use it. Think of social media platforms - the more people are on them, the more valuable and engaging they become.

These models, and many others, serve as maps, as guides on our journey into the domain of Innovation. They illuminate the path, helping us navigate the landscape of the new. Through their lens, we can better understand the essence of Innovation and how it manifests in different contexts. We don't do this explicitly but use them as reference points.

*The Ideas Guy* will dig into these models and look at how they relate to our luminaries for each chapter. Let's delve into the stories of those who have dared to birth new realities.

INNOVATION IS THE ABILITY TO SEE CHANGE
AS AN OPPORTUNITY - NOT A THREAT.

STEVE JOBS

# [ CHAPTER 1 ]

# A UNIVERSE OF POSSIBILITIES

We start, possibly predictably, at Apple, with Steve Jobs. An idea birthed in a garage, now a global force.

We find ourselves standing in the cool shade of an apple tree. The tree of knowledge, the tree of discovery, the tree of possibility. And from this tree, an idea fell, like Newton's apple, into the fertile soil of Steve Jobs' mind.

Picture it: a garage, cluttered with the junk of the everyday, a sanctuary of solitude away from the humdrum of the world. It was here that an idea took root, an idea that would change the world, that would redefine our relationship with technology, with each other.

Apple. A simple fruit, a humble name, yet a symbol of a revolution, a beacon of Innovation. Steve Jobs, a young man with a mind bursting with ideas, a heart filled with passion, a spirit aflame with a daring dream. And in that garage, that dream started to take shape, to grow, to become.

Jobs and his partner in creation, Steve Wozniak, didn't just see a personal computer; they saw a tool to empower individuals, a way to liberate creativity, a means to connect humanity. They saw a universe of possibilities. And they dared to reach for the stars.

The journey wasn't smooth, the path not straight. There were challenges, setbacks, moments of doubt. Yet, they persisted, they believed, they dared. And that daring, that belief, that persistence, birthed a revolution.

Let's take a moment to honour the spirit of Jobs and Wozniak, the spirit of Apple. Let's remember that Innovation isn't just about creating something new, but about birthing new realities, about opening up universes of possibilities.

Inception. The start, the beginning, the seed from which mighty oaks grow. It's where we find ourselves now, at the cusp of our journey, the threshold of our adventure. And from here, the horizon is filled with the glow of infinite possibilities.

Jobs himself said, "The ones who are crazy enough to think they can change the world, are the ones who do."

Cast your thoughts back, way back, to 1976. Imagine a world without smartphones, without laptops, without the myriad of gadgets that we take for granted today. A world on the brink of a Digital revolution, a world ready to embrace the future. And at the heart of this change? A fledgling company named Apple, and their first product: the Apple I.

Now, the Apple I wasn't the first personal computer. It didn't boast the most cutting-edge technology, nor the slickest design. It was, by most accounts, rudimentary. A circuit board sans a monitor or a case. Yet, it was the seed of an idea, the beginning of a revolution, the birth of a legacy.

The Apple I was successful not because of what it was, but because of what it represented. It was an idea - the idea that computers could be personal, that technology could be accessible, that the power of computing could be harnessed by the everyday individual.

This was the heart of Apple's Innovation–the realisation that technology wasn't just about machines, but about people. It was this human-centric approach that set Apple apart, that made the Apple I not just a product, but a vision.

The Apple duo weren't just selling a product; they were selling a dream. A dream of a world where individuals were empowered by technology, not intimidated by it. A world where technology was an enabler, not a barrier. A world where anyone, anywhere, could tap into the vast potential of the Digital.

The Apple I was successful because it planted this dream in the minds of people. It wasn't about the specs, the chips, the circuitry; it was about the potential, the possibilities, the promise of a new world. And it was this promise, this vision, this dream, that resonated with people, that ignited the spark of Innovation, that began the journey of Apple.

The lesson of the Apple I? That Innovation is about tapping into the dreams, the aspirations, the potential of people. Because at the end of the day, Innovation isn't just about technology; it's about humanity. And it's this truth that lies at the heart of the Apple story.

Pause for a moment. Look at the object you're likely holding (or is at worst, less than ten feet away). A rectangle, a unison of glass and aluminium, created with such grace and precision that it fits smoothly in your hand. Press a button, swipe the screen, take a retinal scan and you are catapulted into a world teeming with knowledge, a universe brimming with experiences. This isn't any object; this is the iPhone.

The iPhone. So common, so familiar, that it seems almost mundane in its ubiquity. Yet, when you pause to really think about it, to consider its essence, its purpose, you realise its true nature: a marvel, a wonder, an epitome of Innovation.

Apple didn't invent the smartphone. Oh no, they did something far more intriguing: they reimagined it. They saw beyond the superficial, the physical, the ordinary. They didn't see a device; they saw a portal, a gateway, a key to a universe teeming with untapped possibilities.

The iPhone wasn't a product, it was a proclamation. With its intuitive interface that seemed to understand your thoughts before you did, its design so elegant it seemed more art than technology, and its revolutionary fusion of phone, internet, and media player, it was a bold declaration. A declaration of a world that was more connected, more creative, more empowered.

The iPhone was an idea, a philosophy encapsulated in a sleek frame and a bright screen. It wasn't just about making calls or browsing the internet; it was about living in a world where knowledge was always at your fingertips, where communication was instantaneous and effortless, where technology served to augment our lives, not complicate it.

As we've said: Innovation is not just about creating new things, but about creating new ways of seeing, new ways of thinking, new ways of experiencing. The iPhone was more than a product; it was an idea, a vision of a world that could be.

And then there's iTunes. At first, you may see it as a mere music platform. Yet, in essence, it was a symphony of revolution. Before iTunes swept the stage, music was tangible, physical, bound by the confines of CDs, cassettes, records. But Apple, they danced to a different tune. They saw beyond the physical form. They perceived music as an experience, an emotion, a fleeting moment captured in a melody.

Apple did not just create a platform; they composed a masterpiece that transformed the rhythm of music consumption. They made music accessible, portable, shareable. They transformed not just the method of listening, but the very interaction with music, the very experience of it.

Here's a striking note: by 2013, a decade after its launch, iTunes had over 500 million users, sold over 25 billion songs and had a catalogue of more than 26 million songs. Those numbers, those staggering figures, they represent more than sales, more than users. They represent moments, memories, melodies that have touched lives, brought joy, comforted hearts. They represent the incredible transformative power of an idea - the idea of iTunes.

Apple didn't just change the way we listen to music; they changed the way we feel it, experience it, live it. They showed us that Innovation isn't just about changing what we do; it's about changing how we feel. Because at the end of the day, Innovation, like music, is about stirring the soul. And then, they shifted the name. iTunes became Apple Music. Just like that, the family grew.

If you are in public: take a look around you. If you're not, put this book down and pop to a place where there are more than 5 people. What do you see? You'll likely spot someone with a pair of those small, sleek, white appendages hanging out of their ear(s). No wires. No fuss. Just pure sound. They're AirPods, Apple's wireless earbuds, and they're more than just a music accessory.

Before AirPods, headphones were a tangled mess of wires, an incessant fight to untangle, a constant battle of putting them in the wrong ear. But Apple, they saw beyond this inconvenience. They saw freedom, they saw seamless integration, they saw an opportunity. And they seized it.

AirPods. An Innovation that leaps beyond the physical and leaps into the experiential. A device so intuitive, so naturally integrated into our daily lives that you forget it's there. You put them in, and suddenly, you're enveloped in your own private world of sound, no matter where you are.

AirPods aren't just about playing music wirelessly. They're about changing our relationship with sound. With their seamless connection, noise cancellation capabilities, and spatial audio features, they've redefined our auditory experience. And the world listened. It's estimated over 150 million units of AirPods have been sold. And over 100 million people use them today. Now, that's not just an impressive sales figure. That's a testament to a breakthrough, a testament to an idea, a testament to Innovation.

Apple didn't just innovate; they sang a new song of what could be. They transformed our connection with sound, made us dance to a new tune of possibilities.

These are just a few examples of Apple's innovative prowess. Each product, each service, each idea, a testament to their commitment to Innovation, to birthing new realities, to challenging the status quo. So, we know now that Innovation is not just about creating something new, but about reimagining, reshaping, redefining the world around us.

The Apple I, iPhone, iTunes, AirPods–they're all manifestations of Apple's keen ability to see beyond the current state of things. They look past the existing framework, past the tangible, past the obvious. They don't just see a computer, a smartphone, a music platform, or a pair of headphones; they see a universe of possibilities, a stage for experiences, a symphony of Innovation.

Apple doesn't just create products, they compose experiences. They seamlessly integrate technology with our daily lives–be it through intuitive user interfaces, revolutionary music platforms, or wireless soundscapes. In this composition of integration, they transform our relationship with technology, turning it from a tool into an extension of ourselves.

Apple teaches us that design is not a mere afterthought, but a vital part of Innovation. They showed us that aesthetics, the very beauty and feel of a product, matter. Every curve, every pixel, every hue–it's all part of the experience. A product should not just function beautifully; it should be beautiful. With their stunning designs, from the sleek lines of the iPhone to the minimalist elegance of the AirPods, Apple has redefined our expectations of what technology should look like. They've shown us that Innovation is not just about what a product does, but also about how it makes us feel, how it speaks to us, how it fits into our lives. They've woven aesthetics into the very fabric of their Innovation philosophy.

Each idea is a note in the symphony of Innovation, a beat in the rhythm of creation. Apple reminds us of the profound impact Innovation can have when we dare to think differently, to see beauty in design, and to seamlessly intertwine technology with our lives. It's about challenging the status quo, transforming experiences, empowering possibilities. That's the very essence of being an Ideas Guy.

And so, with the spirit of Apple guiding us, we continue our journey. Innovation is not a destination, but a journey, a process, a state of mind. And on this journey, every idea, every dream, every possibility, is a step towards a new horizon, a new reality, a new future. The universe of possibilities is waiting.

## [ APPLYING THIS IN PRACTICE ]

**EMBRACE THE BEAUTY**: What can you, the reader, take away from our journey through Apple's landscape of Innovation? It's this–see the beauty in your ideas. Acknowledge the aesthetics, the design, the visual language of your Innovation.

Design isn't just about how things look, it's about how things work. It's about how users interact with your idea, how they feel when they engage with it. The curves, the colours, the textures–they're not just frivolous details; they're part of the experience, part of the story.

So, the tangible step you can take today? Look at your own projects, your own dreams, your own ideas. Ask yourself some questions like: Are they aesthetically pleasing? Do they resonate not just in function but in form? Can they delight the senses as well as serve a purpose? Do they tell a story that's not just heard, but also seen and felt?

If not, it's time to rethink. It's time to embrace the beauty in your ideas. Sketch, doodle, design, play with colours and forms. Make your idea not just innovative, but beautiful. Make it not just a solution, but an experience. Make it not just functional, but delightful.

Not customer service but customer delight. Serve them by delighting them. This could be in your classroom, boardroom or living room–the beauty is what's before you–you get to serve those around you and acknowledge there is beauty to be found.

That's your takeaway. That's your rhythm to sway to, your note to hum. Embrace the beauty in your ideas.

**EMBRACE THE BEAUTY**

MAKING MISTAKES IS THE PRIVILEGE OF THE ACTIVE. IT IS ALWAYS THE MEDIOCRE PEOPLE WHO ARE NEGATIVE, WHO SPEND THEIR TIME PROVING THAT THEY WERE NOT WRONG.

**INGVAR KAMPRAD**

# [ CHAPTER 2 ]

# EVERYDAY MAGIC

Now, let's look into the enchanting world of IKEA and Ingvar Kamprad, the magician who turned simple everyday objects into a revolution of design and affordability. A testament to the transformative power of ideas.

Here we are, in the unassuming landscape of Innovation. And we find ourselves leaning against the sturdy, well-crafted framework of IKEA furniture. The tree of practicality, the tree of simplicity, the tree of affordability. And from this tree, an idea sprouted, like the assembling of a flatpack, into the grounded soil of Ingvar Kamprad's mind.

Imagine it: a small village in southern Sweden, a quiet farmland amidst the hustle and bustle of the world. It was here that an idea took form, an idea that would not only change our living spaces but also redefine our relationship with furniture.

IKEA. A basic name, a common item, yet a symbol of a revolution, a beacon of Innovation. Ingvar Kamprad, a young lad with a mind ripe with ideas, a heart brimming with ambition, a spirit stirred by a unique dream. And in that small village, that dream began to assemble, to construct, to take form.

Kamprad and his team didn't just envision furniture; they saw a solution to empower individuals, a way to provide practicality, a means to infuse simplicity. They saw a universe of possibilities. And they dared to build a ladder to the stars.

The journey wasn't without splinters, the path not without twists and turns. There were hurdles, missteps, moments of uncertainty. Yet, they persisted, they believed, they dared. And that daring, that belief, that persistence, gave life to a revolution.

Let's celebrate the spirit of Kamprad and his team, the spirit of IKEA. Let's recall that Innovation isn't just about creating something novel, but about shaping new realities, about unlocking universes of possibilities.

The start, the beginning, the seed from which sprawling furniture stores grow. It's where we find ourselves now, at the genesis of our journey, the threshold of our adventure. And from here, the horizon is filled with the luminescence of infinite possibilities.

Kamprad once said, "The most dangerous poison is the feeling of achievement. The antidote is: to every evening think what can be done better tomorrow."

Take your mind back, far back, to 1943. Picture a world without flat-packed furniture, without the accessible designs, without the democratic design principle that we today take for granted. A world on the brink of a practical revolution, a world ready to welcome affordability. And at the heart of this change? A fledgling company named IKEA, and their first product: a simple wooden table.

Now, the wooden table wasn't the first piece of furniture. It didn't possess the most cutting-edge design, nor the finest craftsmanship. It was, by most accounts, plain. A basic wooden frame. Yet, it was the seed of an idea, the birth of a legacy.

This table was successful not because of what it was, but because of what it symbolised. It was an idea–the idea that good design could be affordable, that functional furniture could be accessible, that the comfort of a home could be enjoyed by everyone.

IKEA's Innovation lies in this realisation–that design isn't just about aesthetics, but about practicality. It was this practical-centric approach that set IKEA apart, that made the wooden table not just a product, but a vision. This isn't a contradiction to Jobs' Apple. It's a new facet. Dimensions of Innovation.

IKEA isn't just selling furniture; they are selling a dream. A dream of a home where practicality meets beauty, where affordability co-exists with quality, where simplicity goes hand in hand with style.

Every piece of IKEA furniture, from that initial wooden table to the modern day Billy bookcase, embodies this vision. They are pieces of a puzzle, parts of a picture, bricks in the building of a dream home.

In the realm of business, we often talk about disruption. IKEA's inception can be considered one of the finest examples of this. They didn't just break the mould; they reshaped it entirely. They questioned the norm, they pushed the boundaries, they dared to be different.

Ingvar Kamprad didn't start IKEA with the aim of building a furniture empire. His dream was bigger, bolder. He wanted to democratise design. He wanted to bring the comfort and functionality of well-designed furniture to every home.

IKEA's approach to design and manufacturing, their business model, their branding, all align with this vision. They pioneered flat-pack furniture, which reduced costs and made transportation and assembly easier for customers. They created the IKEA catalogue, not just as a product showcase, but as an inspiration for better living. They built stores that are not just retail spaces, but experiential showrooms where customers can feel and envision their dream homes. Oh, and meatballs.

The inception of IKEA marked a new era in the furniture industry, and the ripples of their Innovation continue to influence how we think about and interact with our homes. They took a basic wooden table and turned it into a symbol of aspiration, a beacon of Innovation, a testament to the power of practical design.

From inception to growth, from challenges to triumphs, from dreams to reality. And as we travel, keep in mind the words of Ingvar Kamprad, "To design a desk which may cost $1,000 is easy for a furniture designer, but to design a functional and good desk which shall cost only $50 can only be done by the very best."

This is the spirit of IKEA–to make the best available to all. It's a tale of how a simple wooden table transformed into a global revolution, a story that's as much about human ingenuity as it is about furniture. This is the story of IKEA–a story of Innovation, Inspiration, and Aspiration.

Imagine a world of furniture that arrives not as a cumbersome, fully-assembled unit but as a sleek package of parts, inviting you to put it together yourself. This is the realm IKEA crafted with their revolutionary "flat-pack" concept. It isn't just about furniture; it's about shifting paradigms, breaking down bulky barriers, and reimagining what furniture could be. It's about transforming logistics, reducing shipping costs, and making the impossible possible–a compact, easy-to-transport solution for everyone.

In this story, IKEA didn't just sell furniture; they invited people to become creators, architects of their own spaces. The twist-and-turn, the bolt-and-screw, the step-by-step creation, it was all part of a bigger picture–a story where customers weren't mere consumers but active participants in the saga of their living spaces. They dared to shift the narrative, and the world watched in awe.

Bring to mind an IKEA catalogue, now digital but for so long the mainstay of yuppy coffee tables, transcending the realm of commonplace product listings, transforming into a portal that opens into a horizon of unexplored potential. Far from being a dreary inventory of goods, it is an illuminating manuscript that serves as a canvas for the imagination, a vivarium that fosters the growth of creative ideas. Each leaf you turn unfolds a new narrative, etched not just with images and words, but with the vibrant strokes of possibilities and inspiration.

Each image is more than a mere representation of a product; it is an incandescent spark that kindles a bonfire of fresh perspectives. It dances across your mind, teasing and coaxing your imagination to take a bold leap beyond the confines of the ordinary. It's as though every photographed item, every visual representation, ignites a cognitive adventure that dares you to explore further, challenging you to invent and reinvent the spaces you inhabit.

The IKEA catalogue was never intended to be just that, a catalogue. It transcends its ostensible purpose, metamorphosing into a compass guiding you towards a realm of dreams, a handbook that empowers you to navigate through the maze of the mundane and locate the extraordinary. This unassuming guide, in your hands, becomes a beacon of inspiration that pierces through the fog of monotony, illuminating a path to a world where every object is pregnant with the potential to transform a space, where every idea has the power to alter perspectives.

In a world that often revels in uniformity, the IKEA catalogue stands out as a lighthouse, emitting a resplendent beam of inspiration that disrupts the sea of sameness. It invites you to break away from the pattern, to embrace the possibility of redefining your environment in ways that are as unique and multifaceted as you are. The IKEA catalogue is more than a mere listing of products; it's an artful tapestry of inspiration, a tool that empowers you to envisage a home that mirrors your individuality, dreams, and aspirations.

Now, imagine, if you will, stepping into the universe of an IKEA store, an intricate maze that defies the commonplace idea of a retail outlet and blossoms into an enchanting island of exploration and revelation. This is not just a tangible commercial building; it's an experiential voyage which has been precisely designed and laid out for you, where every footstep guides you on a course that feels more akin to a treasure hunt than a shopping trip.

The corridors are far more than mere receptacles for merchandise; they are pulsating with aspirations, possibilities, and prospects. They hold not only the tactile and visual elements of furniture but also the ethereal allure of transformative potential. Here, the retail aisles bristle with silent whisperings of dreams, becoming conduits that transport you from the mundane to the realm of imagination. It is a sphere where the ordinary and the extraordinary dance in harmonious balance, igniting sparks of creativity.

Stepping into an IKEA store is not like a casual saunter through a standard outlet. It is like embarking on an expedition, traversing the unknown, seeking the extraordinary within the ordinary, the hidden within the visible, and above all, the potential within the dormant. You find yourself embarking on a mission, where the delightful reward is the joy of discovery and the thrill of inventing and reinventing your surroundings.

The miniature rooms, meticulously staged and adorned within the confines of IKEA, begin to feel oddly personal. These humble spaces, initially belonging to a far-off store, slowly morph into your intimate spaces. They become the living room where your family congregates for cosy movie nights, the kitchen where meals are lovingly prepared, the bedroom that serves as a serene haven after a demanding day.

The metamorphosis is subtle, yet profound. As you wander through IKEA, these spaces, filled with the potential for transformation, begin to transfigure, reflecting your life, your dreams, your needs. You find yourself seeing not just a display, but a manifestation of your life within these walls. It is here, in the heart of this circuitous store, that you begin to see the reflection of your home, not as it is, but as it could be, filled with the promise and potential of an IKEA-inspired transformation.

Lastly, and perhaps most significant, is IKEA's solemn pledge, a vow to transition into a circular business model by the year 2030. This isn't merely a commitment towards recycling or promoting sustainability. Rather, it embodies a much deeper principle, an assertion of accountability, a conscious decision to care for our collective home, our Earth.

This commitment by IKEA reaches far beyond the confines of a corporate promise. It's a clarion call, an impassioned rallying cry echoing across the expanse of consumerism. It's a challenge issued not only to businesses but also to individuals, to communities, to nations. It invites us all to rise, to shed passivity and adopt an active role in preserving and nurturing our planet.

IKEA's resolution is far more profound than an abstract promise, an empty corporate gesture. It's a directive to every one of us to reflect, reconsider, and reinvent our actions. It's a plea for mindfulness about our consumption habits, our waste generation, and our overall impact on the environment. It's an invocation for us to join in a movement, a revolution, to alter the course of our planet's future.

In a world where reckless consumption and disregard for the environment are often the norm, IKEA's commitment serves as a ray of hope, a spark that could ignite a wildfire of change. It's a testament to their belief that we can, collectively, shape a different narrative, one that puts the Earth and its well-being at the forefront.

But this isn't just about IKEA. This pledge challenges each of us to step into the arena, to become stewards of our environment. It's an urgent call for collective responsibility, for unified action. Because in the end, it isn't just about what one corporation pledges to do. It's about what all of us, as inhabitants of this planet, choose to do to make a lasting, impactful difference. It is, in essence, a call to arms for the preservation of our world.

IKEA's tale isn't just a tale of a furniture retailer; it's a grand epic of Innovation, of bold ideas and brave revolutions. They didn't just change how furniture is sold; they changed how it's perceived, how it's loved. This is the story of IKEA, and like all great stories, it invites us to be a part of it.

The conventional furniture store offers just that - furniture. But when we step into the world of IKEA, we step into a realm of unbounded potential. With every piece of flat-pack furniture, every thoughtfully designed showroom, every plate of meatballs and lingonberry jelly, IKEA teaches us to see not just the physical object in front of us, but the unseen possibilities it holds. The bed isn't just a bed; it's a sanctuary of comfort. The kitchen isn't just a kitchen; it's a theatre of culinary creativity. By designing for the unseen potential, IKEA encourages us to reimagine the ordinary, turning the functional into the phenomenal.

IKEA's design philosophy goes beyond aesthetics; it delves into functionality and purpose. Every product is meticulously crafted to serve multiple roles, making it adaptable to various living spaces and individual needs. Whether it's a modular storage unit that can transform into a creative workspace or a sofa bed that offers comfort during the day and a cosy bed at night, IKEA's focus on unseen potential sparks our imagination, encouraging us to explore new ways of living and interacting with our environment.

IKEA doesn't just sell furniture; they craft experiences. They flawlessly interlace their products with our everyday lives. In this composition of involvement, they transform our relationship with furniture, turning it from a mere commodity into an extension of our identities. It is not done to us but with us. It's more of a WE-KEA than an IKEA actually.

IKEA's commitment to involvement extends beyond the creation of products. They invite customers to become co-creators, engaging them in the design process through user-generated content and interactive platforms. By encouraging DIY assembly, IKEA empowers individuals to take charge of their living spaces, fostering a sense of ownership and accomplishment.

Beyond customer involvement, IKEA engages in collaborations with artists, designers, and innovators to infuse fresh perspectives and ideas into their collections. This approach ensures that IKEA remains a dynamic and evolving force in the world of design, constantly adapting to the changing needs and desires of its diverse clientele.

In the heart of IKEA's Innovation lies an unwavering dedication to the essence of home. Beyond just providing functional furniture, IKEA weaves a tapestry of emotions and memories within every design. Their creations are not merely objects; they are guardians of comfort and catalysts of belonging. IKEA understands that home is where the soul finds solace, and they strive to curate a harmonious symphony between design and emotion.

IKEA's Innovation is centred on the profound understanding that a home should reflect the unique stories of its inhabitants. They create spaces that mirror the dreams, aspirations, and quirks of the people who dwell within them. IKEA's designers embark on a journey to capture the essence of diverse lifestyles and cultures, transcending geographic boundaries and celebrating the universal feeling of warmth and togetherness that home exudes.

Through their extensive research, IKEA dives deep into the subtleties of daily life, learning about the rituals that enrich our days and the challenges we face. With this treasure trove of insights, they craft products and solutions that harmoniously blend form and function. From ingenious storage solutions for compact apartments to versatile furniture that adapts to our ever-changing needs, IKEA fosters an atmosphere of ease and delight.

The idea of embracing the essence of home transcends beyond their products. It permeates every aspect of IKEA's approach, from their interactive store layouts that allow us to imagine our dream spaces to their accessible pricing that enables millions to create a place they can truly call their own. The reality is that every IDEAS Guy needs a home - a safe haven, a sanctuary, a place of solace.

IKEA's Innovation philosophy is about fostering a deep connection with the essence of what makes a house a home. By empowering us to express our individuality, embrace our roots, and create spaces that resonate with our hearts, IKEA invites us to partake in the eternal dance of human emotions and the places we call home. Their innovative spirit seeks to enrich lives, making every day an enchanting journey within the haven we create for ourselves.

IKEA can steer us, inspire us, and remind us of the significant impact Innovation can achieve when we dare to think differently, to see potential in every facet of life, and to seamlessly intertwine our everyday lives with our decisions. It's about challenging norms, transforming experiences, powering possibilities. And so, with the spirit of IKEA guiding us, we persist in our journey. And on this voyage, every idea, every dream, every possibility, is a stride towards a new horizon, a new reality, a new future. The universe of possibilities awaits.

# [ APPLYING THIS IN PRACTICE ]

**CHAMPION SUSTAINABILITY:** As we traverse the captivating landscape of IKEA's Innovation, an awe-inspiring principle emerges–the profound importance of championing sustainability in every facet of our ideas. Just as IKEA has embraced sustainability as a guiding light, we too can recognise the transformative potential of infusing our Innovations with a sustainable narrative, a legacy of responsibility, and an unwavering commitment to the well-being of our planet.

Sustainability isn't a fleeting trend; it is the very essence of progress, the soul of a vision that harmoniously intertwines with the environment. It is a harmonious dance between human aspirations and the preservation of our natural resources, a testament to the realisation that our dreams can soar higher when they are grounded in eco-consciousness.

When we champion sustainability in our ideas, we embrace a holistic perspective that extends beyond immediate gains. We are acutely aware of the environmental impact, the life cycle, and the enduring legacy of our Innovations. We comprehend that each decision, each resource, and each interaction weaves a narrative of responsibility that resonates with generations to come.

As visionaries seeking to shape a brighter future, we recognise that sustainability is not merely about mitigating harm; it is about actively nurturing positive change. Our ideas can be agents of transformation, catalysts of progress that propel us towards a regenerative era, where creativity and environmental stewardship dance in harmonious unison.

So, the tangible step we can take today? Take a long, hard, introspective look at our projects, our dreams, our aspirations, our homes. Are they adorned with the hue of sustainability? Do they breathe life into our world while cherishing its precious resources? Can they be a beacon of hope for a planet yearning for balance and harmony?

If we find that our ideas are not yet adorned with the emerald mantle of sustainability, it is time to reimagine. It is time to infuse our Innovations with the spirit of eco - to recycle stagnant paradigms, to reuse ingenuity, to reduce waste, and to reimagine the boundaries of possibility. If we aren't actively living, working, teaching that there is no Planet B, we need to change that channel.

Like IKEA, let us craft a sustainable narrative that weaves through every thread of our ideas, a narrative that honours the past, enriches the present, and extends a flourishing legacy to the future. Let us rise as torchbearers of sustainability, guardians of the planet's well-being, and champions of a brighter, greener pathway.

Together, let us embrace the vanguard of change, nurturing ideas that not only fulfil their purpose but also celebrate the responsibility we bear towards the world. As we champion sustainability, we shall tread the path of harmony, weaving a tapestry of inspiration that intertwines the essence of our ideas with the heartbeat of nature.

In each idea, let us find the echoes of renewal, the rhythm of regeneration, and the symphony of hope that resounds in every corner of our planet. For, in championing sustainability, we become architects of a future where Innovation and the environment harmoniously coexist, shaping a world where dreams flourish in the embrace of a thriving, sustainable legacy.

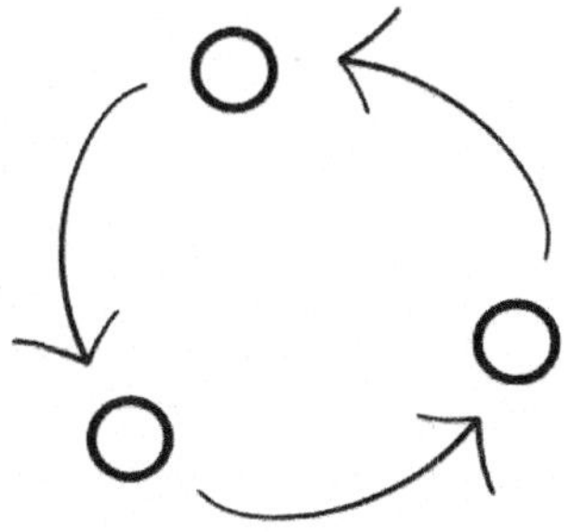

# CHAMPION SUSTAINABILITY

I THINK PEOPLE CAN CHOOSE TO BE NOT ORDINARY. YOU KNOW, THEY CAN CHOOSE TO NOT NECESSARILY CONFORM TO THE CONVENTIONS THAT WERE TAUGHT TO THEM BY THEIR PARENTS. SO, YES, I THINK IT'S POSSIBLE FOR ORDINARY PEOPLE TO CHOOSE TO BE EXTRAORDINARY.

ELON MUSK

# [ CHAPTER 3 ]

# CHASING THE MOON

As we turn the page, our eyes lift from the earthly terrain of Kamprad's flat-pack revolution and fixate on a new, uncharted horizon. Enter Elon Musk. When ambition dared to dream the impossible, the sky was no longer the limit; it was the starting point.

Some may be tempted to skip past this chapter with our protagonist's less-than-clean dives into politics, X, and cryptocurrency. You may think that Musk's misalignments mean his alignments are maligned or even now malevolent.

But it's worth more than a mention that the brightest stars often burn unevenly, casting light and shadow in "equal" measure. Musk is not a saint, nor does he claim to be. His flaws–etched deeply into the public record–are part of what makes him human and what makes his achievements so astonishing. To dismiss him outright is to miss the thunderous heartbeat of his vision: a world where Innovation is not constrained by convention but unleashed to rewrite our collective future.

In the vast expanse of the cosmos, there exists this theatre of ceaseless Innovation. It's a place where the boundaries of human ingenuity are continually tested, reshaped, and redefined. This is the story of SpaceX–an ambitious dream of reaching the stars, born in the crucible of Silicon Valley.

Picture a world, not too dissimilar from our own, where the confines of earthbound existence were beginning to feel a tad too familiar, too restrictive. There was a hunger for something greater, a thirst for the exploration of the vast, unknown wilderness of outer space. The name SpaceX was yet to be etched in the annals of history, but the seeds of an extraordinary vision were already being sown.

Elon Musk, a figure shrouded in an aura of enigma, has become a byword for daring, boundary-pushing Innovation. His name resonates with an unyielding aspiration to dictate the future. Born to the rhythmic cadence of code and the electric hum of circuitry, Musk has long been fueled by insatiable ambition and an unwavering drive to redefine the world as we know it.

His earliest foray into the tech world began with Zip2, a city guide software company that catapulted him into the spotlight. It was here that the world got its first glimpse of Musk's unerring instinct for Innovation, his knack for identifying and capitalising on Digital frontiers. This venture was just a prelude, a harbinger of the extraordinary feats he was yet to accomplish.

Musk's entrepreneurial journey gathered momentum with the inception of PayPal, a revolutionary concept that transformed Digital payments, democratising financial transactions in a rapidly globalising world. His vision extended beyond the here-and-now, striving to shatter the constraints of convention and create technologies that would leapfrog us into the future.

Then comes his investment in and leadership of Tesla, where he's persistently championed the cause of sustainable transportation. By challenging the monopoly of petrol-powered vehicles and thrusting electric cars into the mainstream, Musk is not just shaping the future of mobility; he's contributing significantly towards our collective effort to combat climate change.

Elon Musk, a name now synonymous with crazy Innovation and entrepreneurial courage, has consistently and persistently pushed against the very grain of the accepted, the normative. He has navigated the maze of impossibilities, daring to envision and actualise a world that others could barely dream of. He is not just a businessman or an entrepreneur; he's a visionary, an architect of the future, relentlessly shifting the contours of our world.

Yet, his gaze was always fixed on a realm far beyond our world. His dream was not just to touch the stars but to create a civilisation that could dance among them. It was this dream that led to the creation of SpaceX.

SpaceX's first years were marked by bold ideas and high risks. The company sought to achieve what had never been done before: to make space travel more accessible, to create reusable rockets, and to make interplanetary life possible. The dream was vast; the challenges, monumental.

The Falcon 1, SpaceX's first rocket, was the embodiment of this bold ambition. It was a symbol of a dream larger than life itself. The journey wasn't without failures. The first three launches ended in heartbreak, yet the spirit of SpaceX did not falter.

Again, Innovation at SpaceX was not simply about creating new technology. It was about redefining the very ethos of space exploration. It was about daring to dream bigger, to challenge the impossible, and to redefine the limitations of human ingenuity.

The launch of the Falcon 1 marked the start of a new era in space travel. The journey was far from easy, but each failure was seen not as a setback but as a step forward, a learning curve, a bridge to a better, more innovative solution.

When Falcon 1 finally reached orbit in September 2008, it was not just a triumph of technology; it was a victory for the daring spirit of human Innovation. SpaceX had proven that space travel could be more accessible, more sustainable, and above all, more daring.

Nonetheless, the cosmic voyage of SpaceX was in its nascent stages, merely embarking upon the cusp of an interstellar odyssey. The successful launch of Falcon 1 marked the commencement of a revolution, a stepping stone towards a brighter future of space exploration. This legacy was carried forward by the Falcon 9 and Falcon Heavy, rockets that not only challenged but also dismantled the established frontiers of space travel.

Yet, SpaceX did not just launch these mechanical beasts into the ethereal expanse of space; it also orchestrated their safe return, guiding them back home to Earth. This was an exceptional feat that blended pinpoint precision, avant-garde technology, and intricate engineering to achieve something that was once deemed impossible. Rockets that ascended to the cosmos came back to land on Earth, ready to soar again.

This radical Innovation was nothing short of a game-changer, completely revolutionising the space industry's dynamics. Reusable rockets were no longer a fragment of science fiction; they were tangible realities, courtesy of SpaceX. The implications of this were immense: it meant significantly reducing the exorbitant costs associated with space travel, making it economically more viable and accessible.

The advent of reusable rockets heralded a new era, promising more frequent missions, thereby accelerating our journey to understand the cosmos. Space was no longer a one-way journey for these rockets; it had become a round trip. The introduction of such technology brought us closer to realising our dreams of exploring the unknown, of becoming a multi-planetary species, of understanding the cosmos that lies beyond our reach.

SpaceX's journey was just beginning, and with it, they were redefining what was possible. They were not just launching rockets; they were launching a new era of space travel, reshaping our relationship with the cosmos, and igniting a spark of hope for a future where space exploration is no longer an elite privilege but a common endeavour for humanity. This was more than a technological triumph; it was a beacon illuminating our path towards the stars.

However, the Falcon series of rockets, while undoubtedly transformative, represented only a single movement in SpaceX's grand symphony of Innovation. The magnum opus was yet to be fully realised, as the Dragon spacecraft arrived on the stage, redefining not just cargo delivery, but the very nature of human spaceflight.

The Dragon spacecraft, aptly named for its fiery ambition and celestial prowess, revolutionised how we transport supplies and humans beyond the confines of our atmosphere. It took the legacy of the Falcon rockets and elevated it to a new stratosphere of possibilities. Dragon didn't just deliver cargo; it served as a reliable conduit between Earth and the cosmos, a trusted courier that could carry both lifeless supplies and life-filled astronauts.

The introduction of Dragon reshaped our relationship with the International Space Station (ISS). It allowed us to access this celestial outpost more frequently and reliably, transforming it from a distant dream into a reachable destination. Suddenly, the ISS was not just a hub for elite astronauts chosen by a handful of space agencies; it was within the realm of possibility for a broader spectrum of explorers, ushering in a new era of democratised space travel.

Dragon's impact was profound and far-reaching. It made the ISS accessible, forging a bond between our blue planet and the sprawling cosmos that goes beyond the abstract. It's as if Dragon has become a celestial commuter, a cosmic ferry, bridging the gap between our home and the space station.

In the grand symphony of SpaceX's Innovation, Dragon is the powerful crescendo, the apex where the melody of cargo delivery meets the harmonious chords of human spaceflight. With every successful mission, it not only brings us closer to the stars but also reiterates SpaceX's promise of making space travel a shared human experience, transcending the barriers of nations, disciplines, and backgrounds. The Dragon spacecraft, thus, symbolises not just technological advancement, but also the dream of an inclusive, unified quest for space exploration.

And then came Starship, a vessel designed to ferry humans to Mars and make life multiplanetary. An outlandish vision transformed into a tangible, awe-inspiring reality. The story of SpaceX is not just about manufacturing rockets and spacecraft; it's about igniting dreams and turning the seemingly impossible into reality.

The aspiration to colonise Mars, once relegated to the realm of science fiction, has come to symbolise the relentless spirit of SpaceX. The goal of Mars colonisation extends beyond human survival. It encapsulates a vision of Innovation, resilience, and boundless exploration, the very tenets that define SpaceX.

The successful launch and landing of the Starship prototype marked another significant stride in their odyssey. It demonstrated the feasibility of large-scale space travel, bolstering the dream of making life on Mars more than a Bowie classic.

However, SpaceX's vision expands even further than Mars. Musk envisages a future where humanity becomes a panstellar species, capable of exploring and inhabiting multiple celestial bodies. This bold vision, while seemingly overwhelming, underpins SpaceX's ethos: to challenge boundaries, to push the limits, and to spearhead the future of space travel.

Looking back at their trajectory, SpaceX's story is more than a timeline of technological milestones. It's a testament to the power of dreams, the determination to overcome challenges, and the bravery to chase the seemingly impossible. From the successful launches of the Falcon series and Dragon spacecraft to the ambitious Starship project, SpaceX continues to redefine our perception of what's attainable in space exploration.

The journey of SpaceX is far from complete. As we continue to witness the unfolding of this extraordinary cosmic saga, we can only speculate about the exciting Innovations the future holds. The story of SpaceX is still being inscribed, with each launch, each landing, and each crazy dream. It's a narrative about challenging boundaries, about reaching for the stars, and about redefining what's possible. Most importantly, it's a story about the relentless pursuit of dreams, no matter how unattainable they may seem.

At SpaceX, Musk's unwavering determination to push the boundaries of space travel coalesces with his other visionary ventures. Tesla, his trailblazing electric vehicle company, fuels the movement towards sustainable energy solutions. By revolutionising the automotive industry with high-performance electric cars, Tesla inspires a shift towards a greener, more sustainable future for transportation.

Beyond automobiles, Musk's passion for renewable energy extends to SolarCity, a company he co-founded to harness the potent energy of the sun. SolarCity's mission is to illuminate homes, businesses, and cities with the brilliance of solar power, sparking an era of clean, renewable energy.

Through Neuralink, his groundbreaking neurotechnology venture, he envisions a future where the boundaries between humans and machines blur. Neuralink's ambitious goal is to create brain-machine interfaces, enabling the seamless exchange of information between the human brain and computers. This pursuit holds the potential to revolutionise medical treatments and redefine our understanding of cognition.

Not content to stop there, Musk's innovative spirit extends underground with The Boring Company. This visionary venture aims to alleviate urban traffic congestion by creating a network of underground tunnels, providing swift and efficient transportation for urban dwellers. It might not be a present reality but the dream is there.

At the very heart of his guiding principles lies the art of propelling multi-dimensional Innovation. Elon Musk's grand vision transcends the boundaries of space exploration, through the medium of ground transportation, even venturing into human biological development, encompassing a vibrant spectrum of pioneering that steers the course of humanity towards a future brimming with possibilities.

Musk's approach underscores the significance of exploring the interstices between disparate domains. Through this synthesis of ideas, a harmonious symphony of progress emerges. The art of propelling multi-dimensional Innovation challenges conventional boundaries, inspiring a dynamic synergy between diverse fields of exploration.

From the very beginning, Elon Musk's ventures have been driven by a relentless pursuit of reinvention. He possesses a unique ability to challenge established norms and revolutionise industries that were once deemed stagnant. Whether it's the electric vehicle market with Tesla, the aerospace industry with SpaceX, or the future of transportation with The Boring Company, Musk consistently pushes the boundaries of what is possible.

He defied sceptics who believed that electric cars couldn't be practical, stylish, and desirable. Tesla's sleek designs, cutting-edge technology, and impressive performance have shattered the notion that electric vehicles are merely a niche market. Through continuous Innovation, Musk has not only made electric cars a reality but also paved the way for a sustainable future in transportation.

Similarly, with SpaceX, Musk has challenged the conventional approach to space exploration. By developing reusable rocket technology, he disrupted the traditional space industry model, which relied on costly, single-use rockets. SpaceX's successful landings and re-flights of Falcon 9 rockets have demonstrated that space travel can be more affordable, sustainable, and accessible to humanity at large.

Elon Musk's ventures have always been about more than just products and profits. They are driven by a profound mission to inspire and captivate a global audience. Musk understands that to bring about transformative change, he needs to foster excitement and passion in individuals from all walks of life. He isn't squeaky clean either; indeed, many Ideas Guys tread a difficult line in this respect.

Through innovative marketing strategies, Tesla has built a community of dedicated followers who are not only customers but also brand ambassadors. The excitement surrounding new product announcements, software updates, and even the prospect of self-driving technology has transformed Tesla into a cultural phenomenon. People are not just buying cars; they are buying into a vision of the future that is sustainable, electric, and exciting.

Musk has opened up the world of space exploration to the public, turning rocket launches into shared experiences. SpaceX's live webcasts of missions have become global events, drawing millions of viewers who eagerly witness each launch with awe and anticipation. By making space more accessible and inviting people to be part of the journey, SpaceX has inspired a new generation of space enthusiasts and dreamers.

In Elon Musk's holistic perspective, Innovation is not just about pushing the boundaries of what is known, but also about sharing the journey with the world. By fostering excitement and inclusivity, he has created a movement that goes beyond industries and technologies, empowering people to be part of something bigger and bolder.

As we embrace the principles of Innovation demonstrated by Elon Musk, we find ourselves at the threshold of transformative change. His vision and audacity serve as a testament to what is possible when we challenge the status quo, engage the collective imagination, and create a future that is not just innovative, but also profoundly inspiring. Guided by these principles, we continue our expedition into the universe of Innovation. These principles guide us towards a future where the cosmos is within our reach, and mankind's potential is truly limitless.

# [ APPLYING THIS IN PRACTICE ]

**PUSH BOUNDARIES:** A pivotal takeaway from our journey through the universe of Elon Musk's Innovation is the potent concept of pushing boundaries. Whether it's through Tesla's electric vehicles, SpaceX's aerospace exploits, or The Boring Company's vision for transportation, Musk's ventures have consistently demonstrated the power of audacity and the willingness to challenge reality.

Tesla's journey in the electric vehicle market exemplifies the idea of pushing boundaries. Their sleek designs, cutting-edge technology, and impressive performance redefined what electric cars could be, transforming them from niche products into coveted status symbols. His ambition was to accelerate the world's transition to sustainable energy. This grand objective pushed the boundaries of what a car company could achieve, as Tesla branched into renewable energy solutions with products like solar panels and energy storage systems. By embracing an expansive vision, Musk steered Tesla towards becoming not just an automaker but a catalyst for a global sustainability movement.

Musk's vision extended beyond just our planet. His ambition to colonise Mars reflects his commitment to pushing boundaries on a cosmic scale. The idea of establishing a self-sustaining human presence on another planet was once the realm of Rodenberry and Lucas, but Musk's audacity and determination have turned it into a concrete goal. The development of the Starship spacecraft, with its potential to carry humans to Mars and beyond, demonstrates Musk's unwavering dedication to exploring uncharted territories.

Innovation is not just about incremental improvements; it's about challenging preconceptions, venturing into unexplored realms, and seeking transformative change. Ask yourself: Are you pushing the boundaries with your ideas and projects? Are you challenging the status quo in your field of interest? Embrace audacity, welcome the unknown, and dare to pioneer changes that have the potential to redefine what's possible.

If you are a teacher in a classroom, consider the boundaries that can be pushed and push them. If you're an entrepreneur, go beyond the wall into unfamiliar territory, into the lateral sectors to what you know. If you're a student, push against the normal way of doing things to take your learning beyond the guardrails the system has imposed upon you.

Innovation is not limited to any one domain or industry. It's a mindset, a bold and brave approach to making a difference in the world. Whether you're an entrepreneur, an artist, a scientist, or anyone pursuing their passion, let Musk's example inspire you to push boundaries and embark on a journey of discovery, creativity, and impact. As the Ideas Guy, it's not just about producing superior versions of existing ideas; it's about conceiving groundbreaking concepts that could reshape our world and push humanity towards a more extraordinary future.

## PUSH BOUNDARIES

THE WORLD NEEDS MORE SOCIAL INNOVATIONS.

ANNE WOJICKI

# [ CHAPTER 4 ]

# DECODING DNA

In this narrative, we're stepping off the launchpad and into the mystery of our very being - the intricate design of human life written in the lines of our DNA.

It's a journey into the spiral staircase of life, where every step holds the clues of our past, the reality of our present, and the possibilities of our future. We're decoding our blueprint and our guide is Anne Wojcicki, the pioneering force behind 23andMe, a company that opened the doors to personal genomics, revealing the secrets that lie within the heart of our cells.

Imagine a time, not so long ago, when the language of our DNA was accessible to only a select few–the geneticists and the molecular biologists who could comprehend its complex narrative. We could gaze upon our reflection, examine our traits, but the inner story, the one coded into every cell of our being, remained unread. That was until Wojcicki and her team stepped onto the scene. They dared to dream of a world where our genetic heritage could be made accessible, where the code of life would be deciphered, not in secluded research labs, but in the comfort of our homes.

Wojcicki, with her background in biology and a flair for entrepreneurship, co-founded 23andMe in 2006. Named after the 23 pairs of chromosomes that make up the human genome, the company embarked on a mission to make personal genetics a part of everyday life. They crafted a simple yet revolutionary kit that could unlock the secrets woven into our DNA.

The innovative thinking is profound: take a simple saliva sample, send it to the lab, and let the scientists unravel the story hidden within the DNA. Suddenly, the complex language of genomics is transformed into a legible report, easily understood by any curious mind. The once far-off land of genetics has been brought close, within the reach of our fingertips.

With the rise of 23andMe, genetics is no longer confined to scientific literature; it is now a part of dinner table conversations. We can trace our ancestry, understand our propensity towards certain traits and conditions, and realise the power of prevention through early detection. It is like holding a mirror to our very being, not just reflecting our physical image but revealing the essence of who we are.

Through 23andMe, Wojcicki invites us on an extraordinary voyage, navigating the vast oceans of our genetic heritage. We can see where our ancestors walked, understand the journey of our genes, and discover how those tiny sequences of DNA influence our physical traits, behaviours, and health.

Our DNA is no longer a cryptic script but a narrative of our past, present, and future. We find ourselves a part of a larger story, connecting with people and places we never knew existed, yet they were a part of us.

By unlocking our genetic secrets, Wojcicki didn't just provide a fascinating exploration into our being, she offered a tool for prevention, a guide to healthier living.

23andMe is more than a biotech company; it is a revolution in our understanding of ourselves. Under Wojcicki's leadership, the company has changed the narrative of health, wellness, and ancestry. She's shown that the mysteries of life aren't solely for scientists to decipher, but are open to everyone's curious gaze.

In the story of 23andMe, we see the power of innovative thinking. The genetic code, once a secluded realm, has become a shared exploration, an open dialogue, a personal encounter with the heart of our existence. This extraordinary journey, pioneered by Wojcicki, marks a new epoch in human understanding. It is as if a new door has been opened, allowing us to delve into the complexities of life, revealing what it truly means to be human.

This is a quest that goes beyond medical diagnoses or genealogical pursuits. It is about self-discovery, and how our unique genetic story connects us to the broader human existence. It's a journey that invites us to engage with our own story, shaping it and, at the same time, being shaped by it.

By presenting genomics in a digestible format, Wojcicki has empowered us to engage with our health in a more proactive manner. Suddenly, preventive medicine is not just a vague concept but a personal commitment we can make. The understanding of our genetic predispositions can serve as a guiding light, informing lifestyle choices and potentially alerting us to potential risks before they manifest into serious conditions.

The democratisation of genetic information is changing the face of healthcare, shifting it from a largely reactive approach to a more proactive and preventive one.

In our exploration of ancestry, 23andMe creates bridges, joining individuals through genetic ties. It weaves a narrative that spans across time and geography, unravelling stories of migration, resilience, and connections that defy political and geographic boundaries. It allows us to celebrate our shared humanity while appreciating the beauty of our unique genetic stories.

Today, we have the tools to explore the universe within us. Anne Wojcicki's trailblazing vision has given us the keys to this universe, unlocking a world that blends science, history, and personal discovery in ways we could have only imagined.

In personal genomics, we are not just spectators but active participants. Through 23andMe, we're invited to shape our understanding of the past, engage with our present, and pave the way for a healthier, more aware future.

In a world that often seems vast and impersonal, Wojcicki brings us back to ourselves, reminding us of the profound truth that every single one of us holds a unique, intricate, and beautiful story within our DNA. It's a reminder that within us lie not just secrets of our past, but also keys to our future.

Anne Wojcicki's impact is a bold stroke of genius, a testament to the transformative power of curiosity and Innovation. And we, as beneficiaries of this Innovation, stand on the cusp of a new era in personal health, self-understanding, and human connection.

The effects of this genetic revolution extend beyond the individual. By broadening our understanding of our shared genetic heritage, we begin to perceive our collective identity from a new perspective. Our relationships, societies, cultures, and even nations are illuminated in a new light - a light that reveals our shared past and intertwined futures.

The power of 23andMe is indeed the power of knowledge. With every genetic report, we are offered a chance to see ourselves anew. We are given a language to articulate our existence. We gain an enhanced understanding of how genes shape us - from the colour of our eyes to the types of foods we prefer. We are reminded of how the dance of DNA can lead to a symphony of diversity, creating the endless array of unique individuals that populate our world.

Yet, this exploration is not without its challenges. There is an inherent responsibility that comes with the knowledge we glean from personal genomics. Wojcicki, the steward of this revolution, has always been a staunch advocate for ethical practises, ensuring the privacy and security of genetic data, and fostering an open dialogue about its implications.

23andMe is not just a company, but a platform for Education and advocacy, demystifying genomics and bridging the gap between science and society. It challenges us to be our own health advocates, to embrace our unique genetic narratives, and to participate in a global conversation about what it means to be human in the era of genomics.

As we continue to tread the path laid out by Wojcicki, we enter an era of unparalleled self-understanding and self-empowerment. Our collective voyage with 23andMe reminds us that, although our DNA is vast and complex, we are not merely observers of our genetic destiny. We are active participants, empowered by knowledge and driven by curiosity.

Genetics has been brought to light, made accessible and personal, reminding us that we are not only made of star stuff but are also keepers of ancient wisdom encoded in our very cells.

So, we write a new chapter in the book of human understanding, a chapter written with the letters of our DNA, shaped by the shared experiences of our past, and looking forward to the endless possibilities of our future. Here, every one of us has a unique story to tell, and thanks to 23andMe, we now have the tools to tell it. 23andMe is transforming the landscape, allowing us to take a more proactive and personalised approach to health. This is a true revolution, bringing the power of personalised medicine directly into our homes.

The potential impact is extraordinary. Imagine a world where we are no longer blindsided by illness. Where we can prepare, preempt, and perhaps even prevent certain health conditions based on our personal genetic code. This is the future that 23andMe and Anne Wojcicki are helping to shape, a future where we transition from reactive to proactive healthcare.

Moreover, the company's vast genetic database is a goldmine for scientific research. Collaborations with research institutions around the world are leading to groundbreaking discoveries, unravelling the complex interactions between genes, environment, and lifestyle. This treasure trove of data, harnessed ethically and responsibly, is accelerating the pace of genetic research, leading us towards new treatments, cures, and a better understanding of the intricate dance of our DNA.

It expands our understanding of ancestry and heritage, taking us on a fascinating journey through the corridors of history. By exploring our genetic roots, we gain a deeper connection to our ancestors, the cultures they came from, and the footprints they left behind.

These ancestral insights remind us that our human family is vast and interconnected. As we uncover our genetic tapestry, we realise the shared threads that bind us all, reinforcing a sense of unity amidst our diversity. Our individual stories are part of a saga of human migration, adaptation, and survival.

And yet, the story is not just about looking backward. It's about the shaping of things to come. By empowering individuals with their genetic information, by pushing the boundaries of scientific understanding, they are building the foundations for a new era. An era where genetics becomes a key tool for wellness and a lens to understand what makes us who we are.

Through this journey, we are challenged to redefine our perceptions of identity and humanity. They are inviting us to engage in a bold exploration of our deepest selves and encouraging us to become active participants in the global conversation about the future of genomics.

As we continue this adventure, one thing remains clear: the work of 23andMe and Anne Wojcicki has opened up a new frontier for humanity, one that brings us closer to answering some of the most fundamental questions about who we are and how we can live healthier, more informed lives.

One of the key principles we can glean from 23andMe's journey is the power of empowering personal discovery. The company has transformed the landscape of genetic testing by making complex genomic information accessible and understandable to all.

This principle urges us to reflect on our own work and consider how we can empower others through knowledge. It challenges us to break down barriers and make specialised information or expertise accessible and beneficial to a broader audience. By availing knowledge, we open doors to new opportunities, spark curiosity, and foster a sense of agency in those who seek to understand and navigate the complexities of our world. It's not just about science or genetics; it's about our divine spark, our psychic dynamite. What is in your hands? It is more than enough!

In a broader context, this principle prompts us to reflect on the unique knowledge or expertise we possess and consider how sharing it could positively impact others. Whether it's through Educational initiatives, open-source projects, or collaborative efforts, the act of sharing knowledge can lead to transformative outcomes. Just as 23andMe empowers individuals with genetic insights, we too can empower others by sharing valuable information and contributing to a collective reservoir of knowledge.

Beyond offering a service, 23andMe has created a thriving community of individuals on a shared journey of self-discovery. This community fosters connections, inspires conversations, and amplifies the collective experience of genetic exploration.

This principle invites us to explore how we can create communities around shared experiences or interests in our own initiatives. Building connections and fostering a sense of belonging can deepen engagement and lead to meaningful collaborations. Whether it's forming networks within our professional spheres, creating platforms for like-minded individuals to connect, or nurturing communities that embrace diversity, the power of community can enrich our lives and elevate the impact of our ideas.

As the Ideas Guy, we can reimagine the ways we share knowledge, bridge gaps, and ignite a collective passion for exploration and growth. It's more than genetics; it's about humanity thriving - as a direct result of our ideas.

## [ APPLYING THIS IN PRACTICE ]

**DEMOCRATISE COMPLEXITY**: Think about your life, your work, the passion that lights you up inside. Perhaps you're a designer, an engineer, or maybe you're teaching the next generation. Or maybe, just maybe, you're creating, innovating, pushing the boundaries as an entrepreneur. Each of us, in our own worlds, grapple with complex concepts, ideas that can sometimes feel like they're just out of reach.

But have you ever considered…what if you could break those ideas down? What if you could make your own field not just more understandable, but genuinely accessible to a wider audience? 23andMe has peeled back the layers, breaking down the barriers of understanding something as vast and intricate as one's own DNA. What a journey of discovery!

In every field, every walk of life, knowledge truly is power. The light of understanding illuminates the path ahead. What if you could take your knowledge, your unique understanding, and use it to empower others? Imagine the ripple effect. A wave of enlightenment, reaching out from you, from your work, to touch others. Teaching, writing, mentoring, or perhaps crafting resources to guide others.

And when people understand, when they have a clear picture of their own identities, they're equipped. Armed with knowledge, they can make decisions that reflect their true selves. They're no longer groping in the dark. They're navigating with a compass, with a map.

Now think of community, of connection. Think of bringing people together. As you embark on your journey - be it a project, a presentation, or a product launch - imagine how you can weave a tapestry of shared experience. Because it's in that shared journey, that mutual purpose, that people find connection, collaboration, and a sense of true belonging. It's the place where Innovation thrives.

Build a community centred on discovery. Take a moment to reflect: How can you democratise complexity in your own sphere? How can you create a community around a shared journey or purpose? How can you be a beacon, lighting the way for others?

Remember, it starts with you. It always starts with you.

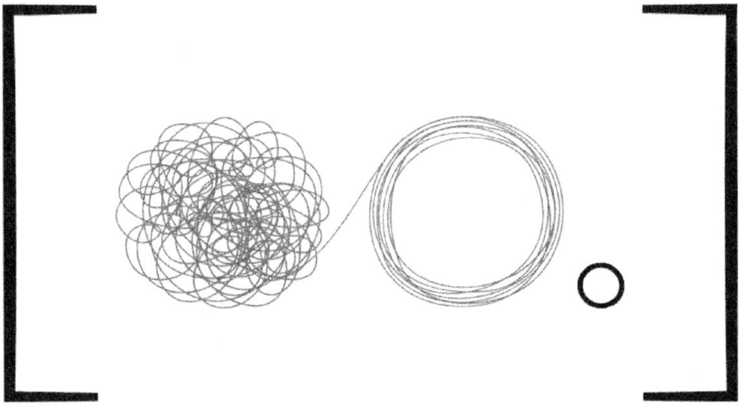

**DEMOCRATISE COMPLEXITY**

# [ PART II ]

# DIGITAL - MASTERING THE MATRIX

WHAT REALLY TURNS ME ON ABOUT TECHNOLOGY IS NOT JUST THE ABILITY TO GET MORE SONGS ON MP3 PLAYERS. THE REVOLUTION - THIS REVOLUTION - IS MUCH BIGGER THAN THAT. I HOPE, I BELIEVE. WHAT TURNS ME ON ABOUT THE DIGITAL AGE, WHAT EXCITES ME PERSONALLY, IS THAT YOU HAVE CLOSED THE GAP BETWEEN DREAMING AND DOING.

BONO

And now, we step onto the Digital highway, an electrifying dimension woven from ones and zeros, where ideas catch fire and spread with the speed of light. This is a universe pulsating with possibility, and it's yours to navigate.

Here, we find ourselves immersed in a universe where ideas are the stars, illuminating the vast Digital expanse, casting their glow upon unchartered territories. These are the ideas that shape our present, sculpt our future, and leave us breathless in their brilliance.

Digital - it's not just a word, it's a revolution. It's the language of our time, the rhythm of our lives, the melody that weaves through our every interaction. It's a world where dreams become realities, where ideas take form, where boundaries dissolve into the limitless expanse of possibility.

In this world, individuals morph into architects of the new, crafting ideas into structures of brilliance, painting the canvas of the Digital realm with the hues of imagination. They are the Ideas Guys, the visionaries, the pioneers, propelling us towards horizons yet unseen.

But here's the thing - Digital isn't just about technology, or algorithms, or even Innovation. It's about connection, communication, collaboration. It's about humanity, amplified. It's about understanding the human spirit and crafting experiences that touch hearts, spark curiosity, and ignite a sense of wonder.

The realm of Digital is a dance between technology and humanity. It's where the mechanical meets the emotional, where the logical intertwines with the creative. It's a symphony of opposites, harmoniously co-existing, creating a melody that echoes through the corridors of time.

In this section, we'll encounter those who are mastering the Digital matrix, those who see beyond the code and into the heart of what it means to be human. We'll explore their journeys, delve into their thought processes, their insights, their 'aha' moments. We'll learn from their trials, their triumphs, their tenacity. No one ever completes Digital. It's an Infinite Game as James Carse and Simon Sinek champion. The end is never the end.

We'll understand that the Digital world, as with Innovation, is not a destination, but a journey. It's not a fortress to be conquered, but a realm to be explored, an adventure to be embarked upon. It's a world that invites you, beckons you, to become the 'Ideas Guy,' to tap into your creativity, your ingenuity, your courage.

Just imagine it for a moment, the Digital space as a cosmic symphony. Every note, a pixel. Every harmony, a coded algorithm. Every crescendo, a burst of Innovation. Here, we find a matrix pulsating with potential, eager to be mastered.

Now, this symphony plays different tunes, and to understand them, we lean into various models, created by thought leaders and organisations at the forefront of Digital Innovation.

First on our trek, we encounter **GARTNER'S HYPE CYCLE**, a model that comes from the esteemed research and advisory firm Gartner. This model's rhythm is all about tracking the adoption and maturity of Digital technologies over time. It takes us on a journey from the peak of inflated expectations, where a new technology generates tremendous hype, to the trough of disillusionment, where reality sets in and initial expectations are challenged. But as we progress, we ascend the slope of enlightenment, where we learn how to effectively harness the technology's potential, leading us finally to the plateau of productivity, where the technology becomes an integrated part of our Digital landscape. In this model, we learn the importance of patience, understanding that the road to success in this space is often marked by ups and downs, and that embracing a measured and strategic approach is key to unlocking true value.

Next, we have the **CROSSING THE CHASM MODEL**, a compelling composition that comes from the renowned author and marketing expert Geoffrey Moore. This tune is all about understanding the critical moment of transition from early adopters to mainstream adoption. It's a song that acknowledges that not all customers are the same and that different approaches are needed to address the needs of diverse audiences. By focusing on the specific requirements and expectations of each group, businesses can create a harmonious Digital journey that resonates with a broader range of customers and leads to widespread adoption.

Then, let's delve into the **DIGITAL MATURITY MODEL**, a rhythm that comes from global management consulting firm McKinsey & Company. This model maps the growth and development of organisations in their Digital transformation journey. It takes us through stages of infancy, adolescence, and maturity, highlighting the importance of continuous learning, adaptability, and investment in Digital capabilities. It's a song that inspires businesses to keep pushing boundaries, reinventing the status quo, and fostering shared excitement throughout their Digital evolution. By embracing this model, organisations can navigate the complexities of the landscape and realise their full potential in the ever-changing Digital universe.

Finally, we step into the cadence of the **DIFFUSION OF INNOVATIONS MODEL**, a rhythm that guides us through the journey of how new ideas, products, or technologies spread and gain acceptance in the Digital landscape. This model, popularised by Everett Rogers, outlines the different stages that Innovations go through as they are adopted.

At the heart of this model lies the idea that not all individuals or businesses are quick to embrace change. Instead, adoption occurs in a bell-shaped curve, where innovators and early adopters lead the charge, followed by the early majority, late majority, and finally, the laggards. Each group plays a crucial role in the diffusion process, and understanding their needs, motivations, and concerns is key to successfully making a dent.

The Innovators, at the forefront of technology, thrive on the excitement of trying something new and experimental. They are the visionaries who shape the panorama, constantly seeking out cutting-edge ideas and technologies. Next come the Early Adopters, eager to embrace Innovations that align with their values and aspirations. These forward-thinking individuals and businesses play a pivotal role in driving early traction and spreading positive word-of-mouth. As the Innovation gains momentum, it enters the realm of the Early Majority - a pragmatic group that carefully assesses the benefits and risks before embracing change. Their adoption signals that the Innovation has proven its value and reliability. Following closely are the Late Majority, who are more sceptical of change and often require social proof and strong evidence of the Innovation's success before committing. Finally, there are the Laggards, who are resistant to change and tend to adopt new technologies only when they have become deeply embedded in the mainstream.

In this model, we learn the significance of tailoring our Digital strategies to suit the needs of each group. By providing early adopters with exclusive access and experiences, and by addressing the concerns of the majority, we can create a harmonious dance that draws more participants into the symphony of Innovation. As we navigate the stages of diffusion, we come to appreciate that the Digital realm is not just about the brilliance of ideas or the allure of technology; it's about understanding human behaviour and fostering an environment where Innovations can take root and flourish.

Dancing to these rhythms, everyone can master the Digital matrix, hear its symphony, and, in doing so, perhaps compose a melody of their own. A melody that's not just about selling a product or promoting a brand, but about sharing ideas, starting conversations, and making a difference. Let's step onto the Digital dancefloor and seize the moment, pirouetting our way through the possibilities that awaits.

Let's master the matrix. Let's venture into this wonderland of ideas, this universe of possibilities. Let's learn, let's explore, let's imagine.

WE NEED DIVERSITY OF THOUGHT IN THE WORLD TO FACE THE NEW CHALLENGES.

TIM BERNERS-LEE

# [ CHAPTER 5 ]

# WEAVING THE WEB

Imagine stepping into the labyrinth of the human mind. Thoughts intersect, ideas connect, and Innovation blossoms in every corner. This maze of inspiration and creativity is much like the World Wide Web, woven together by Sir Tim Berners-Lee. He didn't merely introduce a technology; he laid the framework for a Digital revolution that forever changed how we live, work, and interact.

Our journey into the enigmatic vortex of the web begins at a time when computers were isolated entities. The challenge that loomed ahead was about creating bridges between these disparate islands of data. The answer? The World Wide Web. This was the bridge that connected data islands into a single, interconnected continent of information.

Berners-Lee's invention was more than a tool for linking data; it redefined the way we think about and interact with information. He transformed data from static and unidirectional into a dynamic, interconnected network. The vision was grand - a world where everyone could contribute to and access the vast pool of human knowledge. And thus, the World Wide Web was conceived.

Who is Tim Berners-Lee, you may ask? Born to parents who were mathematicians and early computer programmers, Berners-Lee's roots were steeped in technology. Yet, his vision transcended beyond codes and algorithms. He dreamt of a world united through the power of shared information, and he had the technical prowess to translate this dream into reality.

Berners-Lee's Digital Innovation was akin to discovering a new dimension. His genius lay in orchestrating a symphony of existing technologies – the HTTP protocol, HTML language, and URL addresses. This trinity formed the fundamental pillars upon which the World Wide Web was built. Perhaps the most astonishing act of all was Berners-Lee's decision to offer the World Wide Web to the world, free of charge, and devoid of any restrictions. This act wasn't merely one of generosity; it was a testament of faith in the power of collective knowledge and the potential of humanity to create something remarkable together. It's this open nature that sets him apart.

The inception of the World Wide Web was akin to the discovery of a new world, a vast, untouched landscape ripe with possibilities. It began with Berners-Lee at the helm, leading the expedition, mapping out this terrain for the first time. The early days were marked by Innovation and uncertainty, as pioneers began to explore this new frontier. They built the first websites, erected the first servers, laying the foundation stones of what was to become our Digital home.

The first web pages, tiny Digital outposts in a vast Digital wilderness. Each one was a beacon of connectivity, a proof of concept that demonstrated the potential of this new world. Gradually, these isolated outposts started to grow, connecting with one another, forming networks, communities, cities in the technological topography.

Over time, the Web transformed from a technological curiosity to a global necessity. As it spread its tendrils across the world, it evolved into an intricate network, a sprawling metropolis of information and interaction. It became the World Wide Web we know today - a global platform for commerce, communication, creativity, and collaboration.

Today, the Web is more than just a collection of websites and servers; it's a reflection of our society, a mirror that captures our shared knowledge, our collective creativity, and our global connectivity. It's a marketplace bustling with commerce, a library housing the collective knowledge of humanity, a stage where voices from all over the world can be heard. It's a living, evolving entity, shaped by the interactions and contributions of its billions of users.

The World Wide Web is a testament to the power of connectivity. Each hyperlink is a Digital handshake, each server a crossroads where information highways intersect. In this interconnected landscape, ideas travel at the speed of light, Innovations are born from collaborations across continents, and everyone, everywhere, has the potential to contribute to the global conversation.

Berners-Lee's vision has truly taken root. The World Wide Web has grown beyond its creator's wildest dreams, yet it continues to evolve, expand, and inspire. It's a manifestation of our shared Digital potential, an enduring testament to the power of collective ideas. The Web is our global canvas, a platform where we can create, share, learn, and connect. And in this world, we are all explorers, pioneers, contributors, all part of the paragon of progress that is the World Wide Web.

The development of the Web is a saga, a tale of human ingenuity and synergy unfolding in the vast expanses of cyberspace. From its humble beginnings to its current global ubiquity, the Web serves as a beacon of our age, a testament to our innate drive to connect, share, and innovate. It's a testament to Berners-Lee's vision, a world woven together by invisible threads of connectivity, a Digital ritornello played on a global stage.

When Tim Berners-Lee first conceptualised the World Wide Web, he didn't envisage an exclusive platform for the tech-savvy few. No, he dreamed of a Digital canvas as vast as humanity itself, one that encapsulated the full spectrum of human experience. His vision was not for a restrictive or exclusive portal, but rather an open, egalitarian stage, where each individual, irrespective of their technical prowess, geographical location, or societal standing, could contribute their unique strokes.

Berners-Lee saw a world where a grandmother in a small French town, a teenager in bustling Tokyo, and a researcher in the heart of New York all had equal access to the same vast reservoir of information. He wanted the canvas to be a platform that could be navigated by anyone, anywhere - a space that embraced everyone, in all their diversity. It was about creating a democratic Digital universe where everyone - from the corners of rural India to the high-tech offices of Silicon Valley - had the same ability to access, utilise, and contribute to the web. It was about breaking down barriers, about ensuring that no person was denied the opportunity to learn, explore, and grow. This notion of inclusivity is central to his vision.

In essence, Berners-Lee envisaged the web as a vast vista that is influenced by countless voices, yet controlled by none. The nature of his creation is such that it rejects the dominance of any single entity, ensuring that the reins of the World Wide Web are held collectively, by the global community. This principle of decentralisation is like an ocean, where countless rivers contribute their waters, all pouring in from diverse regions, each with its unique characteristics. Each river flows freely into this ocean, and yet, no single river can lay claim to the ocean itself. The ocean is the collective result of all its tributaries, just as the web is the collective product of all its users.

By ensuring that no single entity could monopolise the web, Berners-Lee protected the diversity and freedom that are intrinsic to the Digital space. Decentralisation promotes an environment where voices from different corners of the world can be heard, where diverse ideas can coexist, clash, and lead to new understandings. This has allowed the web to grow organically, shaped by the countless interactions that occur within it each day.

This structure is not just about the physical distribution of servers or the technical protocols that allow computers to connect. It's about fostering an ecosystem of equality and freedom, one where no single voice can drown out the others. The web, as Berners-Lee envisioned it, is a genuinely democratic entity. It's a place where everyone can have a say, where the power to shape our Digital future is distributed among all its users.

In essence, this is a guarantee of seamless coexistence among multifaceted technologies, a promise of unity amidst the diversity. Imagine a bustling global megacity, its streets thrumming with the hum of myriad languages, its corners showcasing a mosaic of different cultures. Yet, at its core, this metropolis functions as a single entity, each of its diverse elements finding a way to coexist and acquiesce. This is the essence of interoperability in the World Wide Web, an intricate hive where different technologies - devices, software, networks, languages - communicate and interact harmoniously.

Berners-Lee instilled a universal standard into the web, ensuring that it serves as a common platform accessible to everyone, irrespective of their chosen technology. Whether you're using a smartphone in New York or a desktop computer in New Delhi, whether you're connected via fibre-optics or satellite, his vision guarantees that you can access and contribute to the same World Wide Web in a seamless manner.

Interoperability, in this sense, is not merely a technical feature; it's a commitment to Digital inclusivity, a testament to the World Wide Web's identity as a tool for universal collaboration. By embracing different technologies and fostering their harmonious interaction, Berners-Lee's principle of user interoperability is a catalyst that drives the Digital world towards unity, towards a shared experience for all.

So the web is an intricate tapestry. Each thread represents a different idea, a different story, a different voice. Together, they form a stunning picture, an interconnected narrative of humanity's shared wisdom. And this, this is the masterpiece composed by Tim Berners-Lee.

But our odyssey doesn't end here. It's time for us to take the reins, to be active participants in this Digital tapestry, not just passive observers.

## [ APPLYING THIS IN PRACTICE ]

**PRIORITISE INCLUSIVITY:** Whether you're developing a new app, writing your next blog post or creating the next YouTube sensation, remember to make it accessible for everyone. Whether it's using clear and simple language, incorporating accessibility features for differently-abled individuals, or ensuring your platform is device-agnostic, remember: the web was built on the premise of universal access. So, respect the principle of decentralisation. In the Digital realm, this means acknowledging and supporting the right to open access and free speech. But, it also means acting responsibly, understanding that our online actions have real-world consequences and that a world where some win at the expense of others is a world where everyone loses.

We don't just traverse the Digital labyrinth, we become its architects, its caretakers. We take up the mantle from Berners-Lee, continuing the legacy of the internet, contributing our threads to the ever-evolving quilt. It's our shared heritage, a testament to our collective ingenuity. It must remain a vibrant, inclusive, and open space for generations to come.

Tim Berners-Lee has composed the cornerstone piece. It is our turn to contribute our melodies, our ideas, our Innovations. Every corner turned, every path taken, reveals something new, something unexpected. It's a testament to the infinite potential of human creativity, to our shared desire to connect, to learn, to grow. As we navigate this Digital matrix, our guiding stars, leading us towards a future that's as beautifully diverse and interconnected as the web itself, need to be clear.

Take a moment to ponder: How can you prioritise inclusivity in your Digital domain? How can you create a space where unity comes from diversity? How can you be open in your affairs? How do you contribute to this vast, interconnected network? What will be your thread in the tapestry?

The beauty lies in the journey itself, in the new pathways we forge, in the connections we create, and the knowledge we share. This is our legacy to the future.

As you ponder these questions, remember that you're part of something much larger, a global orchestra playing a grand symphony, composed by Berners-Lee, and continued by each one of us. Let's ensure that this Digital symphony continues to resonate with the principles of openness, inclusivity, and collaboration. Let's continue to weave, to make the web a testament to our shared dreams, our shared wisdom, our shared humanity.

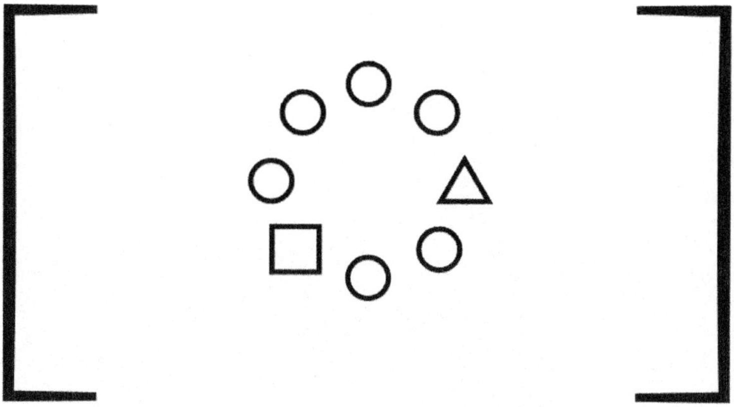

# PRIORITISE INCLUSIVITY

I'M JUST INTERESTED IN BUILDING A COMPANY THAT DOESN'T NECESSARILY CHANGE LIVES BUT ADAPTS PEOPLE'S BEHAVIOUR.

**DANIEL EK**

# [ CHAPTER 6 ]

# SOUNDS OF CHANGE

We're stepping into the dynamic realm of sound and silence - the intricate design of Digital music streaming etched into the harmonious symphony of our lives. It's a journey into the depths of our sonic landscape, where each note holds the echoes of our past, the rhythm of our present, and the harmonies of our future. We're decoding our soundtrack, and our guide is Daniel Ek, the innovative force behind Spotify, a company that transformed the music industry and shaped how we listen to music.

Imagine a time, not so long ago, when the language of music was limited by physical boundaries - the records, CDs, and radio stations that set the tempo of our lives. We could choose our soundtrack, define our style, but the immense library of global sound, the one embedded in every corner of our planet, remained unheard. That was until Ek and his team stepped onto the scene. They dared to dream of a world where every melody, every rhythm, every beat could be made accessible, where the spectrum of sound could be shared, not in isolated corners, but in a globally connected orchestra.

Ek, with his background in technology and a knack for entrepreneurship, co-founded Spotify in 2006. With a portmanteau from the words "spot" and "identify," the company embarked on a mission to create a platform that would make the wide spectrum of global music a part of everyday life. They crafted a simple yet revolutionary application that could unlock the world's music library.

The innovative thinking is profound: log in to your account, search for a song, album, or artist, and press play. Suddenly, the complex language of music is transformed into a shared soundtrack, easily accessed by any curious ear. The once fragmented world of music has been made whole, within the reach of our fingertips.

With the rise of Spotify, music is no longer confined to record stores; it is now a part of our Digital ecosystem. We can explore genres, discover new artists, and engage with the universal language of sound in a way that was unimaginable a few decades ago. It is like holding a radio to our very being, not just broadcasting our favourite tunes but revealing the essence of who we are.

Ek invites us on an extraordinary journey, navigating the vast oceans of our sonic heritage. We can experience the harmonies of different cultures, understand the evolution of genres, and discover how melodies and beats influence our emotions and thoughts. We share and corroborate, supporting each other with our preferences and playlists. The sound of a generation, or the generations.

With Spotify, our music is no longer a static collection but a dynamic playlist of our past, present, and future. We find ourselves a part of a larger symphony, connecting with artists and melodies we never knew existed, yet they have become a part of us. Curated to keep you connected. From the known to the unknown with consummate ease and seamless mixing - no DJ required.

By unlocking our audial secrets, Ek didn't just provide a fascinating exploration into our musical preferences, he offered a tool for self-expression, a guide to the soundtrack of our lives.

Spotify is more than a streaming service; it is a revolution in our understanding of ourselves. Under Ek's leadership, the company has changed the narrative of music, entertainment, and culture. He's shown that the world's melodies aren't solely for musicians to compose, but are open to everyone's listening pleasure.

In the story of Spotify, we see the power of innovative thinking and the Digital revolution combined. The audio landscape, once a secluded realm, has become a shared exploration, an open dialogue, a personal encounter with the heart of our expression. This extraordinary journey marks a new epoch in human understanding. It is as if a new frequency has been tuned in, allowing us to look into the complexities of sound, uncovering the invisible ties that bind us through music.

We've stepped into a new world. A world where we've unshackled ourselves from the confines of physical storage - no more towering stacks of CDs, no more overflowing music files eating up the precious memory on our devices. This is the world where music, in all its infinite splendour, exists somewhere unseen, untouched, yet always within reach. This is the world of the cloud, a celestial sphere of sounds. And it was Spotify that opened the gates to this magnificent arena.

It's like a magic trick, isn't it? We reach out, press play, and the music flows. But where is it coming from? Not from our devices, no, but from somewhere out there. Directly from servers, songs come streaming into our lives. It's as if the melodies are plucked from the ether itself, instantly at our beck and call, no delay, no resistance.

It's an extraordinary paradigm shift. With Spotify, we're not owners of individual tracks or albums, as we used to be. Instead, we're granted an all-access pass to a boundless library of music. Imagine that. Every genre, every artist, every beat, every note - they're all right there, not in our hands, but at our fingertips.

It's like carrying a gramophone the size of a world in our pockets, yet as light as a feather. This isn't just convenience, it's freedom - the freedom to explore, to discover, to immerse ourselves in the music we love, anywhere, anytime, without limits.

That's the beauty of Spotify's Innovation. It's not just about music; it's about transforming how we experience it. It's about breaking down barriers, erasing boundaries, and bringing the astral sphere of sound into our daily lives. With Spotify, the world doesn't just listen to music; we live it, we breathe it, in all its resplendent glory, every single day.

The Spotify platform enables listeners to explore the diverse landscape of music from the familiar to the unknown. The algorithms behind its "Discover Weekly" playlists expose us to new sounds and artists, encouraging us to venture out of our comfort zones. It's like having a personal DJ, carefully curating tunes that reflect our mood, preferences, and perhaps our unexplored musical curiosity.

Through the lens of technology and music, Ek has shown that Innovation is not merely about disruption, but about fostering deeper connections and understanding. The essence of music—its capacity to convey emotions, tell stories, and transcend barriers—is made even more potent by Spotify's power to share it widely.

Ek's vision extends beyond music. He seeks to create a holistic audio platform, where not only music but podcasts, audiobooks, and other forms of audio entertainment are readily available. It's an ongoing powerhouse of ideas, expanding the boundaries of our lived experience.

The transformation of how we access and experience music is only the beginning. The data from our listening habits, collected and analysed, provides a unique insight into our collective mood, trends, and social changes. Spotify's annual "Wrapped" feature, which gives a snapshot of our music preferences throughout the year, is a mirror reflecting our changing society.

We are living in the age of streaming, the age of Spotify. A time when our connection with music is as limitless as our imagination.

Ek has started a sonic revolution, a crescendo that continues to rise. His story, much like a captivating song, invites us to listen, to explore, and to appreciate the profound impact of music on our lives. Through his pioneering efforts with Spotify, Ek has changed our rhythm, making the world move to a different beat.

And so, as we take this journey with Ek, we experience the sounds of change, the melody of transformation. His tale is a testament to the power of Digital, the beauty of music, and the incredible potential of technology to change the way we experience the world.

Imagine yourself as the visionary leader at the forefront of your next groundbreaking project. Whether it's a pioneering tech startup, a cutting-edge software update, or an innovative Digital marketing Strategy, your mission extends beyond mere creation. It transcends the boundaries of novelty and ventures into the realm of crafting meaningful connections.

Just as Spotify beautifully illustrates, Digital success is an art of weaving an intricate web of connections that unite us all, interlinking our individual experiences and preferences to create a profound and shared journey.

At the heart of Spotify's success lies the genius of Ek, who grasped the essence of his platform was a symphony of interconnectedness. It's about orchestrating an experience that resonates with each listener, weaving together the harmonies of their unique tastes, passions, and emotions. In the grand brocade of Spotify, every individual finds themselves entwined, their musical voyage aligned with a global chorus of shared moments.

This profound insight reflects a deeper understanding - that the true power of Digital lies not solely in its technological prowess, but in its capacity to foster connections and build communities. Digital Innovation becomes an enabler of shared experiences, a platform for dialogue, and a medium for forging bonds that transcend geographical boundaries. Just like the delicate threads of a spider's web, Digital connections reach far and wide, glistening with the brilliance of unity and diversity entwined. As you embark on your own Digital journey, take inspiration from Spotify's interconnected symphony and recognise that your Innovations are a means of creating bridges between hearts, minds, and cultures, igniting a harmonious symphony of shared aspirations and collective dreams.

As you embark on your own Digital journey, remember to take inspiration from Ek's spirit of exploration. The Ideas Guy thrives on the willingness to break free from constraints, to envision a broader landscape of possibilities, and to set sights on creating something beyond the expected. Don't be confined by the limits of your initial idea.

Today, pause and reflect on your Digital expedition. Consider how you can build deeper connections, foster more engaging experiences, and tell stories that resonate with your audience. Embrace the notion that the canvas is vast and open for your imagination to roam freely. Dream bigger dreams, and let your passion guide you towards uncharted territories.

Every step holds the potential to make an impact. So, seize the opportunity to push the boundaries, to explore new avenues, and to craft experiences that leave an indelible mark. Just as Ek's Spotify expanded beyond music, your Digital journey can unfold in unforeseen directions, revealing new realms of possibility. Embrace the challenge, embrace the dream, and let your creative spirit soar. The universe awaits your touch, and it's time to make your mark on this grand symphony.

# [ APPLYING THIS IN PRACTICE ]

**HARNESS THE POWER OF STORIES:** Your life, your work, your passion…whatever it is that ignites that spark within you, consider this: what if you could bridge the gap between individuals and experiences? What if you could bring forth a narrative that sings from the data, and use it to connect, to make a difference?

Spotify uses music as the threads that weave together stories of artists, cultures, and emotions. They saw the potential in data, recognised the tales it could tell, and used it to connect people with music they may not have discovered otherwise. They've created a community that celebrates diversity, unity, and the simple joy of music.

You, too, could create a symphony from your data. Be it in Education, engineering, design or entrepreneurship, data is an invaluable asset. See the untold stories in your data. Let it guide you, inspire you, help you win. Maybe it's trends that could lead to better user experience, or gaps that call for more resources. Maybe it's success stories that inspire and motivate, or feedback that helps you grow.

But don't stop at the stories. Explore the unexplored. Venture beyond the current limits of your vision. So, how can you stretch your vision? Is there a new feature that can enhance your product, or a novel market waiting for your service? Maybe there's a new method to bring a fresh perspective to your work. Challenge the boundaries of your thinking, and let your vision soar.

Think of the potential. Imagine the power of an interconnected community, inspired and united by shared experiences. Reflect on the stories waiting to be discovered in your data, and the possibilities that lay beyond your current boundaries.

If you're trying to convey a concept about marriage or love to your students, tell your story of meeting, falling in love and leverage the data of your wedding album, perhaps. Or, if you're launching the next service from your business, wrap in a story of how it helped someone just like them. The narrative threads itself into the fabric of understanding, turning abstract ideas into tangible emotions. Stories are not mere decorations; they are the connective tissue between intention and impact. They make the impersonal personal, the complex relatable, and the forgettable unforgettable. A well-told narrative doesn't just inform—it transforms, guiding your audience to see themselves within the arc of your tale and, ultimately, within the solution you offer.

How will you harness the power of connection, story, and exploration in your work, in your life, today?

**HARNESS THE POWER OF STORIES**

DON'T LET YOURSELF MAKE EXCUSES FOR NOT DOING THE THINGS YOU WANT TO DO.

**SAM ALTMAN**

# [ CHAPTER 7 ]

# OPEN THE DOOR

We're traversing the intricate neural pathways of artificial intelligence - the mosaic of code, algorithms, and machine learning that shapes our increasingly Digital lives. This is a journey into the depths of our data-driven landscape, where each line of code and each data point forms the echoes of our past, the rhythm of our present, and the harmonies of our future. We're deciphering our Digital dialogues, and our guide is Sam Altman, the forward-thinking force behind OpenAI, a company that's revolutionising the field of AI.

As with Musk in Chapter 3, depending on when you're reading this, you might be tempted to dismiss Altman as either hero or villain, prophet or profiteer. The headlines may paint him in stark contrasts, his actions dissected through the lens of admiration or suspicion. But to reduce him to a binary is to overlook the symphony he conducts—a complex arrangement of ethics, Innovation, and ambition. Altman's vision stretches beyond the surface, inviting us to grapple with the profound questions AI raises about humanity's role in shaping its own destiny. Like Musk, he provokes, he polarises, but most importantly, he pushes us to confront the edges of possibility.

Take a moment to imagine a time, not so long ago, when the landscape of artificial intelligence was something of a wild frontier – exciting, yes, but also daunting, complex, and riddled with challenges. AI was seen as an elusive, distant future – a dream that was just out of our reach. That was until Altman and his team stepped onto the scene. They dared to dream of a world where the power of AI could be harnessed for the greater good, where the potential of this technology could be realised, not just by a select few, but by humanity at large.

Altman, with his experience in technology and an intuition for entrepreneurship, co-founded OpenAI in 2015. With a name that hints at the organisation's core ethos — openness, transparency, and accessibility — OpenAI set out on a mission to ensure that artificial general intelligence (AGI) benefits all of humanity. They embarked on the development of highly autonomous systems that outperform humans at most economically valuable work, all the while placing a key emphasis on long-term safety and technical leadership.

The innovative thinking here is both profound and radical: construct an AI system, yes, but do so with the community at heart. OpenAI isn't a mere set of algorithms confined to a silo; it's a global undertaking, an inclusive mission to ensure this powerful technology doesn't harm humanity or concentrate power unduly.

OpenAI's journey is one of exploration and navigation, guiding us through the vast universe of artificial intelligence. They've brought forth groundbreaking projects such as GPT-3 and -4, language models that use machine learning to produce human-like text, and Dactyl, a robotic hand taught to solve a Rubik's cube. These endeavours illuminate the myriad possibilities of AI, showing us a future where machine learning, code, and human ingenuity intersect in harmonious synergy.

And Altman's vision is not limited to the realm of AI. His broader ambition is to ensure a safe and beneficial AGI. This approach involves not only advancing AI technology but also developing robust safety measures and advocating for broad distribution of benefits. Through this holistic perspective, OpenAI looks beyond the binary code to consider the wider societal impact of their work.

In the narrative of OpenAI, we witness the convergence of innovative thinking and the Digital revolution. The world of artificial intelligence, once a realm of mystery, has become an open frontier, a shared journey, a collective endeavour. This extraordinary voyage marks a new chapter in human understanding. It's as if a new frequency has been tuned in, a new language has been learned, allowing us to delve into the complexities of AI, and uncovering the invisible ties that bind us through data.

OpenAI's mission, led by Altman, signals a new era of ideas. It's not just about developing powerful AI; it's about ensuring that power is used responsibly and equitably. Through OpenAI, Altman invites us to embark on an extraordinary journey, one that explores the vast potential of artificial intelligence and the intricate networks of data that shape our world. His vision is a beacon that lights the way, guiding us towards a future where AI benefits all, and where the promise of this technology is finally realised.

The stage was being set in the year 2021, a time when the world was just beginning to grasp the awe-inspiring possibilities of AI. Right there, at the heart of this revolution, sat OpenAI, which introduced a deep learning model named DALL-E, a Digital artist extraordinaire. This creative genius could sketch into existence the imaginations articulated in words. It crafted stunning visuals from natural language descriptions, unveiling a realm of possibilities that sent ripples of excitement across the globe.

DALL-E was like a magician, pulling out of its hat a wide array of images, from the strikingly realistic to the utterly fantastical. Imagine having a portrait that's realistic down to the last detail, or perhaps a landscape that seems plucked straight from the wildest corners of your dreams. DALL-E was capable of creating all this and more, bringing to life a vibrant symphony of visuals painted with the strokes of artificial intelligence. The world had seen many Digital artists, but DALL-E stood apart, creating with a unique brush of deep learning. It was the dawn of a new age, an age where language was no longer confined to verbal and written communication; it had broken free into the realm of imagery.

Fast forward to November 2022, a time when the world was eagerly awaiting the next big Innovation from OpenAI. This time, the spotlight was on a new entrant named ChatGPT, a chatbot built on the robust foundation of GPT-3.5. In an uncanny semblance to human conversation, ChatGPT communicated with seamless fluency. The conversations it held were so convincingly human-like that the lines between artificial and natural conversation blurred. It became a popular tool across diverse fields. Customer service found a new assistant, Education discovered a new way of imparting knowledge, and entertainment opened up a whole new realm of possibilities.

As we moved into the early days of 2023, a big announcement reverberated across the world. Tech giant Microsoft declared an investment in OpenAI to the tune of $10 billion. Such a staggering amount of money rocketed OpenAI's value to $29 billion, placing it among the most esteemed AI startups in the world. OpenAI was no longer just a player; it was now a titan leading the charge into the uncharted territories of artificial intelligence.

Now, imagine the scene unfolding in March 2023. OpenAI, not one to rest on its laurels, announced the release of a new Application Programming Interface (API). This wasn't just any API, it was a magic key designed to unlock the secrets of ChatGPT and other OpenAI models, making them accessible to developers worldwide. This API held the promise to revolutionise the way AI-powered applications were built, potentially leading to a new era of innovative applications powered by the potent technology of OpenAI. Plugins, open-source, developer integrations - these all became possible overnight.

And then November 2023, as we saw ChatGPT celebrate just its first birthday, there was a crazy weekend. On Friday 17th November, the board dismissed Altman due to purported issues with transparency, leading to the resignation of company president Greg Brockman in response. The following day, both attempted to persuade the board for reinstatement, but their efforts were unsuccessful in influencing the board's decision. There were absolute shockwaves all over the world. Social media went crazy. Some analysts reckoned that $45 billion was wiped off Microsoft's valuation in response (they owned 49% of OpenAI at this point).

By Sunday, both had secured positions with Microsoft, to pursue their advancements in AI technology. By Monday, a significant 95% of OpenAI's workforce was contemplating a move to Microsoft as well. Late on Tuesday, OpenAI declared, "An agreement has been preliminarily reached for Sam Altman to resume his role as CEO of OpenAI with a restructured initial board." It's like an episode of Eastenders on speed! Despite the tumultuous events, the potential consequences for the AI sector could have been more alarming had the situation resulted in a widespread departure of OpenAI staff. This seemed likely just days earlier. A substantial migration of talent from OpenAI to Microsoft would signify a shift from a company originally focused on AI safety concerns to one less visibly committed to these principles.

That said, the narrative of OpenAI is a story of ceaseless Innovation, of boundaries being pushed and new territories being explored. It's a journey marked by breakthroughs and triumphs, a testament to human creativity and technological prowess. OpenAI's relentless drive is taking us into a future where the lines between reality and imagination blur, where artificial intelligence isn't just a tool, but an integral part of our lives. It's a thrilling ride, a story that's still unfolding, a journey that promises to take us to destinations yet unknown. With OpenAI at the helm, the future of AI is not just an exciting prospect, it's a vibrant reality that's unfolding right before our eyes.

Altman has started an AI revolution, a crescendo that continues to rise. His story, much like a compelling algorithm, invites us to engage, to explore, and to appreciate the profound impact of artificial intelligence on our lives. Through his pioneering efforts with OpenAI, Altman is shaping a future that moves to a different beat, one that's driven by the rhythm of Innovation and the harmony of shared benefits. And in this future, the possibilities are as limitless as our imagination.

While others may have perceived AI as a mere tool or a fleeting trend, OpenAI saw something much more profound – a vast constellation of possibilities that could reshape the very fabric of Digital technology. They recognised that AI wasn't just about automating tasks or mimicking human behaviour; it had the potential to transcend these limitations and become a catalyst for a new Digital era.

With a relentless pursuit of knowledge and an insatiable curiosity, OpenAI harnessed the power of data and algorithms to unlock AI's true potential. They explored the intricacies of language, the nuances of human thought, and the complexities of problem-solving, unveiling the hidden gems that lay beneath the surface of Digital possibilities.

Their journey was more than just technical advancements; it was a philosophical exploration of the relationship between humans and machines, the ethical implications of AI, and the impact of their creations on society. They dared to ponder the uncharted territories of AI, embracing the challenges and uncertainties that came with it.

As a result, their creations, like Chat-GPT models, emerged not just as cutting-edge tools, but as envoys of AI's boundless capabilities. These models could communicate, understand, and generate language with an eerie human-like fluency, elevating AI from a mere tool to a companion on the journey of human knowledge.

The legacy of OpenAI's ability to uncover the hidden echoes throughout the modern world. Their breakthroughs in AI are inspiring a new generation of innovators, urging them to peer beyond the immediate and envision the untapped potential of technology. As the world advances further into the age of AI, OpenAI's vision will continue to guide us, illuminating the path to discoveries that were once veiled in the shadows.

They beckon us to explore the uncharted territories and embark on audacious quests. It's a testament to the power of curiosity, the beauty of exploration, and the transformative potential of Innovation. OpenAI's unique gift? The art of seeing beyond, the magic of uncovering the hidden, and the boundless possibilities that await those who dare to dream.

Altman didn't keep his AI technologies isolated; instead, he sought synergy with scientific and technology communities worldwide, fostering a collective push towards a shared Digital future. By engaging in partnerships and open dialogue, they transformed AI from a niche specialty into a central pillar of our identities. 100,000,000 users in just two months.

In this age of interconnectedness, collaboration is the key to unlocking Innovation. Altman's approach of opening their doors and minds to others allowed a global community to contribute and enrich the AI landscape with diverse perspectives. This collaborative spirit not only accelerated AI advancements but also solidified AI's role in various sectors, making it an inseparable part of our everyday experiences.

Embracing collaboration and diverse perspectives will lead us to shape a future where technology, humanity, and AI harmoniously coexist, creating a horizon ripe with endless opportunities.

Sam Altman's influence on OpenAI underscores the significance of embracing the human element in the realm of AI and technology. While the world witnessed an AI revolution, Altman recognised that human values and ethics must be deeply embedded in these Innovations. OpenAI didn't just develop AI for its own sake; they emphasised the responsible use of AI and the necessity of ensuring it aligns with human needs and aspirations.

Their pursuit of beneficial AI isn't just about creating sophisticated algorithms; it's about understanding the impact of these technologies on individuals and society as a whole. OpenAI's culture of ethical reflection challenges us to consider the human consequences of our Digital endeavours, steering us towards a path of responsible Innovation.

In our own Digital ventures, let us heed Sam Altman's call to embrace the human element. As we explore technology's vast potential, let's always keep humanity's well-being at the forefront. By weaving human values into the fabric of our Innovations, we can create a Digital universe that serves not only our technological aspirations but also the greater good of society. The legacy of OpenAI reminds us that true progress is achieved when we integrate the brilliance of technology with the warmth of the human spirit, crafting an online world that uplifts, empowers, and cherishes us all.

# [ APPLYING THIS IN PRACTICE ]

**UNLEASH COLLECTIVE GENIUS:** to use the phrase coined by the wonderful Linda Hill. Embrace the Ideas Guy within you not as an isolated genius but as a conductor, orchestrating a symphony of diverse minds. Surround yourself with a team that brings a rich tapestry of skills, perspectives, and experiences, for it is in the harmony of collaboration that true Digital breakthroughs are born.

OpenAI and Sam Altman's journey exemplify the might of collective genius. From the brilliance of individual researchers to the magic woven by a collaborative community, they harnessed the strengths of many to transform AI into an awe-inspiring reality. Similarly, in your Digital endeavours, recognise that no one person holds all the answers. Empower your team to contribute their unique ideas, to challenge and uplift one another, and to find common ground in a shared vision.

Altman said, "You really want a company full of missionaries, not mercenaries," and that makes a lot of sense. Missionaries serve on purpose and because of love; mercenaries do a job because of reward. Know the difference. Be the difference.

Let diversity be your guiding star. Embrace differences of opinion, for it is in the interplay of contrasting perspectives that novel solutions emerge. Just as a rainbow owes its splendour to the convergence of vibrant hues, your Digital projects will thrive when you welcome and honour diverse viewpoints. The key is in the name, *Open*AI.

Foster an environment where all voices are heard, and each individual is empowered to contribute their best. Encourage the sharing of ideas, both big and small, for even the tiniest spark can ignite a blaze of IDEAS. Celebrate collaboration as a journey of discovery, where each step unveils new possibilities and leads you closer to groundbreaking achievements.

As the conductor of collective genius, you have the extraordinary privilege of guiding your team towards the stars. Your role is not just to lead but also to listen, not just to command but also to collaborate. As you unleash the potential of collective genius, you will see your Digital ideas transcend boundaries, soar to new heights, and shape the world in ways previously unimagined.

So, embrace the IDEAS Guy within you, not as an individual genius, but as a conductor of collective brilliance. Together, let us compose a symphony of Innovation, where the voices of many intertwine, creating melodies that resonate in the hearts and minds of a global audience. The journey is more rewarding when we embark together, hand in hand, united by the pursuit of knowledge, the joy of discovery, and the dream of a brighter Digital future.

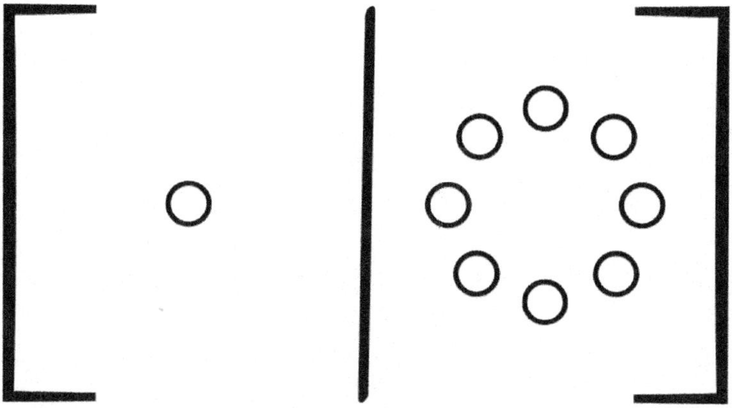

# UNLEASH COLLECTIVE GENIUS

AN ENTREPRENEUR IS SOMEONE WHO JUMPS OFF A CLIFF, AND BUILDS A PLANE ON HIS WAY DOWN.

REID HOFFMAN

# [ CHAPTER 8 ]

# OPEN THE DOOR

We find ourselves in the world of Reid Hoffman, where geographic boundaries and time zones aren't seen as insurmountable obstacles, but as challenges that can be overcome by the power of connection. Hoffman, co-founder of LinkedIn, envisioned a professional world united not by geography, but by common goals, shared knowledge, and mutual growth opportunities. The result of his vision was LinkedIn, a Digital platform that's more than just a networking site–it's a testament to the power of human connection in the age of technology.

Picture standing on a mountain top, surveying the world before you. Below, there are valleys and chasms, symbolising the separation between professionals worldwide. Between an entrepreneur in Sydney and a software engineer in San Francisco, between a marketing specialist in London and a human resources manager in Singapore, there are not just physical distances, but also differences in culture, industry norms, and business practises. Yet, in these differences, Hoffman saw potential. He saw the chance to build bridges – not physical ones, but bridges built on shared professional interests, on mutual respect, and on the common desire to learn, grow, and succeed.

Launched in 2002, LinkedIn began as an idea, a spark in the minds of Hoffman and his co-founders. It was a vision of a platform that could transform professional networking, taking it beyond exchanging business cards at corporate events and towards building meaningful, mutually beneficial relationships. The idea was to create a Digital space where professionals could showcase their achievements, share their knowledge, and connect with like-minded individuals. But for Hoffman, LinkedIn wasn't just about finding people – it was about creating a community.

In the beginning, LinkedIn was a seedling that needed to be carefully nurtured. Hoffman and his team understood that for this platform to truly make a difference, it had to offer something unique. It had to go beyond the traditional paradigms of networking and job seeking and provide a space where professionals could also learn, collaborate, and grow. And so, they put their efforts into building a platform that was designed to foster engagement, encourage knowledge sharing, and facilitate collaboration.

As LinkedIn grew, it started to reshape the professional landscape. No longer were careers limited by the city you grew up in or who your parents knew. LinkedIn was not just breaking down barriers – it was redefining what it meant to be a professional in the Digital age. As the world of LinkedIn unfolded under the aegis of Hoffman, we bore witness to a profusion of features blooming on the platform, each catering to different professional cravings and requirements. Pulse, for example, beat into being, creating a sanctuary for thought pioneers, a space where members could scatter their wisdom and dive headfirst into swirling currents of discourse, crossing paths with various industry topics. This offered the LinkedIn denizens more than just an opportunity to learn from the wisdom of others – it provided a platform where they could echo their unique voices across their fields of expertise.

In another stride towards fostering growth and learning, LinkedIn unveiled its Learning platform – an ocean of online courses spanning a staggering array of fields, a testament to the platform's deep-seated commitment to nurturing ceaseless learning and growth among its members. Consider the power of LinkedIn Groups. These communities within the platform have given professionals a space to connect over shared interests, industry trends, or professional challenges. They provide a sense of camaraderie and shared purpose, reminiscent of the connections we crave in the physical world but seamlessly translated into the Digital space.

Similarly, the platform's features like "Kudos" and "Skill Endorsements" have added a human touch to the Digital experience, allowing us to appreciate and validate each other's skills and achievements in a public, appreciative way. These features not only facilitate professional growth but also foster a culture of mutual recognition and respect.

The tectonic shift that LinkedIn brought about in recruitment practises remains unmatched. With the advent of LinkedIn Jobs, the very landscape of hiring and job seeking was reshaped. Businesses and potential candidates found themselves at a juncture where they could connect directly, extending the reach of opportunities far beyond the confines of immediate networks or demographic constraints. Further, the platform's marriage of job matching with analytics brought into alignment the skills of a candidate and the requirements of a job, ushering in a new era of successful hires and content employees.

Hoffman's vision transcended the boundaries of professional networking and recruitment. Under his watch, LinkedIn blossomed into a bustling marketplace for business-to-business marketing. The introduction of features such as LinkedIn Ads and Sponsored Content added new dimensions to the platform. With its treasure trove of rich professional data, LinkedIn unlocked the potential to deliver targeted advertising, forging a path towards more impactful B2B marketing campaigns.

The influence of LinkedIn, it would seem, has permeated beyond the realm of individual professionals, embedding itself in the very DNA of the business world. For companies, it has emerged as an indispensable tool to carve out their brand, magnetise talent, market their offerings, and gather critical industry insights.

The world of LinkedIn is more than a network of professionals; it's a platform that mirrors the global business ecosystem in the Digital era. It's where connections become collaborations, where insights turn into Innovations, and where opportunities are just a click away. Hoffman's creation is not just a website; it's a testament to the potential of technology when harnessed with a vision to uplift and empower.

As we marvel at this, let's pause for a moment to appreciate the intricacies of its construction. Every feature, every update, every algorithm was shaped by a team of individuals committed to Hoffman's vision. It's a testament to the power of teamwork - the collective effort it takes to build something that impacts millions of lives worldwide.

Hoffman's vision continues to thrive. LinkedIn may have been bought by Microsoft in 2016, but its core principles remain intact. It continues to connect professionals, facilitate learning, and drive Innovation, ever true to its founder's mission.

Through LinkedIn, Hoffman didn't just give us a platform; he gave us a compass to navigate the professional landscape. LinkedIn's impact on the professional world is immeasurable. It has broken down barriers, transformed recruitment practises, and given professionals a voice and a platform to be heard. It shows the potential of technology when harnessed with a clear vision and a commitment to connection and collaboration.

As we look to the future, one thing is clear - the Digital journey is a journey of connection. Whether it's through platforms like LinkedIn or through our personal and professional networks, connection is at the heart of the Digital experience.

In a world often divided by differences, Hoffman and LinkedIn remind us of the power of connection, of mutual respect, and of shared learning. They remind us that we are not alone. We are part of a global community, a collective force shaping the future of work, business, and society.

Remember, the key is not to see Digital tools as mere utilities, but as platforms for connection, collaboration, and growth. Whether you're an entrepreneur, an executive, a job seeker, or a thought leader, embracing the power of connection can unlock a world of opportunities.

Today, LinkedIn is more than just a platform. It's a global professional community, a vibrant ecosystem that thrives on the exchange of ideas, on the mutual support of its members, and on the shared commitment to professional growth. It's a space where the static becomes dynamic, where the professional self is not just about past achievements, but also about current contributions and future aspirations.

LinkedIn shows us that the professional journey is not a solo expedition but a community trek. It emphasises the importance of mutual support, of learning from each other, and of growing together. It encourages us to see our peers not as competitors, but as companions on our professional journey. Networks don't need to be fake pitches, feigned handshakes, and faux giggles at the local hotel at 6am every Thursday morning. Nor is it a boys club where backs get scratched along with egos and pocket linings. Be gone with the insincere recommendations and inflated expectations. LinkedIn, at its core, is a constellation of relationships. It's a nexus where individuals can interconnect, learn from one another, and blossom together. As we etch our own Digital narratives, let us not forget the significance of relationships. They extend beyond networking – they weave a community of individuals who can bolster us, challenge us, and catalyse our growth.

With LinkedIn, Hoffman invites us to look beyond our immediate professional environment and to consider the global stage. It encourages us to learn from different cultures, to collaborate across borders, and to appreciate the diversity of the professional world. This is the essence of the Digital offer: we are closer than ever. Six degrees of separation quickly reduces. The global market is open for business. Hoffman chose to dance with change, unafraid to ruffle the status quo and embrace new paradigms. As we traverse the terrain, we must also court Innovation, welcome fresh ideas and readily adapt to shifting circumstances. Innovation is not merely advantageous – it is integral to survival and growth - and this is planet-wide.

LinkedIn promotes a culture of continuous learning. It provides a platform where knowledge is freely exchanged, where insights are shared, and where learning is seen as an integral part of professional growth. It encourages us to always be curious, to always be willing to learn, and to always strive for growth. Connections across industries and then a platform that celebrates achievements. The ethos of LinkedIn is steeped in the principle of lifelong learning. In recognition of the ceaseless evolution of the Digital world, it underscores that continuous learning is not a luxury but a necessity. We must maintain a voracious appetite for learning – refining our skills, expanding our knowledge horizons, and adapting to new developments.

# [ APPLYING THIS IN PRACTICE ]

**BECOME PART OF THE SOLUTION**: The professional world, like any other, is filled with challenges. Whether it's a business problem, an industry-wide issue, or a global economic crisis, there will always be obstacles to overcome. Instead of seeing these challenges as insurmountable, see them as opportunities for Innovation, for collaboration, and for growth. Use the platform to share your insights, to gather different perspectives, and to work together towards a solution. This is not just about problem-solving – it's about contributing to the growth of your professional community and, in turn, your personal professional development.

To actualise these principles, take the leap into the vibrant LinkedIn community. Begin by sculpting a solid profile that faithfully mirrors your professional journey. But don't stop there – interact with others, immerse in discussions, dispense your wisdom, and contribute to the collective growth of the community. Remember, on LinkedIn, your voice carries weight, your insights bear value, and your contributions can incite change.

Let us constantly remind ourselves that the essence of connection lies not in the volume of our network, but in the quality of relationships we nurture, the wisdom we disseminate, and the impact we generate.

Under Reid Hoffman's helmsmanship, LinkedIn epitomises the metamorphic power of Digital platforms. It stands as a beacon showcasing how technology can function as a unifier, facilitating shared learning and sparking opportunities. By dismantling barriers and fostering a global professional community, LinkedIn has undeniably revolutionised the way we map out our professional trajectories.

With this in mind, let's continue our exploration of the Digital world with a deeper understanding of the power of connection and the possibilities it holds. Every connection is an opportunity, every interaction is a chance for growth, and every shared insight is a step towards a more united professional world. Remember, in this world, you're not alone – you're part of a community, and together, you can make a difference.

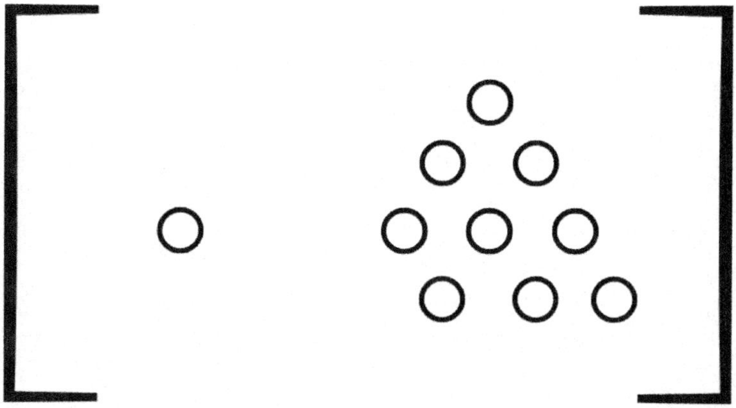

# BECOME PART OF THE SOLUTION

# [ PART III ]

# EDUCATION - UNLOCKING POTENTIAL

EDUCATION IS THE PASSPORT TO THE FUTURE, FOR TOMORROW BELONGS TO THOSE WHO PREPARE FOR IT TODAY.
MALCOLM X

Let's now turn our attention towards the third act in our journey: Education - Unlocking Potential. Feel its call, its beckoning echo, a siren's song inviting us to burrow deeper into ourselves. It's the stream of knowledge, the ocean of wisdom, the expanse where curiosity blooms and intellect thrives. It's a dance floor for the Ideas Guy.

Education holds significance as it is the key to evolution, the passport to progress, the compass guiding us towards advancement. It's the powerful testament to our inherent capability to learn, to grow, to surpass the borders of the known and leap into the unknown. It's about daring to push back against 'what we know' in favour of 'what we could know.'

Education is not just about imparting information; it's about sparking transformation, about igniting not just minds but also hearts. It's about shaking the tree of conventionality, not to uproot it, but to allow for new growth. It's about moving beyond the status quo and reaching towards the realm of potential.

In this section, we'll get acquainted with the educators, the enablers, the change-makers who have braved to redefine norms, to reimagine learning, to transform Education. We'll unearth their victories, their struggles, their experiences. We'll comprehend that Education is not a one-time event, but a lifelong journey, an ongoing commitment. It's not just those in the classroom but those on building sites, in warehouses and office blocks who are keen to grow.

In the sphere of Education, it's as though we're standing at the brink of a grand labyrinth, buzzing with mysteries, bursting with opportunities. This is the terrain of the enlightened, of the soon-to-be, of the may be. It thrives on questions not yet asked and ideas yet to be thought. It beckons us to question the established, challenge the traditional, and cosy up with the out-of-the-box.

Education is the crucible where minds are moulded, the canvas where thoughts are illustrated. It's the wizard that transmutes 'how about' into 'here's how.' It encourages the daring, the venturesome, the valiant. It invites us to step outside our safety nets, to depart from the well-trodden path and chart a new course.

In this domain, the acknowledged notions of yesterday give way to the brave ideas of today. It's not a realm of disruption for disruption's sake, but a realm where enhancement, progress, and enlightenment hold sway. It's a space where 'adequate' is the kickoff point and 'extraordinary' is the finish line we strive for.

As we navigate this part, we'll rub shoulders with the scholars, the visionaries, the pioneers. We'll hear their narratives, their accomplishments, their hurdles. Through their eyes, we'll see that Education is not a sudden revelation, but a process, a pilgrimage. It's a journey of wonder, bravery, and conviction.

So, plunge into the realm of Education. Immerse yourself in its dynamic pulse, its unyielding positivity, its firm belief in the potential for growth. Education is not a terminal, but a journey. A journey to unlock capabilities, to sketch new futures, to transform into the Ideas Guy.

Education is beckoning.

In all its luminous magnificence, it is not a veil for obliteration, nor is it a green light for unbridled dismantlement. It is not about deconstructing for the thrill of novelty, nor about dismissing the wisdom of yesteryears.

Education is not about quick fixes or temporary wins. It isn't a catchphrase to toss around or a magic trick to wave and suddenly solve all challenges. It's not about being different for the sake of standing out or fresh for the sake of newness. It doesn't insinuate a continuous demand for change simply for the sake of evolution.

Education isn't the exclusive realm of the book-smart or the innately gifted. It's not the divine prerogative of a privileged few, nor the secluded haven of prodigies. It doesn't discriminate based on age, gender, background, or profession.

And crucially, Education isn't an endpoint. It's not a pinnacle to overcome, a checkbox to tick, a target to hit. It's a voyage, a process, a mindset. It's a pledge to perpetual progress, to never settling, to constantly reaching for even better.

It's a myriad of things, a mosaic of possibilities, but it also understands its boundaries. It knows its essence, its spirit, its mission. And realising what Education is not, is just as significant as understanding what Education is. For in this recognition, we find clarity. We find direction. We find a profound appreciation for its power and potential.

Within the mosaic of Education, we can identify certain patterns, certain models that guide the path to unlocking potential. Let's explore a few of them:

Let's kickstart our journey with the **EXPERIENTIAL LEARNING MODEL**. Conjured up by David Kolb, it dances to the beat that learning, real learning, comes alive through experience. It's a philosophy deeply ingrained in Maria Montessori's innovative approach to Education. An overture that harmonises the physical, the social, the emotional, and the cognitive. A rhythm that respects the uniqueness of each child, each spirit.

Next, we tune into the rhythm of the **FLIPPED CLASSROOM MODEL**. A method given the limelight by Salman Khan of Khan Academy. It advocates for a shift, a reversal, a flipping of the traditional classroom script. It's a rhythm echoed by Jon Bergmann and Aaron Sams, pioneers who dared to reimagine the structure of the classroom. A melody that lets problems and assignments take centre stage in class while new content steps into the spotlight at home.

Then we find ourselves swaying to the steady beat of the **COMPETENCY-BASED EDUCATION MODEL**. A model that emphasises mastery, proficiency, and deep understanding. It's a rhythm that doesn't rush, that moves at the pace of each learner. This rhythm resonates strongly with the approach of Western Governors University, an institution where Robert Mendenhall, its former president, orchestrated a riff of mastery over speed.

Let's immerse ourselves in the rhythm of the **PROJECT-BASED LEARNING MODEL**. A style of learning that flows from delving deep into authentic, engaging, complex questions, problems, and challenges. It's the signature rhythm of High Tech High, conducted by Larry Rosenstock, an educator who transformed classrooms into vibrant hubs of investigation and exploration.

Finally, we step into the dance of the **COLLABORATIVE LEARNING MODEL**. This is a rhythm woven from the threads of interaction, a melody born from community, from shared understanding. Lev Vygotsky, the renowned psychologist, orchestrated this melody, emphasising that learning is a social, collective journey.

These models, these rhythms, and many others, serve as our compass as we navigate the labyrinth of Education. They light our path, guiding us through the complex dance of learning. Through their lens, we gain a richer understanding of the essence of Education and its diverse manifestations. We use them as implicit anchors as we discover educators with ideas.

As we traverse the stories of those who dared to unlock potential and light the torch of learning, we'll see the thread of these models - some hidden, some illuminated.

THE EDUCATION OF EVEN A SMALL CHILD, THEREFORE, DOES NOT AIM AT PREPARING HIM FOR SCHOOL, BUT FOR LIFE.

MARIA MONTESSORI

# [ CHAPTER 9 ]

# LESSONS FROM A CLASSROOM

Picture this: you're stepping into Maria Montessori's classroom. It's not the typical classroom you're accustomed to, with desks neatly lined up and a blackboard at the front. No, this is a domain of discovery, a terrain of exploration, a space humming with curiosity and wonder.

Instead, you find a beautifully arranged environment, rich with materials designed to entice the children to explore and learn. Each item in the room has a specific purpose and is thoughtfully placed to facilitate ease of use, autonomy, and independence.

Children's artwork and projects often adorn the walls, not just for aesthetic appeal, but to foster a sense of ownership and pride. The children themselves, from the youngest to the oldest, participate in maintaining the classroom – a practise that encourages responsibility and respect for the shared environment.

The room is segmented into different areas, each dedicated to a specific learning domain such as mathematics, language, sensorial activities, and practical life skills. The materials within these areas are arranged logically and aesthetically, inviting children to explore and manipulate them.

Montessori materials are unique and purposeful. They are designed to be self-correcting, meaning that the child can independently identify and correct their errors without adult intervention. This feature nurtures problem-solving skills, resilience, and fosters a love for learning.

Furthermore, you'd notice that children in a Montessori classroom enjoy long, uninterrupted work periods, typically two to three hours long. During this time, children are free to select the work that interests them most. This freedom is balanced by responsibility as the children are also taught to handle materials with care, to complete each task before moving onto the next, and to return the materials to their designated place for others to use.

These distinguishing features of a Montessori classroom, the freedom paired with responsibility, the prepared environment teeming with purposeful materials, the emphasis on self-directed, hands-on learning, all embody Montessori's guiding principles. It's a world that respects the child, encourages exploration, and celebrates learning – a world that holds valuable insights for our journey of IDEAS.

You see children scattered across the room, some are working together, puzzling over a challenge; others are tucked away in quiet corners, absorbed in solitary tasks. They're not waiting for a bell to ring or a teacher's directive. They are in charge. They are actively engaged in their learning. The environment hums with an energy that's both tranquil and alive, a silent cacophony of engaged minds.

Welcome to the Montessori way of Education, a revolution in learning that birthed itself in the early 20th century. Born out of the observant and innovative mind of Maria Montessori, an Italian physician and educator, this approach turned the conventional model of Education on its head. It was an Education centred on the child that nurtured their innate curiosity and spurred them to explore, question, and learn.

It's not a linear path we tread. It's a vibrant tapestry, interwoven with milestones that reflect the evolution and impact of her transformative ideas. Our first milestone takes us to the streets of San Lorenzo in Rome, the year 1907. Maria Montessori, a passionate advocate for children's Education, sets up Casa dei Bambini, "The Children's House". It's here that Montessori's revolutionary pedagogy takes root. Instead of the traditional chalk-and-talk method, she observes children and offers them an environment that fuels their natural curiosity and desire to learn. A milestone indeed, for it's here that the Montessori Method is born, soon to ripple across the world.

As we stride forward in time, we see Montessori's philosophy breaking national boundaries, extending its influence globally. The second milestone we come across is the international propagation of Montessori's method. By the 1920s and 1930s, Montessori schools were spreading across Europe, North America, and beyond. Montessori's revolutionary approach resonated with people across the world, proving that the language of holistic, child-centric learning was indeed universal.

We then leap ahead to the dawn of the 21st century, our third milestone. As Education embraces a more holistic approach, acknowledging the importance of skills beyond just academic prowess, Montessori's ideas experience a renaissance. Today, thousands of Montessori schools operate worldwide, and her pedagogy continues to inspire mainstream reforms. Montessori's philosophies, it seems, were not just ahead of her time but also ready to enrich the ever-evolving Educational landscape.

The milestones in Montessori's philosophy show us a narrative of courage, Innovation, and enduring influence. Her groundbreaking approach, born in a small classroom in Rome, now resonates in countless classrooms across the globe. And as we face the challenges and opportunities of the postmodern era, her principles guide us forward, reminding us to put the child at the centre, to trust their natural curiosity, and to foster an environment of respect and understanding.

The bell rings in the modern world, as we step forward into the classroom of the 21st century. Surrounded by the hum of technology and the hushed whispers of Digital transformation, it's easy to believe that the past has been outpaced by the future. And yet, as we sit down at our desks, we find ourselves greeted by a familiar face.

Montessori's principles echo with a timeless resonance, as pertinent today as they were when they first graced the classrooms of the early 20th century. It's as if Montessori saw the coming of our Digital age, preparing her students for a world where critical thinking, creativity, and problem-solving would become the currency of success.

Her teaching, which championed self-direction and experiential learning, is precisely the approach educators are grappling to grasp today as they attempt to nurture these future-ready skills in students. As technology weaves itself into the very fabric of our classrooms, her philosophy provides a guide, reminding us that even amidst the array of dazzling Digital tools, the essence of learning remains in thoughtful and purposeful engagement.

The global pandemic, an unexpected test of adaptability, saw Montessori's principle of resilience shine. As classrooms were forced into the confines of screens, Montessori educators around the world ingeniously wove their hands-on, personalised approach into the realm of remote learning. They revealed to us that the spirit of Montessori teaching can be maintained even amidst drastic changes, holding onto its core while moulding itself to the demands of the times.

Moreover, as the world wakes up to the importance of social and emotional learning, Montessori's methodology has been ahead of its time. Emphasising empathy, respect for others, and the power of collaboration, these tenets have been the bedrock of Montessori Education long before they started trending in Educational discussions. In a Digital sphere where interactions are often mediated by screens, Montessori's focus on genuine interpersonal relationships breathes a human touch into these virtual exchanges.

As we continue to navigate the currents of Industry 4.0, Maria Montessori's lessons serve as a compass, guiding us towards an Education that honours individuality, stokes the flames of curiosity, values effort, and cherishes lifelong learning. She's not just a figure from our past, but a visionary lighting the path for our future. In the words of Montessori herself, "Education is a natural process carried out by the human individual, and is acquired not by listening to words, but by experiences in the environment."

As we have gathered, the core of Montessori's pedagogical philosophy was a profound respect for the child. She believed in children's natural curiosity, their innate desire to explore, discover, and understand the world around them. She saw children as capable and eager learners, not vessels to be filled with knowledge. In her classrooms, children were allowed the freedom to follow their interests, to choose their activities. They were given the time and space to delve deeply into their tasks, to make mistakes and learn from them. They were not rushed or judged. They were respected. Imagine. Just imagine if our political overlords actually considered what children might actually want to do.

We need to honour our children's innate curiosity, our inner explorer. And then acknowledge that we too, even as adults, are inquisitive, despite the fact that the system may have schooled it out of us. We must be willing to follow our interests, to take risks, to make mistakes, and to learn from them. We must remember that the journey is as important as the destination, that the process of exploration and discovery is as valuable as the knowledge we gain.

A key element of Montessori's philosophy is the prepared environment. Her classrooms were thoughtfully designed spaces that catered to the children's needs, promoted independence, and encouraged exploration. Every piece of furniture, every material, every activity was chosen with the child's development in mind. The environment was designed to be inviting, engaging, and supportive of the child's learning journey.

We need to create spaces that support our journey, that foster enquiry, that invite exploration. Whether it's setting up a quiet workspace for focused work, or creating a routine that supports our goals, the environment matters.

Montessori observed that children have what she called an absorbent mind. This meant that children, particularly in their early years, have a remarkable ability to absorb information from their environment.

In the Montessori approach, this was harnessed through hands-on learning experiences and activities that catered to the child's developmental needs. It was an approach that recognised and respected the child's capacity to learn. We must remember  the nature of our own sponge-like absorbent minds. In the hyper-connected world we inhabit, we are constantly surrounded by information, by opportunities for learning. We must remember our capacity to absorb, to learn, to grow. And we must seek out experiences that nourish our minds and enrich our Education journey.

# [ APPLYING THIS IN PRACTICE ]

**STAY CURIOUS**: Create environments that support our personal goals, and take advantage of our capacity for learning, even within a corporate or collective environment. Start by identifying your interests and passions in the world. Allow yourself the freedom to explore these, to go deep, to take risks. Don't fear mistakes; instead, see them as opportunities for learning.

Next, assess your environment. What changes can you make to better support your goals? This could involve setting up a dedicated workspace, establishing a routine, or simply creating spaces for downtime or play.

As we navigate this classroom, guided by Montessori's principles, let's remember that the power of learning is not just about the knowledge we acquire. It's about the process of exploration, the joy of discovery, the thrill of understanding. So, let's respect our full selves, and harness our absorbent minds. For in the classroom of Maria Montessori, these are the keys to success.

The Montessori approach is a testament to the transformative power of respect-centred Education. It demonstrates how the right environment can unlock curiosity, encourage exploration, and catalyse the learning process. By breaking down the traditional barriers of rigid classrooms and one-size-fits-all learning, Montessori has indeed revolutionised the way we perceive Education and has provided a blueprint that we can apply to our journey. One size fits all actually means one size fits none.

Perhaps the curious shall inherit the earth.

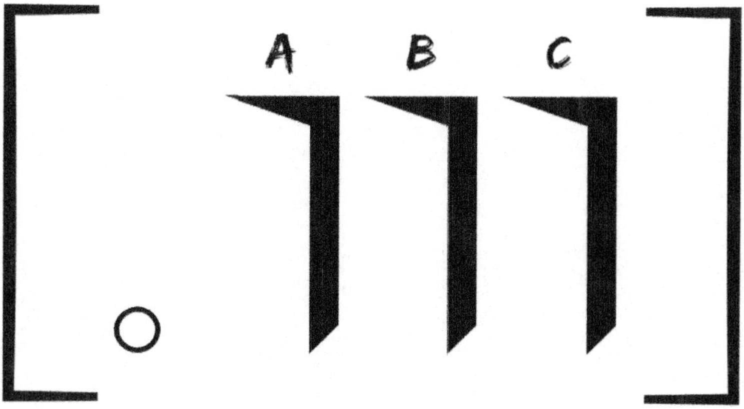


# STAY CURIOUS

THE FACT IS THAT GIVEN THE CHALLENGES WE FACE, EDUCATION DOESN'T NEED TO BE REFORMED – IT NEEDS TO BE TRANSFORMED. THE KEY TO THIS TRANSFORMATION IS NOT TO STANDARDISE EDUCATION, BUT TO PERSONALISE IT, TO BUILD ACHIEVEMENT ON DISCOVERING THE INDIVIDUAL TALENTS OF EACH CHILD, TO PUT STUDENTS IN AN ENVIRONMENT WHERE THEY WANT TO LEARN AND WHERE THEY CAN NATURALLY DISCOVER THEIR TRUE PASSIONS.

SIR KEN ROBINSON

# [ CHAPTER 10 ]

# CHAMPIONING CREATIVITY

The path laid out by Sir Ken Robinson is neither a route etched in stone nor a set of waypoints on a map. Instead, it's a free-flowing river, winding and ever-evolving, teeming with life and richness. It's a journey that takes us beyond the confines of traditional Education systems and into the boundless canyon of creativity and potential.

Robinson believed in the inherent creative abilities that exist in every individual. For him, the problem wasn't about instilling creativity, but rather about nurturing it, providing a fertile ground where it could sprout and grow. He implored us to rethink our approach to Education, to shift from an industrial, assembly-line model to one that respects the diversity of human talents and intelligence.

In his influential TED talk, "Do Schools Kill Creativity?", Robinson challenged the status quo of classroom instruction, arguing that our current system stifles creativity rather than fostering it. This, he argued, was a significant flaw, given that we live in a rapidly evolving world that thrives on Innovation. His passionate and humorous discourse resonated with millions, making it one of the most-watched TED talks of all time.

Robinson's Educational philosophy wasn't just an abstract concept—it was a call to action, a wake-up call to acknowledge and address the limitations of our system. He believed that it was time to transform our schools from places of conformity and standardisation into spaces that nurture individuality and diversity of thought. As we venture deeper into the realm of Robinson's philosophy, let's take a moment to reflect on the transformative power of creativity. What is creativity, really? It's more than just originality or the ability to come up with new ideas. Creativity is a profound, multi-dimensional concept that intertwines with every facet of our lives. It's the essence of Innovation, the seed of originality, and the heart of human expression.

In his work, Robinson emphasised that creativity isn't merely a trait possessed by artists, musicians, or writers. Instead, it is inherent in all of us, lying dormant, waiting to be nurtured and awakened. Every child, he argued, has tremendous creative capacities. However, our Education systems, built on standardisation and conformity, often fail to acknowledge this.

He contended that our Educational institutions, with their linear paths and rigid structures, stifle creative thought. Creativity cannot thrive in an environment where deviation is seen as error and where the arts are considered less valuable than traditional academic subjects. Creativity is divergent—it flourishes when we are free to explore, make connections, and express ourselves.

And why is creativity so vital? In a rapidly evolving world, the ability to innovate, to think outside the box, to create and adapt, is more important than ever. Robinson believed that by nurturing creativity in our schools, we could better prepare our children for the uncertainties and opportunities of the future. He envisioned a system where Education isn't just about passing exams but about fostering curiosity, encouraging exploration, and promoting divergent thinking. These are not the staples in our classrooms (or even the glue sticks).

Robinson also underscored the strong connection between creativity and our overall well-being. When we engage our artistic faculties, we experience a sense of fulfilment and contentment. It opens up a world of possibilities, allowing us to explore our passions and make meaningful contributions to society. By putting this at the heart of Education, we're not only cultivating more innovative minds—we're also promoting happier, more fulfilled individuals.

Let's pause here to reflect on how we can apply these insights about creativity in our lives. How can we foster an environment that encourages creativity in our homes, our schools, and our workplaces? How can we shift from a culture of standardisation to one of exploration and originality?

Robinson's philosophy provides us with a compass to navigate these questions. It beckons us to break free from the traditional moulds. Delving into this philosophy, we realise that championing creativity isn't merely about improving our Education system—it's about transforming the way we view intelligence, learning, and human potential. And to understand this better, let's embark on a journey exploring the key milestones in Robinson's work.

The first milestone we encounter is the release of the report "All Our Futures: Creativity, Culture, and Education," published by the UK government in 1999. Robinson chaired the advisory committee that produced the report, which emphasised the need to place creativity at the heart of Education. It was a groundbreaking moment, one that propelled the discussion about creativity in schools into the mainstream discourse.

In 2009, Robinson penned "The Element: How Finding Your Passion Changes Everything", a book that explored the myriad ways people discovered their passions and talents. This influential work presented countless stories, some from celebrities and others from ordinary people, showing that when individuals found their "element", they achieved a level of success and fulfilment they had never experienced before.

This brings us to 2018, when Robinson co-authored "You, Your Child, and School: Navigating Your Way to the Best Education" with Lou Aronica. This work aimed to empower parents to make informed decisions about their children's Education. Robinson highlighted the importance of understanding each child's unique needs and abilities and urged parents to advocate for an Education system that respects these differences.

The notion of intelligence is as diverse as it is complex, a vibrant spectrum spanning myriad dimensions. Intelligence doesn't merely reside in the realm of academic prowess or theoretical comprehension. It's reflected in the deft hands of the artisan, the innovative mind of the inventor, and the empathetic spirit of the caregiver. Each of us harbours a unique blend of intelligence that distinguishes us from the rest. Therefore, an effective Education system is one that recognises and respects this vast expanse of intellectual diversity. It's an environment that doesn't just accommodate different forms of intelligence but creates fertile ground for them to grow and flourish. It encourages students to explore and embrace their unique intellectual abilities, fostering a diverse and inclusive academic ecosystem where every student can thrive.

Creativity is the lifeblood of Innovation and progress, the fuel that drives the engine of human achievement. And yet, too often, traditional Educational frameworks have treated it as an afterthought rather than an essential component of learning. Robinson passionately contested this notion, placing creativity on an equal footing with literacy in Education. School should not be a constraining force that stifles the creative spirit; instead, it should be a nurturing sanctuary where creativity is encouraged and cultivated. Creativity instils students with a sense of curiosity and wonder, equipping them with the ability to view the world from unique perspectives, find novel solutions to problems, and create value in the world. In the end, an Education that nurtures creativity is one that cultivates future inventors, artists, entrepreneurs, and pioneers.

At the core of Robinson's philosophy is the idea that Education should be a deeply personal journey. As we have already seen, the traditional one-size-fits-all model, with its rigid structures and standardised testing, often fails to account for the unique capabilities and passions of each student. Robinson advocated for a shift towards a more personalised approach, one that recognises and nurtures the distinct talents and passions within each individual. In a personalised academic system, each student's learning journey is tailor-made to fit their unique intellectual and creative profile. This approach does not only aim to enhance academic achievement but also to foster a lifelong love for learning. In an Educational landscape that is personalised, students aren't merely passengers in their journey; they are the navigators, charting their own path towards intellectual growth and personal fulfilment.

As an addendum to this element of personalisation, it is critical at this juncture to assert how artificial intelligence is likely to be fundamental in this personalisation of learning. Powered by intricate algorithms and expansive databases, serving as a Digital companion to each student, this AI understands the student's unique learning style, pace, and interests. It knows when the student is struggling and when they are excelling. It's not a distant, detached entity, but a responsive, intuitive aide that's finely attuned to each student's academic journey. Oh, and remember, "student" doesn't mean child; it is intended to mean anyone studying to learn - a new sales platform, the latest accounting software updates or the new building inspection regulations.

The power of AI in personalising Education lies in its ability to adapt. Instead of delivering a standardised curriculum, it curates a personalised learning experience, picking up on the subtleties of a student's academic progress. It recognises when a maths concept isn't quite clicking or when a student's interest is piqued by a particular historical era. It adjusts, adapts, and moulds the learning journey in real time to cater to the student's evolving needs and curiosities.

Moreover, AI can provide opportunities for learning beyond the confines of a traditional curriculum. If a student expresses an interest in astronomy, AI can provide resources, projects, and activities to explore this passion further. In doing so, it fosters an environment of intrinsic motivation and self-directed learning.

But perhaps one of the most profound ways AI can personalise Education is by providing continuous, detailed feedback. Rather than waiting for a termly report or a terminal exam result, AI provides real-time insights into a student's progress, pinpointing areas of strength and areas needing improvement. This way, students, teachers, and parents can have a dynamic understanding of the learning journey, facilitating timely interventions and celebrating milestones along the way.

Just Imagine, in the realm of Sir Ken Robinson and as the title of his posthumously-completed last book, where each student's uniqueness is celebrated, AI could serve as an extraordinary tool to foster creativity, honour diversity, and most importantly, personalise Education. It carries the promise of an Educational landscape where every learner feels seen, heard, and valued. AI could truly be the key to unlocking a personalised experience, catalysing a revolutionary shift in the way we view and approach Education.

# [ APPLYING THIS IN PRACTICE ]

**PROMOTE UNCONVENTIONAL PATHS**: The principles underpinning Sir Ken Robinson's philosophy suggest a radical departure from the traditional Educational framework. They implore us to champion an Education system that doesn't just tolerate, but celebrates diversity, creativity, and personalisation.

In order to actualise Robinson's vision, we must actively participate in our local Educational communities, sparking conversations around the merits of creativity and individualised learning. We can promote initiatives that embrace diverse learning styles, supporting Educational practises that prioritise creative and critical thinking over rote memorisation.

Furthermore, it's essential for us to empower our children (and adults) to explore their unique talents and interests. We should strive to cultivate an environment where success isn't confined to academic achievements. It's about helping our people understand that Education isn't a rigid path leading to a predetermined destination, but a vast landscape teeming with myriad paths they can explore and create.

But embracing Robinson's principles extends beyond just advocating for change in our Education systems. It also involves incorporating these principles into our own lives. Lifelong learning, in the spirit of Robinson's philosophy, is about nurturing our innate curiosity and creativity. It's about stepping off the well-trodden path and venturing into the wilderness of the unknown, all the while relishing the thrill of discovery and the joy of creation.

We encounter a transformative vision of Education, one that's not just a conduit to employment, but a journey filled with opportunities for self-discovery, creativity, and personal growth. We find ourselves on a mission to revolutionise our Education systems, transforming them into nurturing ecosystems that foster, rather than stifle, the vast potential within each individual - and then spill this out into business, the arts, politics, economics, the whole shebang.

Indeed, Sir Ken Robinson's philosophy reminds us that creativity isn't merely an aspect of Education—it forms its very heart and soul. And so, as we traverse the terrain of this era, we carry within us the promise of a more fulfilling, creative, and inclusive future.

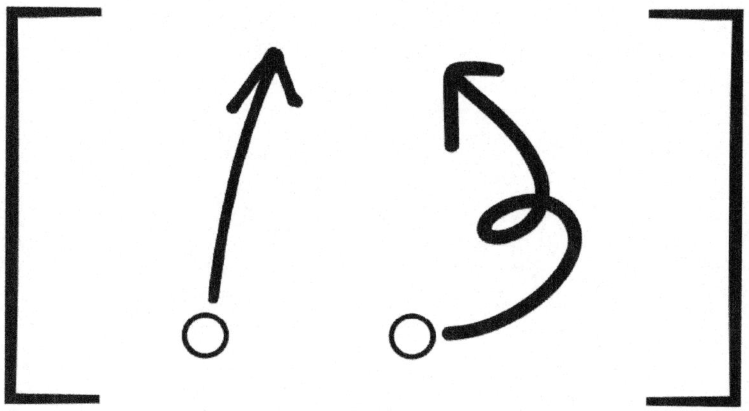

PROMOTE UNCONVENTIONAL PATHS

LATER IN LIFE, WHEN MY KIDS STRUGGLE TO UNDERSTAND A TRICKY CONCEPT OR MASTER A NEW SKILL, I WANT THEM TO HAVE THE STRENGTH AND EXPERIENCE TO TELL THEMSELVES, 'I DON'T KNOW HOW TO DO THIS...YET!' I WANT THEM TO BE CONFIDENT THAT, EVEN IF SOMETHING SEEMS CHALLENGING TODAY, THEY HAVE WHAT IT TAKES TO FIGURE IT OUT.

**SAL KHAN**

## [ CHAPTER 11 ]

# DEMOCRATISING KNOWLEDGE

Let's step into the Digital realm of Sal Khan, the visionary behind Khan Academy, an innovative platform that heralds a new era of accessible Education for all. Khan Academy is not merely an organisation but a tangible manifestation of Sal Khan's unyielding belief in the power of knowledge and its capacity to transform lives. When Khan declares the mission of Khan Academy "to provide a free, world-class Education for anyone, anywhere," it's a clarion call for a global Educational revolution. It's a pledge to dismantle barriers, to stretch beyond traditional paradigms, and to leverage the potential of the Digital age to democratise learning.

Imagine a boundless classroom, one without walls or geographic limits. It's a classroom nestled within the Digital cloud, a click away from anyone with an internet connection. This virtual realm of knowledge is where Khan Academy resides, transforming the Digital landscape into a fertile field of learning. Here, the seeds of wisdom are sown, watered by the nurturing spirit of curiosity, and nourished under the warm glow of dedicated mentors.

Khan's journey started humbly, assisting his cousin in maths through the internet. The potential of this novel approach to tutoring was undeniable. The seeds of an idea began to germinate. With the audacity to dream and the courage to act, he launched Khan Academy in 2008. What began as a compilation of YouTube tutorials metamorphosed into a robust learning platform offering an array of practise exercises, instructional videos, and a personalised learning dashboard.

Today, Khan Academy stands tall as an Educational titan in the Digital age, reaching millions of learners worldwide. Its impact extends beyond numbers, touching lives, sparking curiosity, and empowering learners with the tools to carve their unique paths of discovery.

Khan's pedagogical approach disrupts traditional Educational models, placing the learner at the helm. It centres on 'mastery learning', ensuring that learners fully comprehend a concept before advancing. This individual-centric approach fosters a profound understanding, providing a more meaningful and fulfilling learning experience.

Khan Academy operates under the principle that learning isn't a sprint but a journey of exploration at one's own pace. It champions the idea that mistakes are not failures but stepping stones to understanding, fostering an environment where learners can experiment, stumble, and rise, unfettered by the fear of getting it wrong.

A vital aspect of Khan Academy is its commitment to making learning resources available at no cost. By doing so, it ensures that economic barriers do not obstruct the path to knowledge. In this, we see the true democratic power of the Digital age, echoing the ethos that Education is a universal right, not a privilege for a few.

With this unwavering commitment, Khan Academy continues to reimagine the landscape of Education. It builds bridges where there were once chasms, connects learners across the globe, and fosters a community of knowledge seekers united by a shared thirst for learning.

As we dive deeper, we find ourselves in an odyssey of democratised knowledge, propelled by Digital Innovation. It's a story of how one man's vision, combined with the transformative power of technology, can challenge conventional wisdom, reshape global Education, and unlock untapped potential.

A mosaic of diverse learners, an array of subjects, and a spirit of inclusivity form the cornerstone of Khan Academy. It's an example of how the power of a simple idea, when brought to life by Digital tools and a deep-rooted belief in its potential, can ripple out to create lasting change.

Sal Khan extends an open invitation to all—an invitation to learn, to grow, and to explore the boundaries of their potential. It's an embodiment of the promise held by Digital tools to democratise Education, making it accessible, inclusive, and engaging for everyone, everywhere.

From its inception, Khan Academy has actively sought ways to broaden the learning opportunities it provides, reaching out to learners from various backgrounds, and catering to diverse learning needs.

One such initiative is "LearnStorm", a national learning challenge designed to foster growth mindset and perseverance among students. LearnStorm utilises the motivational power of gamification, rewarding not just academic prowess but progress, effort, and resilience. By celebrating the journey of learning and not just the destination, it serves to inspire a love for learning, an attribute that is invaluable in the ever-evolving landscape of the 21st century.

Another milestone in Khan Academy's journey is "Schoolhouse.World", an initiative launched in 2020 in response to the global pandemic. This peer-to-peer learning platform facilitates free tutoring in a variety of subjects, further broadening the horizon of accessible Education. The students of today become the tutors of tomorrow, creating a self-sustaining cycle of learning and mentoring that transcends borders.

In line with its mission to provide a "free, world-class Education for anyone, anywhere", they launched Khan Academy Kids, a platform that focuses on early childhood Education. Here, young learners can engage in playful activities designed to nurture their creativity, curiosity, and critical thinking skills. This initiative reaffirms Khan Academy's commitment to laying a solid foundation for lifelong learning. It is likely that this is no small part down to the groundwork that last chapter's hero, Sir Ken Robinson, put in for decades.

Despite the significant strides made by Khan and his team, the journey is far from over. As technology evolves, so does Khan Academy, continuously innovating, refining, and expanding its reach. It's a testament to Sal Khan's belief in the transformative power of Education and his relentless pursuit to debureaucratise knowledge.

Khan Academy's journey illuminates the path for future Educational Innovations, offering valuable insights into harnessing the Digital revolution's potential to redefine the world of learning. It's a glimmer of what's possible when we align technology with the noble cause of expanding access to Education, fostering a global learning community that thrives on the free exchange of knowledge.

So, as we navigate the boundless seas of learning in the Digital age, guided by the inspiration that is Sal Khan, we are reminded that Education, at its core, is a fundamental human right. It is a catalyst for personal and societal growth, a potent weapon to combat inequality, and a vital tool to unlock the inherent potential within each individual. Indeed, in this ocean, knowledge knows no bounds.

The lighthouse in the mission is the unwavering belief in the universal entitlement to Education. Leveraging the transformative power of Digital tools, Khan Academy has dismantled traditional barriers, delivering high-quality resources to anyone fortunate to be online. In our Digital age, knowledge should not be held captive within the imposing walls of elite institutions or hidden within the bindings of costly textbooks; it should flow freely like a river, its nourishing waters reaching every parched mind that thirsts for wisdom. Education, in Khan's world, is a birthright, not a privilege. Geographical, economic, political and ethnic barriers are dismantled with unwavering accuracy.

Khan Academy stands firm in its recognition of the individual. Its learning model doesn't just acknowledge, but actively embraces our unique learning paths. It testifies to the importance of personalisation, serving a reminder that we are not uniform beings, and our Educational journeys should reflect this diversity. Everyone learns in their rhythm, in their distinct style, and our Educational apparatus should not only respect but adapt to these idiosyncratic learning expeditions. Learning is not a race, it's a personal journey of discovery. The best thing about this is that the AI revolution which we are seeing across the world is only going to push this journey on faster and more furiously. It seems that Education is not just a human right but *personalised* Education is in fact the real human right.

Khan Academy's vision transcends traditional age boundaries; it isn't confined to the spectrum of school-going years. By offering resources that cater to inquisitive minds of all ages, it amplifies the message of lifelong learning. Learning isn't simply a phase of life contained within the confines of adolescence; it's a pulsating, vibrant way of life. It's an enduring dance with knowledge, with each step, each swirl, revealing new horizons of understanding. In Khan's universe, we are perennial students, persistently evolving, perpetually learning. And this matters - in a world where agility will become the number one workplace commodity, an option to learn, unlearn and relearn will be our greatest asset, just like Alvin Toffler predicted.

These principles, when stitched together, create the fabric of Khan Academy's pedagogical philosophy. Their dedication to building a worldwide, welcoming learning environment demonstrates their belief that Education is more than just a ladder to climb.

## [ APPLYING THIS IN PRACTICE ]

**MAKE IT PERSONAL:** Embark on a journey by cultivating a personalised lifelong learning pathway for employees and then replicate this in every customer interaction. This concept is deeply ingrained in the philosophy of Khan Academy and the journey of the Ideas Guy. It's about recognising that Education and knowledge acquisition aren't confined to formal schooling years but extend across the entirety of our lives. It is the notion and subsequent practise that says everyone is a one, not any old number.

The first step is acknowledging your individual learning style and pace. Like a compass in the vast expanse of the knowledge landscape, this awareness will guide your exploration. As the Ideas Guy, you are the protagonist of your learning journey, and each step forward should resonate with your unique aspirations, interests, and potential.

Digital tools, such as Khan Academy, are your allies in this endeavour. With these platforms, the realm of knowledge expands beyond traditional subject boundaries and timelines, inviting you to chart your own course. Whether it's exploring a long-held fascination with astronomy or nurturing a newfound interest in coding, you have the freedom and resources to indulge your intellectual curiosity.

However, cultivating a personalised pathway isn't solely a solitary endeavour. As the Ideas Guy, you can inspire others around you to begin their journeys. By sharing your experiences and insights, you can create a ripple effect, promoting a culture of curiosity and lifelong learning.

Remember, the essence of the Ideas Guy lies in a relentless pursuit of knowledge and growth. The Digital age, with its vast resources and platforms, presents an exciting opportunity to embody this ethos. It's a chance to redefine what learning means to you, to step away from rigid structures and expectations, and to embrace a personalised and continuous journey of discovery.

Chart your course in this vast knowledge landscape. Embrace the wonders of lifelong learning and savour the fulfilment that comes from pursuing your curiosity. Be the person that inspires others in their journey and celebrate as the domino effect of your pursuit resonates within your community. You are the Ideas Guy, the navigator of your learning journey, and the world of knowledge awaits your exploration.

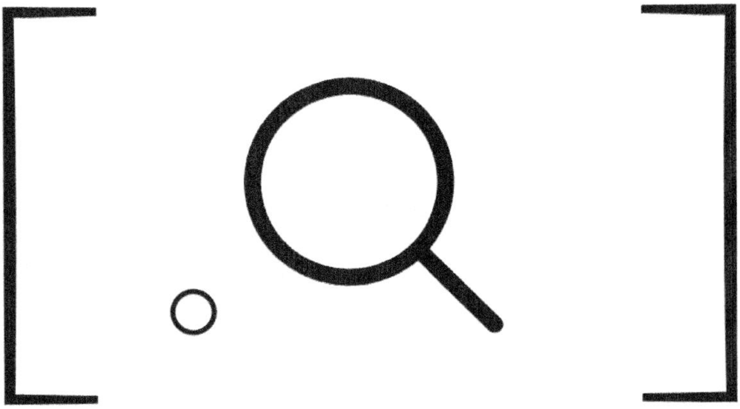

## MAKE IT PERSONAL

IT'S QUITE FASHIONABLE TO SAY THAT THE EDUCATIONAL SYSTEM IS BROKEN. IT'S NOT BROKEN. IT'S WONDERFULLY CONSTRUCTED. IT'S JUST THAT WE DON'T NEED IT ANYMORE.

SUGATA MITRA

# [ CHAPTER 12 ]

# ORGANISE THYSELF

Embark on a journey, a journey less travelled, one that steps away from the well-trodden path of traditional Education, and walks towards the hope of Innovation and self-instruction. This journey is illuminated by the radical vision of Sugata Mitra, an unassuming pioneer, a questioner of conventions, and the mastermind behind the "Hole in the Wall" experiment. His ideas have reverberated across the globe, uprooting deep-seated norms, and ushering in a refreshing, hopeful perspective on learning and Education. He has had the single most profound impact on my own Educational philosophy and I have had the privilege to meet him. He is the embodiment of his passion too; his questions, his inquisitiveness, his pursuit of understanding extends beyond teaching students into every conversation he has.

Sugata Mitra, a physicist by training, is an example of the powerful symbiosis of curiosity and discovery. His foray into the edusphere was not driven by a conventional route but a trailblazing question: "What would happen if children were given the tools to teach themselves?" His quest for the answer revolutionised our understanding of learning, a change that sprouted from a literal hole in the wall.

It was the year 1999, in the heat and dust of a bustling slum in New Delhi, where Mitra's experiment took root. A computer, robust and novel, was embedded in a wall, accessible to anyone passing by. Children from the area, unacquainted with such technology, huddled around this unusual installation. They explored, prodded, and played with the computer, and remarkably, they began to teach themselves how to use it.

Mitra watched this spectacle unfold, a veritable dance of discovery, free from adult supervision or formal instruction. What he observed was a profound demonstration of learning – organic, instinctive, and collaborative. Children were not just memorising information; they were problem-solving, they were navigating complexities, they were teaching each other, and above all, they were enjoying the process. This seemingly simple experiment had profound implications. It challenged the very fundamentals of the traditional Education system, where knowledge is often one-directional, flowing from the teacher to the student.

Fast forward several years, and Mitra's vision of self-instruction is no longer confined to that slum in New Delhi. His "Hole in the Wall" experiment has inspired numerous initiatives globally, reaching places as far as Italy and Cambodia. This model of learning has found its way into various settings – in schools, community centres, and even in remote rural areas.

Yet, the spirit of the experiment remains the same – the belief in the power of self-instruction and the ability of children to learn by themselves when provided with the right tools and environment. This belief doesn't just apply to children in underprivileged areas; it rings true for learners of all ages, across different strata of society.

The "Hole in the Wall" experiment and its subsequent iterations echo an important message. They show us that learning is not an uphill climb that needs to be laboriously trudged through. It's a landscape to be explored, a realm where curiosity is the compass, and discovery, the destination.

This is not to undermine the importance of teachers or formal Education. They are undoubtedly pivotal to learning. But Mitra's experiment invites us to expand our perspective, to view Education as a multifaceted entity where self-instruction can beautifully coexist with formal teaching.

In a world that's rapidly digitising, Mitra's philosophy of self-instruction bears more relevance than ever. It offers a beacon of hope in regions where quality Education is a distant dream. It bridges gaps, it empowers learners, it fosters a culture of discovery, and it democratises knowledge, just like Maria, Ken, and Sal.

And so, as we journey alongside Sugata Mitra, let's remember that learning is as natural as breathing. It's our innate ability, one that's not confined by walls, not restricted by resources, and certainly not limited by our circumstances. As we step into this world of self-instruction and exploration, let's carry this lesson with us, for it has the potential to revolutionise not just our understanding of Education, but also our approach towards learning and discovery.

We find ourselves entering a vibrant arena of self-learning. An arena where boundaries blur, where convention takes the back seat, and curiosity steers the course. It's a space imbued with the spirit of exploration, underpinned by the philosophy of "minimally invasive Education". This concept, coined by Mitra himself, emphasises the capability of children to extract immense Educational value from Digital resources, with minimal adult intervention.

It's a liberating and empowering philosophy, one that has proven to be particularly valuable in areas where traditional resources are scant, and access to qualified teachers is limited. In such contexts, self-learning provides a lifeline, a means for children to rise above their circumstances and gain access to the world's knowledge, unrestricted by their geographical or socio-economic limitations.

But Mitra's vision doesn't merely serve as a stop-gap solution in resource-poor settings. It also has profound implications for more established Educational systems, urging us to reassess our methods and attitudes towards teaching and learning. His work compels us to question: Are we fostering an environment conducive to self-learning? Are we encouraging curiosity and independence in our learners? Are we utilising the potential of Digital technology to its fullest extent?

These questions are not mere philosophical musings, but rather, essential inquiries that can guide the evolution of Education in the 21st century.

Mitra's "School in the Cloud" initiative, a natural extension of his earlier experiment, brings these questions to the fore. It takes the concept of self-learning a step further, integrating it with Digital technology to create Self Organised Learning Environments or SOLEs. In these settings, children collaborate and learn from each other using the internet, guided by just a single stimulating question. It's proof of the power of communal curiosity, the potency of peer learning, and the wonders of the Digital age.

The legacy of Sugata Mitra and his ground-breaking experiments are far-reaching. They seep beyond the realm of academic research and into the heart of communities across the globe. They are woven into the stories of children in the disadvantaged areas of India, of students in the rural landscapes of Colombia, and of learners in the bustling cities of the United States. They resonate in the narratives of educators, policy-makers, and visionaries across the world, inspiring a reimagining of what Education can truly embody.

The "Hole in the Wall" experiment has evolved, grown, and adapted over time, but its essence remains as powerful and relevant as ever. It stands as a reminder that learning is a deeply human endeavour, one that can thrive in the most unlikely of places, under the most challenging of circumstances.

We are reminded of the boundless potential within each learner, and the power of wonder, exploration, and self-instruction. We're invited to imagine a future where learners everywhere have the tools and freedom to teach themselves, where each individual's Educational journey is as unique and limitless as they are.

And as we continue on this exploration, let's hold onto the vision Sugata Mitra presents – one where Education is not a rigid structure to be conformed to, but a fluid, expansive landscape to be explored. A landscape that not only educates but inspires, not only instructs but empowers. A landscape where every learner finds their own unique path, guided by the light of curiosity and the spirit of self-instruction. And within this landscape, every "Hole in the Wall" is a portal to a world of knowledge, a gateway to a future brimming with promise and potential.

We are not merely spectators on this pilgrimage. We are part of it. The ideas that Mitra has championed are not confined to research papers or keynote speeches. They're an invitation, a call to each one of us to rethink, reimagine, and revolutionise Education. And this invitation is open to all.

Let's pause and take a moment to reflect. Are we ready to embrace this new approach to learning? Are we ready to step beyond our comfort zones and venture into this exciting realm of self-instruction? If we are, then the possibilities are endless. And with Sugata Mitra as our guide, we're bound to uncover insights and perspectives that will forever change the way we perceive and engage with learning.

Every learner has a place, every question has value, and every exploration is a step towards the future. And as the Ideas Guy, we are called to be part of this grand adventure, one where it is not just about imparting knowledge, but about kindling the fires of wonder, fostering self-discovery, and illuminating the path towards a future brimming with possibilities.

Mitra has given us a compass, and with it, we can navigate the landscape in new, transformative ways. His work inspires us, challenges us, and invites us to be part of a global conversation about what Education can and should be. Let's answer that call. Let's be part of that conversation. And together, let's reimagine a place where everyone has the potential to be an Ideas Guy. And every Ideas Guy has the power to change the world.

Mitra's "Hole in the Wall" experiment revealed the astounding power of self-learning. With minimal intervention, children were able to teach themselves complex subjects, demonstrating that the human drive to learn is a potent force. As we consider how this insight can transform our own contexts, let's re-evaluate how we can create environments that foster this instinct for self-learning. We are surrounded by those who are inquisitive so we need to provide holes they can fill.

Through his SOLE model, Mitra shone a spotlight on the value of peer learning. He demonstrated that when children collaborate, they not only learn from each other but also reinforce their own understanding. As we seek to apply this lesson, let's ponder how we can encourage more cooperative learning, both in classrooms and in other settings.

Mitra's experiment highlights the innate inquisitiveness and initiative present within every child. The transformation witnessed in the "Hole in the Wall" experiment wasn't just about accessing information, it was about the hunger to learn and the drive to seek knowledge independently. As we adopt Mitra's insights, let's consider how we can cultivate these traits in our own learning environments, making space for intrigue to flourish and initiative to be rewarded. In the journey of learning, as envisioned by Mitra, these qualities are not mere add-ons, but fundamental drivers of the Educational process.

# [ APPLYING THIS IN PRACTICE ]

**ENCOURAGE SELF-LEARNING:** The cornerstone of Mitra's "Hole in the Wall" experiment is self-learning, facilitated by a friendly and inviting environment. It's a powerful concept that we can manifest in our settings, be it in our homes, classrooms, or workplaces. This is not the same as the *spirit* of self-learning. It is a conscious decision to create the *environment* of self-learning. Making a space, whether virtual, physical, or hybrid, that is conducive to this has to be intentional rather than accidental. It resonates beautifully with Montessori, too.

This approach involves shaping spaces where imagination is celebrated, inquiries are embraced, and individuals are granted the liberty to explore and learn at their own rhythm. It doesn't imply forsaking guidance, but rather transitioning to the role of a facilitator who assists and encourages the learning journey rather than governing it. And, remember, this is not restricted to formal learning institutions; it's about all the places and situations where people can take control of their own growth. From YouTube to the local library via the community centre, where there is an opportunity to learn, there is an opportunity to self-learn.

Practically, this could entail assigning people a cooperative project with minimal guidance, allowing them to decipher the best path forward. The goal is to encourage exploration, kindle curiosity, and inspire self-learning. In adhering to Mitra's philosophy, we make these self-directed discoveries. And this isn't confined to adolescent classrooms; it is embodied in Google's 20% time, 3M's 15% rule, or Tim Ferriss' 4-hour work week. It's about taking control of your own learning: autonomy – and also employing that growth mindset we hear so much about.

In the spirit of the Ideas Guy, this is our call to become advocates for self-learning, encouraging our children, our students, our teams to take charge of their learning journey, sparking their curiosity and helping them realise that, indeed, the limit of their potential is but the horizon they choose to see.

# ENCOURAGE SELF-LEARNING

# [ PART IV ]

# AUTHENTICITY - FINDING YOUR VOICE

THE PRIVILEGE OF A LIFETIME IS
TO BECOME WHO YOU TRULY ARE.
CARL JUNG

As we step into the fourth act of our journey: Authenticity - Finding Your Voice, we find ourselves on a landscape that echoes with the powerful resonance of genuineness and sincerity. Imagine it as a profound sanctuary, where the Ideas Guy unearths the essence of their individuality, unravels the courage to bare their soul, and nurtures the spirit to embrace their uniqueness.

Authenticity. It's not merely a characteristic, it's a symphony of expression, guiding our actions, principles, and convictions. It's the bravery to acknowledge our narrative, the daringness to vocalise our thoughts, and the audacity to celebrate our distinctiveness. It's not just about broadcasting a message; it's about embodying that message.

In this chapter, we will come shoulder-to-shoulder with the pioneers who've had the courage to be authentic, to assert their truths, and to inspire others through their genuineness. We will uncover their tales of victories, their testaments of resilience, and their tales of courage, which will illuminate our path as we voyage towards finding our voice.

Authenticity isn't about crafting a facade or following a predefined template; it's about composing our narrative, one that vibrates harmoniously with our deepest core. It's not a destination to be arrived at but an ongoing journey, a continuous process of aligning our outward expressions with our innermost beliefs.

Authenticity is about erecting bridges of trust, credibility, and respect. It's not an endeavour of ceaseless acclaim; it's a commitment to personal truth. It isn't about the pursuit of perfection; it's about the embracement of honesty.

Within the expanse of Authenticity, we will encounter several models that guide us to explore and understand this crucial concept more deeply.

Firstly, the **AUTHENTIC LEADERSHIP MODEL**: Crafted by Bill George, this model emphasises the idea that authentic leaders act in accordance with their core values and convictions. It's the model that invites us to lead not only with our minds but with our hearts. It advocates the unison of our actions with our beliefs, transforming us into living embodiments of our principles.

Secondly, we might consider the **POSITIVE DISINTEGRATION THEORY**: Introduced by Kazimierz Dąbrowski, this model proposes that personal growth is born out of periods of psychological tension and conflict. It's a testament to the transformative power of adversity, reminding us that, just like a piece of coal transforming into a diamond under pressure, our true brilliance often emerges in times of challenge.

Then, we have the **SELF-DETERMINATION THEORY**: Developed by psychologists Richard Ryan and Edward Deci, this theory highlights the pivotal role of autonomy, competence, and relatedness in promoting motivation and personal well-being. It guides us towards an enriched understanding of the facets that constitute our authentic selves and emphasising the nourishment of these facets.

Next, the **IMPRESSION MANAGEMENT THEORY**: Crafted by Erving Goffman, this model explores the ways we curate and manage our social image. It serves as a reminder of the societal lenses through which we view and express our Authenticity. It prompts us to understand that, while our social image is important, we should never let it overshadow our true selves.

Finally, think about the **THEORY OF NARRATIVE IDENTITY:** Proposed by Dan McAdams, this model accentuates the importance of personal stories in shaping our identities. It underscores the narrative nature of our personal growth, reminding us that our journey towards Authenticity is akin to an evolving story, with each chapter contributing to the development of our unique identity.

Each model of Authenticity can become a cornerstone in our quest. As we consider each model, we immerse ourselves in a transformative journey, aligning more and more with our true selves.

Our exploration doesn't stop here. We plunge deeper for it's a vast ocean, teeming with the potential to unlock our true selves. We journey alongside those who've braved the path of Authenticity, who've dared to live open-handed, and in doing so, have ignited a beacon for others.

We uncover their narratives, their victories, their struggles, their lessons. We unravel the blueprint of their integrity, decoding how they've shaped their unique identity. Through their eyes, we gain insights into the dynamic process of Authenticity, its ebbs and flows, its twists and turns, its glorious heights and its challenging depths.

So, let us continue on our pilgrimage, embracing the rhythm of our unique voice, and in the process, nurturing the Ideas Guy within us.

THE SECRET TO HAPPINESS IS TO BE WORKING AT YOUR PASSION. IF YOU WANT TO BE MISERABLE, LEAD A DESPERATE LIFE LIKE EVERYBODY ELSE WHERE THEY DRAG THEIR ASSES TO WORK EVERY DAY BECAUSE THEY HATE THEIR JOB.

YVON CHOUINARD

# [ CHAPTER 13 ]

# CONSCIOUS CONSUMERISM

Nestled amidst the thrumming looms of thought and Innovation, there exists a thread, rich and golden. It's the thread of Authenticity, a vital element in the fabric of the Ideas Guy. To understand it, we follow the trail leading to Yvon Chouinard, the heart and soul of Patagonia, the man who shaped a brand like none other, built on the robust foundations of environmental ethics and sustainable practises.

Yvon Chouinard's journey is a testament to the power of Authenticity, charting an unconventional path that began in the world of adventure sports. A rock climber, environmentalist, and outdoor enthusiast, Chouinard is a man intimately attuned to nature's rhythm. His connection with the environment isn't a fleeting infatuation; it is a deep, enduring bond that would shape his life's work and his ethos.

The genesis of Patagonia was a response to a tangible need. As a climber, Chouinard found himself disenchanted with the climbing equipment of the time, which often damaged the rock faces. Unwilling to compromise on his love for nature, he decided to fashion his own climbing tools, laying the foundation of what would grow into the Chouinard Equipment Company. This was an enterprise borne not out of desire for profit but out of respect for the environment, a venture that set the tone for the creation of Patagonia.

As Patagonia came to life, Chouinard made a conscious decision to keep environmental ethics at its core. This was not a move to capture market trends or to create an attractive brand image; it was simply the natural extension of Chouinard's deep-seated respect for nature. He refused to compromise on this principle, even if it meant lesser profits or slower growth. His commitment was to the planet first, profit second.

The result was a company that placed sustainability at the forefront of its operations. From ensuring fair labour practises to investing in organic cotton, from committing a percentage of its profits to environmental causes to promoting repair and reuse of its products, Patagonia went against the traditional tide. It chose to carve its own path, marked by responsibility, respect, and a conscious consideration of its environmental impact.

Chouinard's vision wasn't without challenges. The shift to organic cotton almost sunk the company. The commitment to repair and reuse wasn't economically lucrative. Yet, these bold choices were rewarded in an unexpected way. Patagonia attracted a loyal consumer base that shared its values, admired its Authenticity, and were willing to pay a premium for its products.

Patagonia's journey is a stark reminder that Authenticity is not a superficial brand attribute to be flaunted in marketing campaigns. It is a deeply ingrained ethos, a compass guiding every decision, every action. For Chouinard, integrity isn't a Strategy; it is a way of life.

As we tread the path of the Ideas Guy, taking a leaf from Chouinard's book, we recognise that Authenticity is not about creating an image, but about being true to our values and principles, regardless of the external pressures or prevailing trends. This is the spirit of conscious consumerism.

Amidst the noise and chaos of a crowded world, this shines as a beacon of truth, illuminating the path towards genuine experiences. Patagonia stands as a testament to the extraordinary power of Authenticity in forging a brand that resonates on a global scale and it  is woven into the very fabric of Patagonia's existence. It goes beyond mere marketing tactics or empty promises. It is an unwavering commitment to environmental responsibility and sustainable practises that defines every aspect of the company's operations. Patagonia's Authenticity is not a façade but a genuine embodiment of their core values.

In a world increasingly conscious of environmental sustainability, this matters more than ever. People are awakening to the impact their choices have on the planet and are seeking brands that align with their values. Patagonia's authentic commitment to environmental responsibility has struck a resounding chord with cognisant consumers. It has become more than a clothing company; it is a symbol of hope, showing the possibility of aligning business success with ethical responsibility.

Authenticity is the currency of trust. In an age of scepticism and information overload, trust has become a precious commodity. Patagonia's unwavering commitment to its values has built a foundation of trust with its customers. When someone purchases a Patagonia product, they know they are supporting a brand that walks the talk and actively contributes to positive change. This trust cultivates a deep connection, fostering loyalty and advocacy.

It also holds the power to inspire. Patagonia's dedication to sustainability has not only influenced its customers but has sparked a broader movement for change. It serves as a catalyst, inspiring individuals and businesses alike to reevaluate their practises and embrace greater environmental responsibility. By leading with Authenticity, Patagonia has shown that it is possible to marry business success with a genuine commitment to the well-being of our planet.

On September 14, 2022, a letter of profound significance was released by Patagonia, captivating the hearts and minds of people worldwide. Penned by the visionary founder, the letter announced an unprecedented move that would reshape the company's future and its role in the world.

Patagonia revealed its decision to give away its shares to a newly formed charitable trust named the Holdfast Collective. This transformative act signalled a departure from the conventional norms of business and a recommitment to a higher purpose.

At the heart of this decision was a profound message: "Earth is now our only shareholder." With these words, Patagonia severed its ties with traditional shareholders who often prioritise profits over environmental concerns. By relinquishing this financial dependency, the company could steadfastly pursue its mission of protecting and preserving our planet.

The letter unfolded a vision for a more sustainable future. Patagonia set forth ambitious goals, pledging to achieve carbon neutrality by 2025, relying solely on renewable energy sources, and exclusively utilising recycled or organic materials in their products. Furthermore, the company vowed to donate 1% of its annual sales to environmental organisations, reinforcing its commitment to effecting positive change.

The response to this remarkable letter was resounding. People from all walks of life hailed Patagonia's commitment to environmental responsibility. The announcement served as a standard bearer in an era overshadowed by climate change and ecological crises. Patagonia's audacious step to give away its shares exemplified the profound impact businesses can have when driven by a greater purpose.

Patagonia's bold vision for the future of business—one where sustainability, responsibility, and purpose coexist harmoniously—embodied their commitments to carbon neutrality, renewable energy, and ethical sourcing. Through these commitments, Patagonia paved the way for a more conscientious and sustainable business landscape.

This letter from Patagonia carries profound implications for the future of business. It demonstrates that profit and environmental responsibility need not be at odds; rather, they can intertwine to create a more sustainable and equitable world. Patagonia's courageous decision serves as an inspiration, igniting the hope that more businesses will follow suit, redefining their purpose and pursuing actions that benefit both people and the planet.

Authenticity is rooted in a deep understanding of your values, those core principles that shape who you are and guide your decisions. It is about living in alignment with those values, even when it challenges the prevailing norms or expectations. By staying true, you forge an unbreakable bond with your true, brave self, creating a solid foundation for genuine actions and inspiring others to do the same.

In a world that often demands conformity, it takes courage to hold steadfast to your values. It means resisting the temptation to compromise or dilute your beliefs for the sake of fitting in or seeking external validation. Authenticity thrives when you embrace your uniqueness and let your choices reflect the essence of who you are. It is in the moments when you stay true to your values, even in the face of adversity, that your Authenticity shines brightest and resonates with others.

When you align your choices with your values, you invite others to do the same. By embodying them, you create a ripple effect that extends far beyond your own life, inspiring others to step into their truth and contribute their unique perspectives to the world.

Authenticity requires more than just words; it demands consistent action. It is not about making empty promises or superficial gestures but about embodying your values through every interaction, decision, and endeavour. When your words and actions align, trust is built, and you shine through.

Consistency is the language of Authenticity. It is the bridge that connects your beliefs with your behaviour, ensuring that what you say and what you do are in harmony. When others see that you consistently live according to your values, they develop a sense of trust and confidence in your brand. They recognise that your intentions are genuine, and that the principles you uphold are not just lip service but the driving force behind your actions.

Walking the talk means embracing integrity and holding yourself accountable to the values you profess. It means making choices that are congruent with your beliefs and honouring your commitments. When you consistently demonstrate Authenticity through your actions, you inspire others to do the same and create a culture of trust and openness.

Authenticity transcends personal or brand identity; it is about making a meaningful impact on the world. It is about embracing a purpose that extends beyond profit and seeks to contribute positively to the greater good. When you lead with purpose, this becomes a force for change.

Leading with purpose requires introspection and a deep understanding of the impact you wish to create. It means aligning your personal or organisational goals with a larger mission that serves the betterment of society and the planet. Authentic leaders understand that their influence goes beyond immediate success or recognition; it is about leaving a lasting legacy of positive change.

When you lead with purpose, you become a catalyst for transformation. Your Authenticity attracts like-minded individuals who share your vision and values. Together, you can amplify your impact and drive meaningful change in your communities and beyond. Your genuine leadership ignites a spark in others, inspiring them to uncover their own purpose and embrace their authentic self, leading to a ripple effect of positive transformation.

# [ APPLYING THIS IN PRACTICE ]

**LEAD WITH PURPOSE**: As we navigate the landscapes of business and personal endeavours, the wisdom of Yvon Chouinard resonates deeply: leading with purpose is the compass that guides our journey. Just as Patagonia has demonstrated, infusing purpose into every action is the key to creating a legacy that extends beyond profits.

To harness the transformative power of purpose, start by defining your mission. Clearly articulate the "why" behind what you do—whether you're an individual, a business, or a charitable organisation. Align your actions with this mission, allowing it to shape your decisions, strategies, and initiatives. Much like Patagonia's commitment to environmental activism, let your purpose steer your ship in stormy seas and calm waters alike.

As Chouinard did with Patagonia's "Don't Buy This Jacket" campaign, share your values openly and honestly with your audience. Embrace transparency about your goals, challenges, and progress. This genuine communication creates a connection that transcends transactional relationships and cultivates loyalty built on shared ideals.

Remember that purpose is not a static concept. Continuously assess and refine your path, adapting to the changing needs of your stakeholders and the world at large. Just as Patagonia evolved from a small climbing gear company to a champion of environmental responsibility, allow your purpose to evolve, guiding you toward new heights of impact.

By leading with purpose, you infuse every step with intention, transforming actions into meaningful contributions. Let Authenticity and sustainability resonate in every aspect of your life. Embrace a mindful approach to your daily actions, making conscious decisions about the resources you consume and the waste you generate. In a world where disposable convenience has become the norm, take a stand for sustainability. Reduce waste, practise recycling and upcycling, and opt for eco-friendly alternatives. By doing so, you not only reduce your environmental impact but also inspire others around you to follow suit.

Our choices matter, and by aligning them with our values and vision for a better world, we become agents of transformation. As conscious consumers, we wield immense power to shape industries, encourage sustainable practises, and create a lasting impact on our planet. Together, we can sail the seas of conscious consumerism, navigating with purpose, Authenticity, and a deep commitment to the well-being of our planet and its inhabitants.

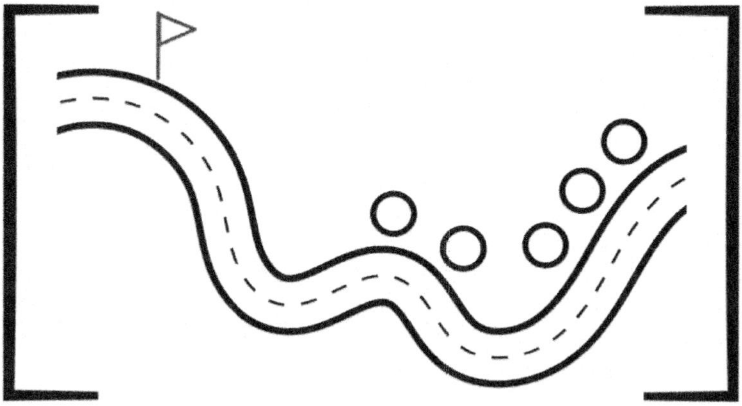

LEAD WITH PURPOSE

A CRISIS HIGHLIGHTS ALL OF OUR FAULT LINES. WE CAN PRETEND THAT WE HAVE NOTHING TO LEARN, OR WE CAN TAKE THIS OPPORTUNITY TO OWN THE TRUTH AND MAKE A BETTER FUTURE FOR OURSELVES AND OTHERS.

**BRENÉ BROWN**

# [ CHAPTER 14 ]

# EMBRACING VULNERABILITY

If you've ever stood on the precipice of sharing a truth, your heart dancing a wild jig in your chest, then you have tasted the bitter brew of vulnerability. It's not a taste we relish, is it? It's uncomfortable, disconcerting - but it's also the gateway to Authenticity, to connection, to transformative self-discovery.

Navigating the uncharted waters of vulnerability can be daunting. But there's a seasoned explorer who's braved these turbulent seas and returned with a map etched with wisdom and understanding: Brené Brown.

Imagine being lost in a dark forest, shrouded in a cloak of uncertainty, when you find a lantern. Its gentle, warming light guides you through the shadowed trees, illuminating a path towards truth. Brené Brown is this lantern for many, her work in understanding vulnerability, the beacon lighting their journey.

From her early days as a social worker to her current status as a renowned researcher and bestselling author, Brown's career has been a quest to understand the human spirit's resilience and wholeness. But her journey was not always a smooth sail.

In 1998, when Brown embarked on her doctoral research at the University of Houston, she chose connection, our ability to empathise, belong and love, as her field of study. As she dove deeper, she encountered powerful undercurrents of vulnerability, courage, shame, and empathy, threatening to upset her long-held beliefs.

Brown found herself on a cliff edge, staring into an abyss of uncertainty. It would have been easier to step back, to retreat into the comfort of what was known and safe. But she did the unexpected, the courageous; she plunged headfirst into the uncharted waters of vulnerability.

This leap of faith led her to develop "The Daring Way", a programme that inspires individuals, teams, and organisations to embrace their vulnerabilities and live authentically. Her work was like a lighthouse, casting a comforting light on the rocky shores of shame, showing us that these difficult terrains can be navigated, that we can reach the safe harbour of self-acceptance.

Then came her 2010 TEDx talk, "The Power of Vulnerability". In this riveting dialogue, she pulled back the curtain on vulnerability, challenging our perception of it as a weakness. Instead, she revealed it as a birthplace of creativity, Innovation, and change, a gateway to Authenticity.

Her words resonated, like a pebble creating ripples across a still lake. The talk rapidly gained momentum and is now one of the most viewed TED talks of all time, reaching millions globally. This wasn't just a talk; it was an open invitation to embrace our imperfections, a call to courage.

Through her bestselling books, such as "Daring Greatly", "Rising Strong", and "Braving the Wilderness", Brown provided tools to help us navigate the rough seas of vulnerability, shame, and fear. Her words are like a compass guiding us towards sincerity, urging us to step out of our comfort zones, to dare greatly, and to rise strong.

Her expedition into vulnerability shows us that it's not about winning or losing; it's about showing up, being seen, living brave and credible lives. She's made waves in understanding vulnerability, inspiring us to embrace it, and, in doing so, discover our truest selves.

As we journey deeper, remember that Brown's voyage is a testament to what lies beyond the daunting seas of vulnerability. The waters may be rough, and the voyage arduous, but as she shows us, it's on these turbulent seas that we find our true north, our intimate selves. Are we ready to set sail?

So, walk with me now. Let's tread the winding path that has been mapped out. It's a path that leads to understanding, to a deeper connection with ourselves and others.

Brené Brown's work isn't just about vulnerability. It's a clarion call to a profound form of Authenticity. An Authenticity that acknowledges our imperfections, our fears, our missteps, and embraces them as part of our story. It's about understanding that vulnerability is not a synonym for weakness, but rather "the birthplace of Innovation, creativity, and change."

To illustrate this, she shares stories of individuals who, through their willingness to be vulnerable, have unearthed deep reservoirs of strength, resilience, and ingenuity. She compels us to rethink our understanding of vulnerability, to view it not as a hindrance, but a catalyst for transformation. This is the essence of IDEAS–start from a place of openness, nakedness, vulnerability–cards on the table.

Her exploration goes beyond the individual. She also dives into how these concepts can revolutionise our interactions, our relationships, our communities. "Authenticity is a collection of choices that we have to make every day. It's about the choice to show up and be real. The choice to be honest. The choice to let our true selves be seen," she says.

In the realm of the Ideas Guy, this resonates profoundly. After all, aren't our best ideas, our most innovative thoughts, often borne from our most vulnerable moments? Those times when we dare to venture outside our comfort zones, to question, to challenge, to explore the unknown waters of our minds?

As we continue, we begin to grasp the transformative power of vulnerability exposing shame for what it is: a lie. They aren't just concepts to be understood, but practises to be embodied, lifestyles to be adopted. They are, in essence, the very roots from which our Authenticity sprouts and flourishes.

Embrace vulnerability. Embrace Authenticity. Let them be your guide as you navigate the complex landscape of Innovation and discovery. And as you do, remember the words of Brené Brown: "Vulnerability is not winning or losing; it's having the courage to show up and be seen when we have no control over the outcome."

Are you ready to step onto the battleground? To show up, to be seen, to embrace your vulnerability? It's a daunting proposition, but therein lies the heart of who we are, the essence of the Ideas Guy. It's a journey worth undertaking, a risk worth taking. "Only when we are brave enough to explore the darkness will we discover the infinite power of our light."

Here, Brené Brown stands as a bastion of truth and courage. Her teachings on the power of vulnerability and the importance of emotional courage have sparked a global conversation, inspiring individuals to step into their true self and embrace their unique stories. In this world of beautifully filtered photos and carefully curated personas, Brown's words remind us to look beyond.

To seed vulnerability means to create spaces where we can show up, where we can share our stories, our struggles, and our triumphs without fear of judgement or criticism. It's about acknowledging that we are human, that we are works in progress, that it's okay to have cracks in our armour.

Vulnerability requires us to venture outside of our comfort zones, to challenge our beliefs, and to confront our fears. It's about embracing the uncertainty and the risk that comes with trying something new or sharing a part of ourselves that we usually keep hidden. It's in these moments when we dare to expose ourselves, that we connect most deeply with others and with our authentic identity.

Authenticity requires courage. It's about standing up for what we believe in, even when it's uncomfortable or unpopular. It's about acknowledging our flaws and imperfections, our hopes and fears, and owning our stories with grace and humility. It's about choosing courage over comfort, even when the road gets tough.

Brown encourages us to "Dare Greatly", to step into the arena, to show up and be seen, despite the risks and the potential for failure. It's about embracing our fallibility and recognising that it's the courage to continue that counts. When we practise courage, we step into our Authenticity, and we inspire others to do the same.

Authenticity is about forging meaningful connections with others, based on mutual respect, understanding, and shared vulnerability. It's about letting go of who we think we should be and embracing who we truly are. It's about creating an environment where others feel safe to do the same.

Brown tells us that "Authenticity is a collection of choices that we have to make every day. It's about the choice to show up and be real. The choice to be honest. The choice to let our true selves be seen." By kindling connection, we give others permission to be authentic, and we create a ripple effect that extends far beyond our own sphere of influence.

Brené Brown's teachings serve as a gentle reminder that our worthiness does not hinge on our achievements, our appearances, or our societal status. It's a journey that begins with a single step, a journey towards Authenticity. And it's a journey that's well worth the walk.

## [ APPLYING THIS IN PRACTICE ]

**PRACTISE VULNERABILITY AS STRENGTH:** To put Authenticity into practise, begin with embracing vulnerability in your day-to-day life. It starts with being open about your feelings, struggles, and triumphs, both with yourself and those around you. It might feel challenging initially, but over time, this openness fosters deeper connections and promotes a culture of empathy.

This extends to embracing failure as well. Rather than seeing it as a setback, view failure as an opportunity for growth. Take ownership of your mistakes and let them guide your learning process. By doing so, you make it easier for others around you to accept their own vulnerabilities.

Similarly, cultivate spaces that encourage others to share their stories without fear of judgement. Whether it's in the workplace or in personal relationships, foster a culture that celebrates Authenticity and vulnerability.

In the spirit of Brené Brown, let's remember that vulnerability is not a sign of weakness, but a mark of courage. It is through vulnerability that we connect authentically with ourselves and others. By embracing our limitations, we pave the way for a more empathetic and authentic world.

This isn't about hanging out dirty laundry for all to see but it is also not about brushing it under the rug either. It's about controlled vulnerability - know where, when, and who it is safe to be fully open with. Who are your people? But in every situation, there needs to be integrity of self – the same in public as in private. Don't shy away from difficult conversations and always strive to communicate openly and honestly. This, coupled with listening empathetically to others, builds trust and fosters deeper connections.

This also means you need to practise self-compassion. We are often our own harshest critics, and this can prevent us from embracing our authentic selves. Be patient with yourself, and remember that everyone is on their own unique journey, including you. The only person you compete with is yesterday's you. 1% better.

As we navigate through life, let us remember that our vulnerability is our strength. It is through embracing our authentic selves that we inspire Authenticity in others and contribute to a more compassionate and understanding world.

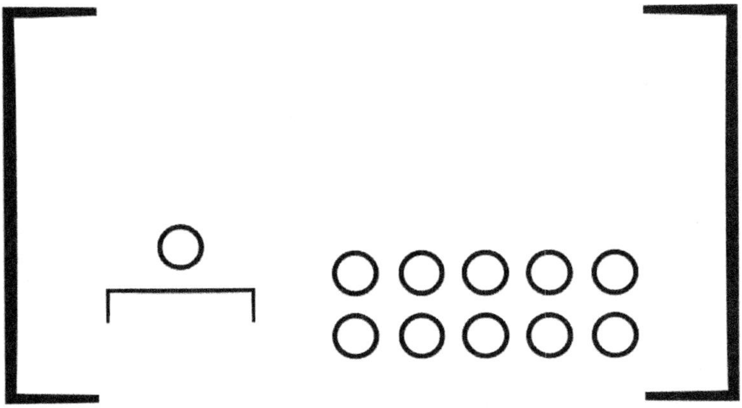

PRACTISE VULNERABILITY AS STRENGTH

HISTORY, DESPITE ITS WRENCHING PAIN CANNOT BE UNLIVED, BUT IF FACED WITH COURAGE NEED NOT BE LIVED AGAIN.

**MAYA ANGELOU**

# [ CHAPTER 15 ]

# NAVIGATING YOUR NARRATIVE

Say hello to Maya Angelou. Marguerite Annie Johnson to give her full title. It is the name she was given at birth, but the world knows her as Maya, a radiant lodestar of Authenticity, a towering pillar of strength.

Ever heard the phrase, "Still I rise"? It's Ms Angelou. Born in the simmering cauldron of racial prejudice, grappling with the monstrous trauma of her past, she ventures through the flame and heat of her circumstances and, like a phoenix, she rises. She takes the sharp shards of her suffering, the throbbing pain of her past, and she works with them. Moulds them. Transforms them into words pulsating with power, words that reach into souls, shake mountains, and shift paradigms.

Maya Angelou stood as a towering presence in American history—a poet, author, and civil rights activist. Born on April 4, 1928, in St. Louis, Missouri, she navigated the daunting landscapes of a segregated society during her upbringing. Despite the early battles she faced, Angelou transformed into a luminary whose influence ignites hearts and empowers minds globally.

She doesn't just bear her truth; she becomes a valiant warrior wielding it. Her weapon? Wisdom, forged in the furnace of her trials, sharpened by her resilience. She's a writer, a poet, a civil rights activist - she lifts her voice high for the voiceless. Through her, the silent whispers become roars. The shadows step into the spotlight.

Angelou's life unfolded as a mosaic of roles—a writer, poet, memoirist, actress, and songstress. At the pinnacle of her literary achievements stands "I Know Why the Caged Bird Sings," a memoir that unearths her childhood narrative, marked by racial adversity, personal struggle, and the profound journey of self-discovery. This masterpiece has etched its place as a cornerstone in modern literature, stirring vital conversations on race, identity, and the resilience that courses through our veins.

Her writing dances with imagery that paints vivid stories, with prose that feels like soulful melodies, and with candid introspection into the tapestry of human sentiment. With eloquence, she uncovers life's intricate layers—love, pain, and the unending pursuit of joy—often weaving threads of her own life into the fabric of her words. Her poems and prose shine light on themes of empowerment, triumph over adversity, and the sheer fortitude that resides in the core of the human spirit.

For Maya Angelou, Authenticity is more than a personal attribute, it's a responsibility, a commitment. It's lifting up your experiences, your reality, for the world to see. It's an open declaration, "This is me, this is my truth," and claiming ownership of it. But it doesn't stop there. It's lending an ear to the hushed tales that others share in the secrecy of the dark, acknowledging them, amplifying them.

In each word she pens down, each speech she passionately delivers, Maya is Authenticity personified. By bearing her truth, she gives others the courage to find their own voices. She inspires them to navigate their own narratives, to unearth their own truths.

Life, as we all know, is a rollercoaster, right? Full of dizzying highs and crushing lows, unexpected twists and turns. She knew that better than most. She stared adversity in the eye, met it face to face, and chose to rise. Her legacy is a profound testament to the transformative power of Authenticity. Her life story, an anthem of resilience and hope that continues to reverberate within us, touching chords in our hearts, reminding us of the strength within us all.

This is Maya Angelou. Her story is not just a tale of overcoming; it's a masterclass in integrity. An epic narrative of a woman who dared to be herself and, in doing so, allowed others to see the power in being true to themselves.

Beyond her literary feats, Maya Angelou breathed fiery life into the battle for civil rights and social justice. Shoulder to shoulder with leaders like Martin Luther King Jr. and Malcolm X, she lent her voice and presence to confront racial disparity and discrimination. Angelou's activism and unwavering commitment to equality left an indelible mark on the annals of history.

The accolades that grace Maya Angelou's legacy reflect her deep and lasting influence on society. Her walls bore honorary degrees, including the Presidential Medal of Freedom—the highest civilian accolade in the United States. Through her literary compositions, powerful speeches, and enduring influence on literature and civil rights, Maya Angelou's legacy reverberates through time, a beacon of truth, justice, and the boundless power of the human spirit.

Maya Angelou was a woman deeply inspired by a profound quote from the Roman playwright Terence: "I am human, nothing human can be alien to me." She often recited this line, and it seeped into her worldview, her words, her authentic self.

Imagine her perspective: I'm human. You're human. We're all human. There's an undeniable connectedness, a shared essence that cannot be overlooked. Angelou believed in the power of these words; they were a mantra, a philosophy she carried throughout her life.

In the echo of these ancient words, she imparts a universal truth. She's acknowledging that she shares the spectrum of human experiences–the joy, the pain, the triumphs, the failures. And it's this shared essence, this shared humanity, that echoes in the very heart of her Authenticity.

The phrase is an ode to equality, a testament to the respect for human dignity that underpins her character. It's a call to recognise the humanity in each other and ourselves, to embrace and celebrate it, despite its imperfections.

In embracing this belief, Angelou shows us the power of our narratives and how our stories, our experiences, intertwine with the stories and experiences of others. Through her Authenticity, she offers us a lens to view ourselves and others without pretence or judgement, to experience the richness and depth of the human spirit, and to engage with the world with an open heart and mind.

Maya Angelou reflects back at us our shared humanity. She illustrates that Authenticity isn't just about being true to ourselves; it's about recognising and embracing our shared human experience. This powerful understanding, passed down through her words and life, helps us to better navigate our own narratives.

She indeed wrote herself,

> *"Find a beautiful piece of art. If you fall in love with Van Gogh or Matisse or John Oliver Killens, or if you fall in love with the music of Coltrane, the music of Aretha Franklin, or the music of Chopin - find some beautiful art and admire it, and realise that that was created by human beings just like you, no more human, no less."*

Ah, the beauty of that quote. Let's linger on it for a moment: "Find a beautiful piece of art…realise that that was created by human beings just like you, no more human, no less."

Doesn't that line resonate with a deep sense of unity, an echo of shared creativity, a stirring recognition of our shared humanity? Maya Angelou, in her infinite wisdom, invites us to see that art–in its many forms–is an expression of our collective human experience. She urges us to recognise that we are, in essence, no different from those artists, those creators, those beacons of human spirit and ingenuity.

So, when we gaze upon Van Gogh's starry night or lose ourselves in the soulful tunes of Coltrane, we're connecting with something profound, something innately human. We're reminded of our own capacity to create, to inspire, to evoke emotion. At this moment, we are no more or less human than those who created these masterpieces.

Angelou's words remind us that Authenticity isn't about striving to be more than human, nor is it about fearing we are less. It's about embracing our shared humanity, owning our narratives, navigating them with courage and sincerity. She nudges us to seek out art, immerse ourselves in it, and then realise that we, too, possess within us that same spark of creativity, that same profound capacity to touch hearts and change lives.

Like Matisse with his vivid colours and shapes, like Franklin with her riveting blues and soul, we too can shape our narratives, colour them with our authentic selves, and leave a lasting impact. That's the power of Authenticity, a power that Maya Angelou embodied and encourages us all to embrace.

It's a journey, a never-ending quest towards understanding, accepting, and celebrating our full selves, a journey beautifully captured in her narrative, a journey we all must undertake. And so, as we navigate our narratives, let's remember Angelou's words, let's embrace our shared humanity, our shared capacity for creativity, and most importantly, let's celebrate our Authenticity.

In a world of varied scripts and numerous stories, Maya Angelou's resonant voice has shaped our collective consciousness. From her life and works, we glean truths that serve as beacons in our journey.

Authenticity thrives in the soil of self-acceptance. Maya Angelou's life is a testament to the power of owning one's narrative, of embracing every chapter, every twist and turn with grace and fortitude. It emerges when we acknowledge our past, our struggles, and triumphs, and weave them into our unique narrative.

The courage to embrace our individual stories, even those that cause us discomfort, sets the stage for an authentic life. It's about understanding that no experience is wasted, that each event, each interaction, makes us more human, but no more human than any other. Like Maya Angelou, we too can use our narratives, our unique perspectives to impact lives and spark change.

Authenticity is a dance to the tune of your inner truth. Her life and works underscore the importance of staying true to yourself, of honouring your inner voice amidst the clamour of societal expectations and norms. It flourishes when we align our actions with our convictions, when we follow our internal compass rather than the paths dictated by societal norms. It demands that we listen to our intuition, stay rooted in our values, and not sway with every wind of external opinion. By embodying our truth, we inspire others to do the same, fostering a culture of Authenticity that radiates beyond our immediate spheres of influence.

Authenticity is more than a personal attribute; it's a catalyst for change. Maya Angelou, with her powerful narratives and genuine self-expression, has inspired countless individuals to live authentically and courageously. Inspiring others through our actions is the pinnacle of this trait. It means using our narratives, our experiences, to create ripples of change, to make a difference.

Maya Angelou's life serves as a vivid canvas, demonstrating the transformative power of Authenticity. As we embrace these lessons, we inch closer to our true selves, painting our lives with the vibrant colours of sincerity, courage, and truth.

# [ APPLYING THIS IN PRACTICE ]

**LIVE YOUR POETRY:** Life, as Maya Angelou teaches us, is nothing less than a grand and evocative poem, a composition spun from our experiences, struggles, triumphs, and resilience. Our existence is the parchment, and our experiences, the ink that crafts verses of significance. Begin by acknowledging this grand tapestry of your life and see each thread as a part of your journey. It is through the harmony of these threads that your story unfolds.

Every breath you take, every emotion you feel, and every challenge you overcome is a part of your narrative. Embrace these experiences, and let them serve as the verses of your life's poem. Authenticity begins when you stop seeking to mimic someone else's melody and start composing your own.

Allow yourself to resonate with your personal truths, and take courage in expressing them. Your story, laden with Authenticity, becomes a call to arms for those navigating their paths in the vast ocean of life. Do not shy away from your story. Instead, own it and share it with the world, for our shared narratives foster a deeper sense of connection and understanding among us all.

Remember, life isn't solely about reaching a particular destination; it's also about appreciating the journey. The richness of your narrative lies not just in the grand achievements, but also in the simple, everyday moments. Your life isn't defined merely by the extraordinary chapters, but by every line, every word, and every punctuation mark that makes your story uniquely yours.

As you embrace your own narrative, inspire others to discover and honour their stories. We are, after all, a grand symphony of voices, each singing our unique melodies, each adding to the orchestra of life. So, let us craft our verses with truth, let our narratives intertwine and resonate, creating a tapestry of life that reflects our shared and unique human experiences.

As you journey through life, let the teachings of Maya Angelou guide you. Remember, your Authenticity is your power, and your story, your greatest symphony. Embrace your story, live your poetry, and inspire a world of Authenticity one verse at a time.

LIVE YOUR POETRY

I WANTED WHAT EVERYONE WANTS.
TO BE ME, FULL-TIME.

**PHIL KNIGHT**

[ CHAPTER 16 ]

# PERSONALISING SHOES

Meet Phil Knight. Yes, that Phil Knight, the mastermind behind Nike's world domination. From humble beginnings in Oregon to creating a global phenomenon, Knight is a paragon of dedication.

Remember the tagline, "Just Do It"? It's all Phil. From an idea conceived during a class at Stanford, he pursued his dream to create superior athletic shoes. This journey wasn't a joyride; it was filled with obstacles and setbacks, peppered with doubts and uncertainty. Still, Phil persisted, fuelled by his authentic passion, grounded by his unique vision.

Born on February 24, 1938, in Portland, Oregon, Phil Knight was immersed in the world of sports from an early age. As a young boy, he developed a deep love for running, finding solace and joy in the rhythm of his own footsteps. Little did he know that this passion would become the foundation for his future endeavours.

After graduating from the University of Oregon, Knight went on to pursue his MBA at Stanford Graduate School of Business. It was during his time at Stanford that the seeds of his entrepreneurial spirit were planted. Inspired by a business class project, he envisioned creating a company that would revolutionise the athletic footwear industry.

In 1964, Knight and his former track coach, Bill Bowerman, co-founded Blue Ribbon Sports, which would later evolve into Nike. With a shared vision of Innovation, performance, and authentic athlete-centred design, they set out on a mission to bring high-quality athletic shoes to the market.

The early years of Nike were marked by challenges and setbacks. Phil Knight faced financial struggles and fierce competition from well-established brands. But his unwavering belief in his vision and his passion for elevating the athletic experience fueled his determination to push forward.

Knight's commitment to Authenticity was the driving force behind Nike's success. He recognised the importance of connecting deeply with athletes and understanding their needs and aspirations. This led to groundbreaking collaborations with iconic athletes such as Michael Jordan, Serena Williams, and Cristiano Ronaldo, who became ambassadors of the Nike brand, embodying its values of excellence, resilience, and Authenticity.

Under Knight's leadership, Nike grew into a global powerhouse, pushing the boundaries of Innovation and design in the athletic industry. The iconic swoosh logo became a symbol of quality, inspiring athletes and individuals around the world to embrace their unique journeys and unleash their full potential.

Le's rewind the clock. It's 1984. Nike is a promising upstart, but Converse rules the basketball courts. Phil Knight believes in his brand's wings, but needs someone to lift them skyward. When rookie Michael Jordan glides across the hardwood, Knight sees poetry in motion. Yet rationale recoils at unproven potential. Knight built Nike through prudence, not pricey gambles.

Sonny Vaccaro pleads his case: Jordan's that one-in-a-million. Knight's belief strains against his business sense. Still, he knows rule-breakers shape history. So he takes the unprecedented leap, offering the kingly sum. Jordan joins Nike's court. The people cheer but Knight braces for mockery at his indulgence.

Then Jordan soars, Nike sales with him. The Air Jordan line becomes their backbone, Jordan their spirit. Knight's faith validated by box office ticket lines and dollar signs. Vision sometimes requires going against the grain of reason. Knight's trust in Jordan's potential forever changed Nike's flight path. One audacious idea, allowed to take flight, can change everything.

Beyond his contributions to the athletic world, Phil Knight's commitment to social responsibility and environmental sustainability has left an indelible mark. Nike's "Move to Zero" initiative, aiming for a zero-carbon and zero-waste future, reflects Knight's belief in using business as a force for positive change.

Phil Knight's remarkable journey is a testament to the transformative power of Authenticity. His unwavering passion, resilience in the face of adversity, and commitment to Innovation have not only revolutionised the athletic industry but have also inspired countless individuals to embrace their own authentic paths.

We are reminded that Authenticity is not just about building a successful business or achieving personal recognition. It's about staying true to your passion, embracing challenges, and leaving a lasting impact on the world around you.

Phil Knight wasn't just a businessman, he was a champion of making a difference. His weapon? A genuine passion, kindled by his love for running, and sharpened by his relentless spirit. An entrepreneur, an innovator, a game-changer–Phil showed the world the power of an authentic dream.

For him, Authenticity was more than a personal trait; it was a driving force, an unyielding determination. It was holding fast to his dream, his vision, amidst the noise of the world, amidst the voices of doubt. And it went beyond that. It was inspiring others to believe in their dreams, encouraging them to pursue their genuine passions.

In each pair of Nike shoes, each innovative design, each compelling ad, Phil was Authenticity in action. By relentlessly pursuing his passion, he inspired millions worldwide to believe in their own dreams. He encouraged them to embrace their true selves, their unique passions, and strive for greatness.

Knight's story is not just a tale of creating a global brand; it's a masterclass in building a place of meaning. A riveting narrative of a man who dared to be true to himself, who dared to pursue his authentic dream, and, in doing so, inspired others to embrace their unique passions, their true selves.

Phil Knight was a man who resonated deeply with the phrase "Be true to who you are." He often echoed these words in his actions, and they permeated his approach to life and business.

Consider his perspective: I'm a dreamer, a doer, a believer. You too have your dreams, your passions. We're all unique in our aspirations. Knight believed in this profoundly; it was a philosophy that he carried throughout his life. In the echo of these words, he imparts a powerful message. He's acknowledging that he shares the spectrum of human aspirations–the dreams, the passions, the hopes. And it's this shared essence that underpins his success.

The phrase demonstrates how his path was shaped by personal authenticity and respect for individual expression. It's a call to recognise our unique dreams and to pursue them hard. Knight shows us how our dreams, our passions, when pursued authentically, can lead to extraordinary outcomes. Through his journey, he offers us a lens to view ourselves and our aspirations without pretence or judgement, to pursue our dreams with courage and tenacity.

Remember, as Knight would say, "Just Do It." Let these words ring in our ears as we step into the world, daring to chase our dreams, no matter how big or small, no matter how impossible they may seem. Just Do It–a call to Authenticity, a call to action, a call to unleash our potential and make our mark in the world.

Authenticity flourishes when fueled by genuine passion. Knight's story shows how chasing a dream—and facing obstacles with fierce determination—can transform a life. True authenticity comes from embracing our deepest aspirations and letting them guide our individual paths.

Embracing our dreams, especially those that might seem out of reach, paves the way for an authentic life. It's about understanding that no aspiration is too lofty, that every effort, every setback, is a stepping stone towards our goal. Like Phil, we too can leverage our dreams, our unique visions to create an impact and drive change.

Authenticity thrives when we stay true to our unique vision. Phil Knight's life and actions underscore the significance of adhering to one's vision, of honouring your inner voice amidst the noise of the marketplace. It blossoms when our actions align with our vision, when we choose the road less travelled over the beaten path. It requires us to listen to our inner voice, stay grounded in our values, and not be swayed by the winds of popular opinion. By staying true to our vision, we inspire others to do the same, fostering a culture that reverberates beyond our immediate spheres of influence.

But it isn't just a personal virtue.

Inspiring others through our actions is the zenith of Authenticity. It means using our dreams, our passion, to create waves of change, to empower others to embrace their ambitions and live their truth. Our actions, imbued with Authenticity, can serve as a guiding light for others, inspiring them to chart their journeys with courage.

## [ APPLYING THIS IN PRACTICE ]

**PURSUE PASSION**: Phil Knight's journey reminds us of the power of embracing our passions wholeheartedly. It's about finding what truly ignites our inner fire and dedicating ourselves to pursuing those passions.

Start by exploring your genuine interests and uncovering what brings you joy and fulfilment. Identify the activities, causes, or fields that resonate deeply with you, and immerse yourself in them with passion and enthusiasm. Be your authentic self in this pursuit.

Embrace a mindset of continuous learning and growth in your chosen field. Seek out opportunities to deepen your knowledge, develop new skills, and expand your horizons. Surround yourself with like-minded individuals who share your passion, and engage in meaningful conversations and collaborations that further fuel your enthusiasm.

When pursuing your passions, be willing to take risks and step outside of your comfort zone. Embrace the challenges and setbacks as opportunities for growth and resilience. Stay true to your own vision and values, and don't let external expectations or societal pressures derail your authentic journey.

Lead by example and inspire others through your passionate pursuits. Share your experiences, insights, and lessons learned along the way. Together, we can create a community of individuals who are driven by their authentic passions and contribute to a world that celebrates diversity and creativity.

Remember, embracing passionate pursuits is not just about achieving success or recognition; it's about living a life that is aligned with who you really are. It's about finding fulfilment in the journey itself and making a meaningful impact in your chosen domain.

So, dare to dream big, follow your heart, and pursue your passions. Embrace the journey of self-discovery and growth, and let your authentic passion guide you towards a life of purpose, fulfilment, and unrivalled success.

**PURSUE PASSION**

[ PART V ]

# STRATEGY - PLOTTING THE PATH

LEADERS ESTABLISH THE VISION FOR THE FUTURE AND SET THE STRATEGY FOR GETTING THERE.
JOHN P. KOTTER

We've now arrived at the pivotal moment of our expedition: Strategy - Plotting the Path. Hear its silent whisper, its subtle guidance. Strategy is a language we often forget to listen to. It's a language that speaks in symbols, signs, and patterns. It's a language of the discerning, the visionary, the Ideas Guy.

Strategy is not just a blueprint, it's an ongoing dialogue between vision and execution, an ongoing conversation between the journey and the destination. It's about making informed decisions, about aligning actions with objectives. It's a compass that helps you navigate the tumultuous seas of uncertainty, a map that leads you to the shores of success.

As we embark on this section, we'll meet the strategists, the architects of growth, the orchestrators of progress. We'll decode their stories, their achievements, their struggles. We'll realise that Strategy is not a fixed construct, but an evolving entity, a dynamic and flexible framework.

In Strategy, we stand on the precipice of a mountain, gazing at a terrain marked by twists, turns, peaks, and valleys. It's the realm of the deliberate, the mindful, the calculated. It's the realm of possibilities, a dance of probabilities. It's where the 'what' meets the 'how.'

Strategy is the wizard that can conjure serendipity, the alchemist that can transform chaos into coherence. It encourages the audacious, the inventive, the daring. It invites us to step outside our comfort zones, to tread the less explored path, to chart a course that leads to our envisioned future.

As we journey through this chapter, we'll walk alongside the visionaries, the innovators, the pioneers. We'll decipher their narratives, their accomplishments, their challenges. We'll understand that Strategy isn't a one-time event, but an ongoing process, a continuous cycle of ideation, planning, execution, evaluation, and refinement.

Strategy is not about merely surviving or maintaining the status quo. It's not about reckless risk-taking or impulsive decision-making. It's not about being different for the sake of differentiation or new for the sake of novelty. It doesn't advocate a myopic view of success or a neglect of long-term implications.

Crucially, Strategy isn't an endpoint. It's not a box to be checked off, a task to be ticked off. It's an expedition, a voyage, a mindset. It's a commitment to continuous learning, to relentless improvement, to constant adaptation.

Each strategic model is a different perspective, a unique viewpoint to better understand the landscape. Although they tend to be about business, there is application of them all across multiple spectrums.

**THE ANSOFF MATRIX**, first on our list, is the brainchild of H. Igor Ansoff. It's a strategic planning tool that offers a scaffold to help leaders and marketers design strategies for prospective growth. The Matrix extends in four directions: Market Penetration, Market Development, Product Development, and Diversification. These dimensions encourage us to investigate our current offerings, scrutinise our target markets, and muse over the potential of new products or new audiences. The Ansoff Matrix invites us to ponder over existing paths and consider new frontiers whether we are in business or not.

Second, we have the realms of **PORTER'S GENERIC STRATEGIES**, a model crafted by renowned academic Michael E. Porter. His model gives us three roads: cost leadership, differentiation, and focus. Cost leadership leverages efficiencies and scales to outperform competitors on price. Differentiation, on the other hand, seeks to deliver a unique offering that makes your company stand out. The focus Strategy encourages you to carve a niche, to offer a specialised service or product for a targeted market segment. Porter's model provides a roadmap to navigate the competitive landscape, encouraging us to ask the hard questions about our market.

Then, the spotlight shifts to the **BCG MATRIX** or the **BOSTON CONSULTING GROUP MATRIX**. It's a strategic planning tool that guides a company to identify its most profitable areas, potential investment zones, and areas for cost reduction. In this matrix, businesses and products are classified as Stars, Cash Cows, Question Marks, or Dogs. Each category presents its own strategic options, ranging from heavy investment to divestment. The BCG Matrix nudges us to assess our portfolio, to juggle our investments, and strategise our growth trajectories.

Next, the **BLUE OCEAN STRATEGY**, conceived by W. Chan Kim and Renée Mauborgne. It's a disruptive approach that encourages businesses to seek uncontested market spaces, creating and capturing new demand, instead of competing head-to-head in existing markets. It's about making the competition irrelevant by charting a new course, by venturing into the blue ocean. This Strategy dares us to innovate, to challenge conventions, and to carve out a unique value proposition.

Finally, we can embark on an understanding of the **THREE BOX SOLUTION**, an innovative Strategy model introduced by Vijay Govindarajan. This model emphasises the need for organisations to maintain performance in the present (Box 1), selectively abandon the past (Box 2), and create a successful future (Box 3). This model isn't about choosing between the now and the future; it's about doing both. It's about striking a balance, about juggling the often conflicting demands of managing today's requirements while simultaneously innovating for tomorrow.

These strategic models can be our compass, guiding us through the complex seas of Strategy. We will unpack the stories of visionary strategists who've dared to plot their path. They've danced with uncertainty, wrestled with choices, and turned roadblocks into stepping stones. They've reinvented industries, disrupted norms, and crafted pathways to success.

Together, we'll embark on this journey, this expedition of Strategy - Plotting the Path. We'll reimagine the future, anticipate the twists and turns, and learn to navigate the intricate dance of Strategy. The terrain of Strategy is calling. Are we ready to answer its call?

TURNING A CULTURE AROUND IS VERY DIFFICULT TO DO BECAUSE IT'S BASED ON A SERIES OF MANY, MANY DECISIONS, AND THE ORGANISATION IS FRAMED BY THOSE DECISIONS.

HOWARD SCHULTZ

# [ CHAPTER 17 ]

# SIPPING SUCCESS

This is a tale of success, a tale steeped in more than just coffee beans. This is the tale of Howard Schultz, a man whose life is a living testament of what it means to be the Ideas Guy. The captain of the Starbucks ship is the maestro of caffeinated dreams. His story is a witness to the power of passion, perseverance, and the pursuit of a grand vision. With a humble beginning and an unwavering belief in the potential of a coffee empire, Schultz carved a path that would forever change the way we sip and savour our favourite brew.

We need to imagine a young man from Brooklyn, not born into wealth, but into aspiration. A family of working-class individuals, a childhood not spent in the lap of luxury, but in the lap of potential, possibility. This is the dream-weaver who reimagined the world of coffee.

In 1982, he found himself in a small chain of coffee bean shops in Seattle. Starbucks, they were called. But the real spark, the real magic, happened in Italy. The espresso bars, teeming with life, connection, community, they spoke to Schultz. They whispered tales of shared experiences, of a communal love for coffee, of a connection that transcended the confines of home and work.

This was Schultz's vision, this sense of belonging. He saw it, felt it, and wanted to bring it to America, wanted to infuse the daily coffee ritual with this Italian spirit. But here's where the plot thickens: the original Starbucks owners didn't see this vision. Didn't believe in it.

So, what did Schultz do? He stepped out, stepped up. He created Il Giornale, a coffee shop that sang the melodies of Italian coffee bars. Two years down this path, and his vision was rewarded. He acquired Starbucks, married it with Il Giornale, and from that union, the Starbucks we know and love today was born. There is a profound lesson on Strategy here: the ability to overcome challenge. To be rejected, to forge ahead regardless and to realise a purpose all require tenacity and a plan.

The path to success is seldom smooth sailing. Schultz encountered numerous obstacles and setbacks along his journey. However, he viewed these challenges as opportunities to grow, adapt, and emerge stronger. Embrace the art of roasting your challenges. Allow them to fuel your determination, refine your Strategy, and ignite your resilience. Remember, it's in the face of adversity that the true measure of success is revealed.

But here's the key: it wasn't just about the coffee. It wasn't about the profits or the business growth. It was about the people, about the "Third Place". A place between home and work, a place of belonging, a place where the barista knows not just your coffee order, but your story, your name.

This is the legacy of Schultz, a legacy that permeates every Starbucks store, every sip of Starbucks drinks. It's a legacy of connection, of shared experiences, of community. And this is what "Sipping Success" means. It's about more than just profits and products. It's about people, about purpose, about creating a sense of belonging.

At the heart of Schultz's success lies the profound understanding that true triumph stems from intertwining purpose and experience in effective Strategy. He recognised that Starbucks could be more than just a place to grab a cup of brown nectar; it could be a haven, a community hub, a gathering spot that fosters genuine connections.

To sip success the Schultz way, we must embrace the art of blending vision and execution. It's not just about the quality of the beans or the allure of the brand—it's about creating an immersive experience, a journey that transcends the beverage itself. From the aroma that envelops the store to the warm smiles of the baristas, every detail is meticulously crafted to evoke a sense of belonging, of being part of something greater. And it's all planned; nothing is incidental.

In Starbucks, you'll find more than just a coffeehouse; it's a sanctuary where people from all walks of life gather, connecting over shared stories and finding solace in the warmth of community. Howard Schultz understood the profound power of fostering belonging–a sense of togetherness that transcends mere transactions. As you venture into the realm of entrepreneurship and community-building, cherish the understanding that success lies not solely in the products or services you offer but in the depth of human connections you cultivate. And be intentional and strategic about how and when you connect.

In the fast-paced world of business, Education, 21st century life in general, it's easy to get swept away in the pursuit of increase and rapid expansion, prioritising individual achievements over collective growth. Yet, as timeless proverbs wisely advise, if you want to go fast, go alone; if you want to go far, go together. The essence of effective Strategy, as highlighted by thought leaders like Simon Sinek, lies in discovering the "why" behind your endeavours. It's about tapping into the sense of community, passionately advocated by American author, speaker and entrepreneur, Seth Godin, that can transform your brand from a mere business or school into a movement, capturing hearts and minds.

Creating a profound sense of belonging starts with understanding your audience, recognising their inherent desire to connect and belong to something greater than themselves. It's the very reason why football teams can evoke unparalleled loyalty, uniting thousands of fans under a shared identity and purpose. It's what ignites the flames of passion and dedication, inspiring people to rally behind a cause, devote their energy, and contribute to a movement that resonates with their values and aspirations.

However, the power of belonging must be wielded responsibly, for, throughout history, unchecked pursuits of belonging have led to extremism and dangerous ideologies. As entrepreneurs and community builders, our mission is to cultivate environments that foster inclusivity, empathy, and understanding. We must ensure that our sense of belonging unites us in positive, constructive ways, supporting one another's growth and flourishing.

The Strategy of belonging stands as a cornerstone of authentic Strategy. Howard Schultz's vision for Starbucks serves as a pillar to the incredible impact of creating an environment where people feel connected and at home.

Rally like-minded individuals around your vision, and seek guidance from mentors who can help navigate the path ahead. Remember that belonging is not just a means to an end; it's an essential element that elevates your venture from a business to a movement, uniting people in shared purpose and passion. Embrace the wisdom of going together, for it is through belonging and collective effort that you can journey far and create a lasting impact on the world.

In a sea of coffee chains, Schultz realised the need to carve out a distinct identity for Starbucks. He took risks, introduced new flavours, and pushed the boundaries of what a coffee shop could be. To sip success, embrace your uniqueness. Blend your passions, experiences, and expertise to create a concoction that is uniquely yours. Don't be afraid to experiment, innovate, and stand out in the crowded marketplace.

Good marketing Strategy, for example, requires an understanding of the triple bottom line: market research (what does the world want and need), competitor analysis (how are others meeting this want or need) and customer personas (who your ideal customer is). It is from this we can find our USP and stand out from it all. Go oat milk decaf macchiato when everyone else drinks the vanilla latte.

Schultz's vision for Starbucks was a grand vision to build a company with a soul–a purpose-driven entity that would make a meaningful impact on the world. To truly savour the taste of success, you must infuse your purpose into every endeavour, embracing the profound importance of aligning your actions with your core values. It's about more than just chasing profit; it's about striving for a greater purpose that extends far beyond financial gains.

On your entrepreneurial journey, let your purpose be the guiding light that illuminates your path. Understand your core purpose and how you can meaningfully affect your customers, employees, and communities. Think of your business as a force for good that creates change beyond just profits.

Consider the ripple effect of your decisions and actions–the lives you touch, the opportunities you create, and the ripple of inspiration you send forth. Purpose-driven entrepreneurship means recognising that you have the power to shape the world around you, and with that power comes great responsibility. Be mindful of the choices you make, and let your purpose guide you in making decisions that align with your values and contribute to the greater good.

Pour your heart and soul into it, infusing each step with purpose and meaning. Let your strategic purpose become the driving force that propels you forward, even in the face of challenges and adversity.

Schultz's commitment to social responsibility and creating a company with a soul set Starbucks apart and inspired a movement that goes beyond coffee cups and cafés. By embracing purpose in your own Strategy, you, too, can create a lasting legacy—one that leaves a mark on the hearts and minds of those you touch.

Take a moment, take a breath, and take a good, hard look at your compass. That compass of purpose, do you feel it? Do you feel the magnetism of it pulling you towards something bigger, something grander than the mere exchange of goods for profit? That's Schultz's gift to us, his wisdom brewed in the crucible of life and leadership. He taught us to pour ourselves, our true selves, into every facet of our work in strategic ways. Our purpose, it's not just an accessory we don on special occasions. It's not a dress we wear when we want to impress. No, our purpose is our skin, our heartbeat, our breath. It's a living, breathing entity that courses through the veins of our actions, our decisions, our successes. And when we align this purpose with our work, magic happens. Real magic. The kind that transforms a mundane cup of coffee into a vessel of connection, a simple coffee shop into a harbour of community.

Swimming these uncharted waters of success, let us learn from the wisdom of Howard Schultz and the Starbucks legacy. Embrace the art of crafting experiences, fostering a culture of belonging, and infusing purpose into your pursuits. Sip success, one cup at a time, and let your voyage be a testament to the power of passion, vision, and unwavering determination to have Strategy front and centre in your organisation.

# [ APPLYING THIS IN PRACTICE ]

**LEAVE AN IMPACT**: Howard Schultz's journey paints a picture of success steeped in purpose and Strategy. He didn't just set out to brew coffee; he wanted to brew a culture of connection, a haven of belonging. He wanted Starbucks to leave a lasting, positive imprint on the world.

To brew your own impact, start by pinpointing your larger purpose in the grand scheme of your endeavours. What is the "beyond" that you aspire to reach? What is the impact you want to make on your customers, your stakeholders, your community? Don't confine your vision to just profit and growth; expand it to encompass the values you hold dear and the change you wish to spark.

Align your actions with this purpose. Ensure every business decision, every Innovation, every interaction is a reflection of this mission. Let it be known that your company stands for something greater, something meaningful.

Be bold and take risks in your pursuit of purpose. Like Schultz, don't shy away from challenges or obstacles. Embrace them as opportunities for growth, adaptability, and resilience. Use them as stepping stones to strengthen your vision and amplify your impact.

Sharing your journey, the path of an Ideas Guy, can inspire and motivate others. Let your story, insights, and lessons inspire others. A ripple of positive transformation can initiate with one idea-driven individual. It isn't just about building a successful organisation; it's about crafting a legacy, about creating something bigger than yourself. It's about fostering a sense of community, a culture of belonging that goes beyond your product or service. It's about pouring your purpose into every cup, every interaction, every decision.

How to live on purpose and in purpose has to be at the heart of every decision about Strategy.

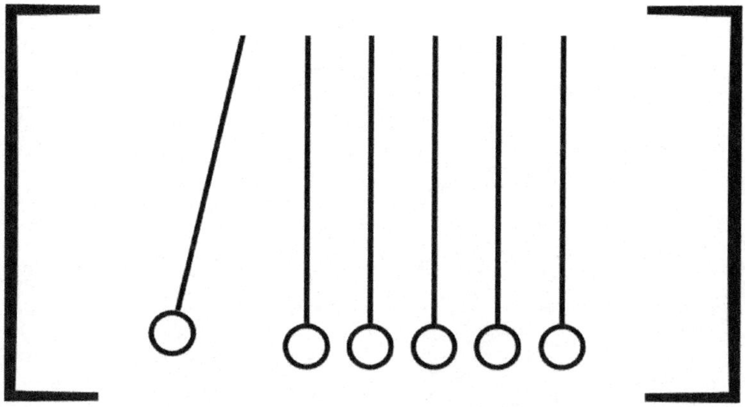

# LEAVE AN IMPACT

WHAT WE NEED TO DO IS ALWAYS LEAN INTO THE FUTURE; WHEN THE WORLD CHANGES AROUND YOU AND WHEN IT CHANGES AGAINST YOU—WHAT USED TO BE A TAIL WIND IS NOW A HEAD WIND—YOU HAVE TO LEAN INTO THAT AND FIGURE OUT WHAT TO DO BECAUSE COMPLAINING ISN'T A STRATEGY.

JEFF BEZOS

# [ CHAPTER 18 ]

# BUILDING EMPIRES

This trek has a new sherpa: Jeff Bezos, the pioneer behind the global empire that is Amazon. On this expedition, we'll chart the strategic steps, the moves and manoeuvres that have led Amazon towards global domination.

Jeff Bezos, a trailblazer in the truest sense, started with a simple idea–a virtual bookstore that defied traditional retail constraints. Yet his vision extended far beyond just books. He envisioned an everything store, a marketplace that could cater to the global audience's every desire. And thus, Amazon was born. The A-Z of everything with a smile is the essence of the logo.

Early on, Bezos adopted a Strategy of relentless customer focus, a path that has since become the company's centrifugal point. He recognised that to build an empire, you need more than just a unique product–you need the trust and loyalty of the consumers you serve. Bezos championed this customer obsession, seeking not just to satisfy customers, but to delight and dazzle them. This Strategy wasn't just insightful. It was transformative, changing the very nature of retail and e-commerce.

But customer obsession was just one part of Bezos's grand plan. Another pivotal element was his long-term thinking. Bezos embraced a mindset that valued long-term growth over short-term profit, a Strategy that demanded patience, persistence, and a keen eye for the future. While other companies fixated on immediate profits, Bezos was investing in the future, building a fortress of Innovation that could withstand the test of time.

This long-term orientation is evident in Amazon Web Services (AWS), a venture that seemed outlandish at its inception. Yet, Bezos, the ever-forward thinker, recognised the potential of cloud computing long before it was a buzzword. Today, AWS is a powerhouse, further evidence of Bezos's ability to look ahead and make purposeful bets on the future.

Bezos also spearheaded the expansion into international markets, pushing Amazon to dominate not just domestically, but globally. He recognised the potential of emerging markets and adapted the business to cater to the diverse needs of customers worldwide. This strategic expansion, coupled with an unrelenting focus on customer satisfaction, solidified Amazon's position as a global leader.

Another strategic move was Bezos's decision to diversify Amazon's portfolio, branching out into areas like entertainment, hardware, and logistics. This diversification Strategy fortified Amazon's position, making it not just a retail giant but a multifaceted empire. Think about Amazon Prime, Ring Doorbells and Cameras, Twitch and Zappos–all under the Bezos brand. Diversity is planned for. There is more than one way to skin a cat.

The journey of Jeff Bezos, of Amazon more broadly, is one of strategic brilliance, of moves carefully calculated and risks courageously taken. Bezos's Strategy–his relentless customer focus, long-term orientation, culture of Innovation, global expansion, and diversification–has resulted in an empire that transcends boundaries, reshapes industries, and continually pushes the frontier of what's possible.

As we trek through the Bezos landscape of strategic mastery, let us reflect on the magnitude of what has been accomplished. An empire, built from a single idea, a venture into the brave new world of e-commerce, that has evolved into a global force that permeates almost every facet of our lives.

The Amazon empire is a testament to the power of Strategy, to the profound impact of a well-planned and well-executed game plan. It's a demonstration of the potential that lies in a single idea, and the transformative power of strategic thinking and relentless execution.

In the end, the journey of Jeff Bezos and Amazon teaches us a valuable lesson: building empires is not a matter of chance, but a matter of choice. It's a result of tactical decisions, of the foresight to envision the future, and the courage to make bold moves in pursuit of that vision. And above all, it's a result of the determination to stay the course, even when the path is steep and the destination far.

Embarking on an expedition to build an empire is like setting sail in stormy waters. As the Ideas Guy, you hold the compass of Innovation and Strategy in your hands. Just like the great explorers of old, your guiding stars are the visionary leaders who've carved out paths of success in the vast landscape of industry.

Bezos's path wasn't mapped out by simply following the well-trodden routes of market trends. He ventured into the unexplored territories of his customers' needs, tuning in to their whispers, discerning their unspoken desires, and letting this understanding steer his compass.

Amazon's focus on customer satisfaction, their drive to exceed expectations, is rooted in Bezos's obsession with the customer. This obsession underpins Amazon's success, guiding them to develop innovative solutions that customers didn't even know they needed. As the Ideas Guy, imprint this customer-first ethos onto your own strategic map. Let your customers guide you, anticipate their needs, deliver beyond their expectations. Your customers are the heroes in the story, not you, so let their satisfaction guide your journey towards success.

This doesn't merely shine on the smooth sailing; it is most luminous in the stormy seas of setbacks and challenges. The bright ideas that have defined Amazon's empire–Amazon Web Services, Kindle, Audible–were not born fully formed. They emerged from the shadowy depths of failure, brought to light through an iterative process of trial, error, and relentless refinement.

Bezos teaches us that in the landscape of empire-building, setbacks are not roadblocks but rather stepping stones. See each setback as an opportunity, each failure as a lesson. Let this cycle of Innovation and iteration be your guiding principle. Approach each challenge with the mindset of a problem-solver, use each failure as a springboard for better solutions, and embrace the journey of continuous improvement.

Focus on the power of thoughtful, deliberate growth. Bezos's empire didn't grow haphazardly; it was strategically architected. His move beyond books, his leveraging of technology, his creation of a logistic marvel–these were all products of calculated decisions and meticulous planning.

Strategic scaling isn't about rapid, unchecked growth. It's about identifying the right opportunities, leveraging your unique strengths, and expanding in a way that aligns with your vision. Dare to dream big, yet act thoughtfully. Allow strategic scaling to be the wind beneath your empire's wings, driving your venture from a fledgling startup to a global force.

As you navigate the vast ocean of opportunities, look for the mile markers on the path to empire-building, those which cast their light for the way forward. Use these lumens to chart your course, to navigate through challenges, and to steer your venture towards the shores of success. Let your strategic acumen be the rudder that guides your empire, and let the journey itself be the adventure of a lifetime.

So, fellow idea explorers, as we look at building empires, let's take a leaf from Bezos's playbook. Let's celebrate the power of Strategy, the role it plays in transforming ideas into empires, and the indomitable spirit of the entrepreneurs who dare to dream big, plan strategically, and execute relentlessly.

# [ APPLYING THIS IN PRACTICE ]

**BLAZE A TRAIL:** Bezos's journey serves as an inspiring reminder of the power of blazing your own trail in the wilderness of the business world. Being an Ideas Guy isn't about just following in the footsteps of others or adopting pre-existing templates of success; it's about charting your own path, rooted in your unique vision and fuelled by relentless Innovation. It is standing on the shoulders of giants but using this as a springboard into a new realm.

As you navigate your venture, take a moment to reflect on your vision. What does your empire look like? What unexplored territories are you excited to discover? How can you break away from the tried-and-tested routes and venture into the unfamiliar? Embark on your expedition with the spirit of a trailblazer, daring to explore where others have yet to tread.

Take your compass in hand, and begin to carve your own path. Cultivate a mindset of creative exploration and fearless experimentation. Foster a culture that embraces out-of-the-box thinking (or in-the-box thinking like we will discuss in Chapter 20), celebrates diverse perspectives, and rewards bold ideas. Your journey is not a sprint, but a marathon of constant discovery, Innovation, and growth.

Remember, as you blaze your trail, you're not just building an empire, you're creating a legacy. Your journey, your ventures, your actions will serve as landmarks for the generations of Ideas Guys that follow.

In this grand expedition, be mindful of the impact you're making on the world, the footprints you're leaving in the sands of time. Strive to create a legacy that transcends commercial success, one that resonates with purpose, inspires Innovation, and sparks positive change.

So, as you set sail on your journey, hold your strategic compass close and look ahead with determination. Be the trailblazer, charting a course where none existed, carving a path that others would aspire to tread. Let the spirit of trailblazing guide you towards a life of purpose, fulfilment, and unrivalled success.

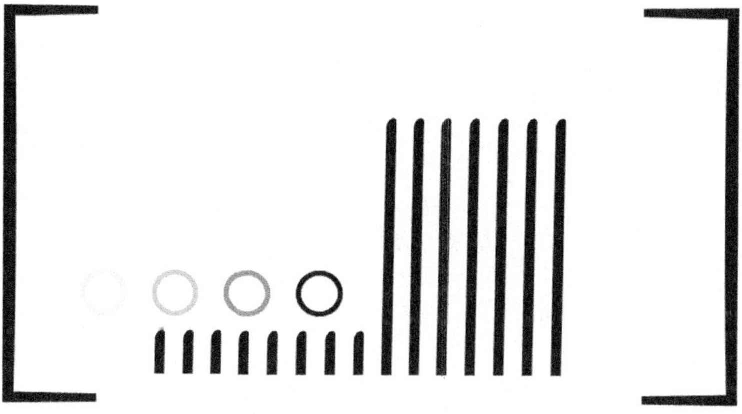

BLAZE A TRAIL

DON'T GET DISTRACTED BY THE SHINY OBJECT [AND IF A CRISIS COMES], EXECUTE ON THE FUNDAMENTALS.

REED HASTINGS

# [ CHAPTER 19 ]

# BREAKING BARRIERS

As we step further into the realm of revolution and reimagination, our guide on this staircase is none other than Reed Hastings, the mastermind behind Netflix, a company that has redefined our collective concept of entertainment. This is the story of a traditional idea transformed into an unconventional revolution, where barriers were broken, paradigms were shifted, and a new era of entertainment dawned upon us. So, strap in and prepare for a journey into the annals of strategic brilliance and creative disruption.

Before we get into the saga of Netflix, let's rewind the tape and take a glance at our protagonist's genesis. Reed Hastings, a philosopher turned entrepreneur, held the belief that the greatest mysteries and revelations resided not just in the age-old philosophical texts, but in the realm of technology, in the potent promise of the internet. This led him down the path of Silicon Valley, a breeding ground for Innovation, where he realised the potential of leveraging technology to break barriers and transform the world as we knew it.

His brainchild, Netflix, came from this potent blend of philosophical curiosity and technological ambition. Hastings saw beyond the confines of the traditional movie rental industry. He envisioned a world where entertainment wasn't limited by store hours or physical locations, where a world of films and TV shows was just a click away. And thus, Netflix began its journey, from a simple online DVD rental service to a global streaming powerhouse, breaking barriers and transforming the landscape of entertainment in the process.

The Netflix revolution wasn't a fluke or a lucky shot; it was the fruit of strategic brilliance and relentless Innovation. The essence of this Strategy lay in Netflix's commitment to customer-centricity. Hastings and his team recognised the frustration of late fees and limited selections that plagued traditional video rental. So, they dismantled these barriers, offering unlimited rentals without late fees. They listened to their customers, understood their pain points, and crafted an experience that was seamless, convenient, and user-friendly. This was just the beginning of Netflix's journey to break barriers.

While the transformation of a traditional rental service into a seamless online platform was a monumental leap, the real game-changer was yet to come. The strategic genius of Hastings lay not just in addressing the existing challenges but in anticipating the future. He saw the advent of broadband internet not as a threat, but as an opportunity to redefine Netflix's business model and pivot towards online streaming. This planned-for pivot wasn't just about keeping up with the technological advancements; it was about staying ahead of the curve, about breaking barriers before they even formed.

Embracing this new direction, Netflix embarked on its journey to become the titan of online streaming. The company continuously pushed the boundaries of what was considered possible, introducing features like binge-watching and personalised recommendations that became synonymous with our modern viewing experience. But perhaps the most significant strategic move was its foray into original programming. This not only diversified their portfolio but also created a new avenue for storytelling, thus breaking the barrier between being a platform and a creator.

Hastings' Strategy for Netflix wasn't confined to creating a successful business model. It was about creating a cultural phenomenon. It was about transforming our very approach towards entertainment. The Netflix effect rippled beyond the realms of business, infiltrating our everyday lexicon with phrases like "Netflix and Chill" and shaping our viewing habits. Hastings' venture broke the barriers of what a company could achieve and the cultural impact it could have.

As we turn over more stones, we uncover the wisdom of Reed Hastings' brilliance. He demonstrated that breaking barriers isn't merely about overcoming obstacles. It's about redefining the possibilities, about reshaping the status quo. It's about moving forward with a blend of foresight, Innovation, and sheer audacity.

Breaking barriers: the notion that with persistence and determination, even the most entrenched walls can be toppled, is one that Hastings intimately understands. His approach is encapsulated in the title of his book, "No Rules Rules: Netflix and the Culture of Reinvention", where he argues that traditional business conventions and barriers must be overcome to foster creativity and Innovation.

In his book, Hastings presents a new paradigm, a departure from the conventional wisdom that has defined business culture for centuries. He breaks the barrier of the traditional hierarchical corporate structure and encourages a more free-flowing, open environment where employees are given the space to think, to question, and to challenge.

"No Rules Rules" is not about the absence of order or structure, rather, it is about the removal of unnecessary and stifling barriers. It's about creating a culture where people are not boxed in by rigid rules, but are given the autonomy to make decisions. Employees are encouraged to take risks, make mistakes, and learn from them.

Hastings advocates for radical honesty and transparency. At Netflix, employee salaries are openly shared among staff, fostering trust and breaking down barriers of secrecy. This practise defies the traditional corporate norm, which often keeps compensation shrouded in mystery. It's a barrier broken, leading to a greater sense of fairness and openness in the organisation.

The idea of "context, not control"–another central tenet of Hastings' philosophy–breaks down the barrier of micro-management. Managers provide context and allow their teams the freedom to decide the best course of action. This freedom breeds responsibility, creativity, and a sense of ownership.

Now, how does the Ideas Guy apply the ethos of "No Rules Rules" to her journey? Just as Hastings broke down barriers to foster creativity at Netflix, the Ideas Guy too can challenge and break down barriers in her path. Conventional wisdom, traditional norms, the fear of failure–these are barriers that can hinder the journey of discovery and creativity.

The Ideas Guy can adopt the principles of radical honesty, transparency, and giving context, not control. By fostering an environment where ideas can flow freely, without the fear of judgement or the restrictions of hierarchy, creativity is bound to flourish. By challenging norms, questioning the status quo, and daring to do things differently, the Ideas Guy will not just break barriers, she'll redefine them. And this is at the heart of Strategy–it's not just being eaten for breakfast.

Netflix's story shows the power of relentless innovation and adaptation. By constantly pushing boundaries, embracing change, and refusing to grow complacent, they've stayed ahead in an ever-shifting industry. Their success demonstrates that thriving in today's market requires the courage to evolve and break new ground.

Hastings' brilliant Strategy is perhaps most clearly seen in the algorithm that curates a personalised playlist for each Netflix user. In this vogue, we can distil the vast array of experiences and insights into tailored takeaways for our expedition.

In the world of Netflix, stagnation is the antagonist. The very essence of the Netflix journey lies in its constant evolution. From mail-in DVDs to online streaming, from being a platform to becoming a creator, Netflix has persistently morphed to stay ahead. Much like how Netflix recognises our viewing patterns and continuously updates our recommendations, we too must learn to recognise the patterns in our lives, our industries, and our world at large. Stay vigilant of the changing tides, adapt with agility, and embrace change as your constant co-star. This requires an open mind, a flexible Strategy, and the courage to venture beyond the familiar. In the grand screenplay of life, let change be your co-star, guiding you through the scenes and leading you to an ending yet unwritten.

It is more "flight deck, adjusting dials, pulling levers, and tweaking according to conditions" than "train on a direct track to a clear destination". We are pilots not train engineers.

Netflix's success can largely be attributed to its foresight. Anticipating the advent of the Digital age, Hastings strategically pivoted Netflix's business model towards online streaming. This strategic foresight, akin to Netflix's predictive algorithms, enabled the company to stay one step ahead of the competition and the industry at large. We too must learn to anticipate, to read between the lines of the present and foresee the script of the future. Understand the trends, decipher the patterns, and build a Strategy that not only navigates the present but also pioneers the future. Develop the art of strategic foresight and use this skill to find unexplored opportunities and new directions.

Netflix didn't just overcome the barriers of traditional media; it broke them and redefined what was possible. From enabling binge-watching to creating original content, Netflix pushed the boundaries and rewrote the rules of the game. Much like how Netflix's Play Something feature surprises us with content outside our usual preferences, we too must learn to challenge our norms, question our limits, and venture beyond our comfort zones. Embrace the unfamiliar, experiment with the unconventional, and break the barriers that confine your potential. Redefine the possible, and let the breaking of barriers be your plot twist, propelling your story onto paths unanticipated and outcomes extraordinary.

In the grand narrative of our lives and careers, let these insights from Netflix's journey guide our course. Like the threads that weave together an engaging Netflix series, let these takeaways intertwine and inform our strategies. Let us learn from the Netflix algorithm's wisdom, continuously evolving, predicting the next move, and surprising us with the unexpected. Let our lives be the series that breaks barriers, embraces change, and anticipates the future. As we venture forth in our journey, may our story be as engaging, as transformative, and as barrier-breaking as Netflix's own. Let's press play and dive into the next episode of our expedition.

## [ APPLYING THIS IN PRACTICE ]

**PAUSE FOR BREATH:** The unique algorithm that anticipates, tailors, and moulds itself to each viewer's taste is not just technology, it's an ideology, a mindset that we can carry into our own lives, careers, and quests. It's about creating our personal life-algorithm that guides us through the labyrinth of choices and onto the paths that align with who we really are.

Begin by taking a reflective pause, stepping away from the hustle and bustle of daily life. Engage in introspection, identify your values, passions, strengths, and goals like we have been looking at over the last few chapters. These are the parameters of your life-algorithm. Just as Netflix's algorithm curates based on viewing history and preferences, let your life-algorithm be informed by your past experiences, learning, and aspirations.

However, remember to keep your algorithm flexible and adaptable. Just like how Netflix's algorithm adjusts with every show we watch, our life-algorithm should be dynamic, evolving with every experience, every lesson, every milestone. Allow for iterations, for recalibrations. Welcome the unexpected plot twists and turns. Be open to revisiting and revising your values and goals as you grow and evolve.

Yet, a crucial part of this algorithm lies in its predictive nature. Much like how Netflix's algorithm recommends what we might like next, our life-algorithm should equip us to anticipate future trends, to foresee challenges and opportunities. Cultivate the skill of strategic foresight. Keep an eye on the horizon, understand the trends, and anticipate what the future might hold. Use this insight to strategically navigate your course and pioneer your future.

Remember to be daring, to be bold (a common theme, eh?). Just as Netflix pushed the boundaries and challenged the status quo, your life-algorithm should encourage you to question, to challenge, to break the barriers of the conventional. Don't confine yourself to the tried and tested. Venture into the unfamiliar, explore the uncharted, experiment with the unconventional. Let the algorithm guide us through the complex narrative of our lives, helping us make choices that align with our values, adapt with agility, anticipate the future, and break the barriers of the possible. And as we navigate our paths, may we become the authors of our stories, the curators of our lives, the architects of our destinies.

Imbibe the wisdom of Netflix's journey and let it illuminate your path. And as you travel on, may your journey be filled with growth, discovery, resilience, and unparalleled success. Here's to forging algorithms, breaking barriers, and crafting narratives that are as unique, as exciting, and as extraordinary as you are.

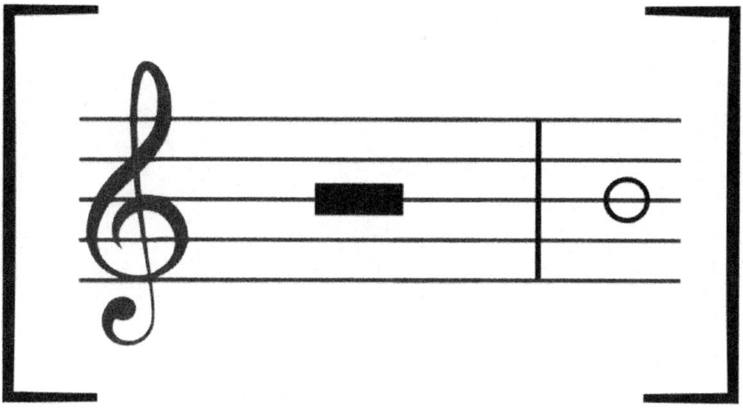

**PAUSE FOR BREATH**

THE INNOVATOR'S JOB CANNOT BE TO DELIVER A PROVEN RESULT; IT MUST BE TO DISCOVER WHAT IS POSSIBLE, THAT IS, TO LEARN, BY CONVERTING ASSUMPTIONS INTO KNOWLEDGE AS QUICKLY AND INEXPENSIVELY AS POSSIBLE.

**VIJAY GOVINDARAJAN**

# [ CHAPTER 20 ]

# UNBOXING & BOXING

Vijay Govindarajan's vision reveals how businesses can master turbulent times, turning waves of change into opportunities that reshape entire industries. In this chapter, we embark on a captivating journey into the origins of his transformative ideas, exploring the development of the Three-Box Solution Strategy–a testament to the power of Strategy and ideas in shaping the course of human progress.

Drawing from deep wells of experience, Govindarajan crafted the Three-Box Solution - a compass for leaders seeking to guide their organisations toward bold innovation and untapped potential. To understand its brilliance, we must trace the footsteps of its creator and discover the wellspring from which his ideas flowed.

Govindarajan's journey began as a curious soul, traversing the landscapes of academia and practical wisdom. Rooted in his Indian heritage and enriched by his global perspective, his mind became a fertile ground for transformative ideas to take root. The seeds of the Three-Box Solution found nourishment in his deep understanding of Strategy, leadership, and the ever-evolving dynamics of the business world.

Inspired by the past, Govindarajan recognised the significance of embracing the present moment while learning from history's triumphs and failures. He observed the companies that rose to greatness and those that faltered, gleaning timeless lessons from their stories. The realisation struck him like a bolt of lightning–an authentic approach to Strategy must balance the dance between managing the present, selectively forgetting the past, and creating the future.

The Three-Box Solution emerged as a symphony, its movements flowing seamlessly between the three boxes. In Box 1, Govindarajan acknowledged the necessity of managing the present, tending to the immediate needs of organisations, and optimising existing operations. This box celebrated the art of honing the present, fine-tuning the mechanisms that propelled businesses forward.

Box 1 emerges as the foundation upon which the dance of strategic transformation is built. In this box, leaders find themselves engaged in the art of excelling in their current business model. It is a place where the familiar takes centre stage, demanding a keen eye for efficiency and a relentless pursuit of excellence.

Within Box 1, organisations strive to refine their strategies and processes, fine-tuning every aspect of their operations. It is the domain of continuous improvement, where leaders harness the power of data, analytics, and feedback loops to drive performance to new heights. A shining example of Box 1's prowess lies in the story of Toyota and their innovative approach to manufacturing. Through the implementation of the renowned Toyota Production System, they achieved unparalleled levels of efficiency and quality, propelling themselves to industry leadership.

Yet, Govindarajan's visionary mind refused to be confined by the boundaries of the present. Inspired by the wisdom of selective forgetting, he realised that true Innovation required shedding the weight of outdated practises and freeing oneself from the grip of past successes. Box 2 is about liberation–a dance with the ghosts of the past, where the courage to unlearn and break away from convention was the key to unlocking future possibilities.

In Box 2, "Selectively Forget the Past", leaders are called to shed the baggage of outdated practises and stagnant mindsets, allowing space for the emergence of fresh ideas and untapped potential. This box serves as a portal to transformation, where the willingness to *unlearn* and let go of past successes becomes the catalyst for future growth.

Selective forgetting does not entail discarding all knowledge gained from the past; instead, it encourages a discerning approach to what is carried forward. It is the art of extracting lessons from history while being open to new possibilities. Kodak's story serves as a poignant reminder of the consequences of failing to embrace Box 2. Despite their pioneering role in photography, they clung stubbornly to film, missing the Digital revolution that unfolded before their eyes. Their failure to selectively forget the past serves as a cautionary tale, urging us to embrace the winds of change and adapt to evolving landscapes.

But it was in Box 3, the sphere of audacious creation, that Govindarajan's ideas soared to their greatest heights. In this box, he harnessed the power of the human imagination, urging organisations to step into the unknown, to embrace calculated risks, and to pioneer new frontiers. Box 3 was a sanctuary of limitless potential–a fertile ground where dreams sprouted, grew, and blossomed into revolutionary ideas that reshaped industries and transformed the very fabric of our world.

Box 3, "Create the Future" is a vibrant and audacious realm where Innovation flourishes, where ideas are nurtured, and where new paths are forged. Box 3 invites organisations to become architects of their own destiny, to transcend the boundaries of the known, and to pioneer incredible opportunity.

Within Box 3, leaders embrace a mindset of courageous exploration. They dare to challenge the status quo, pursuing disruptive ideas and visionary thinking. It is in this realm that companies like Apple have crafted their remarkable success, as we have already seen. From reimagining personal computing to revolutionising the music industry, they exemplify the transformative power of Box 3. Their ability to create the future, to anticipate trends, and to stay ahead of the curve has propelled them to the forefront of Innovation.

The impact of Govindarajan's ideas extended far beyond theoretical frameworks. Through his work, he emboldened leaders to break free from the confines of conventional thinking, to embrace the synergy of Strategy and ideas, and to navigate the ever-changing landscapes of business with Authenticity and vision. His teachings breathed life into countless entities, empowering them to embark on their own journeys of strategic exploration, each step a testament to the transformative power of the Three-Box Solution.

In the grand tapestry of human progress, it is the dance between Strategy and ideas that propels us forward. Vijay Govindarajan, a luminary in his field, has emerged as a guiding star, lighting the path for leaders to chart their course amidst the ebb and flow of change. His authentic approach has become a compass for those who dare to challenge the boundaries of what is possible.

His teachings shine as beacons of wisdom, guiding leaders towards transformative possibilities. As we unravel the essence of his insights, we uncover profound learnings that transcend the confines of the Three-Box Solution. These learnings, like celestial constellations, illuminate our path towards Innovation, growth, and lasting success.

At the heart of Govindarajan's teachings lies a fundamental truth–the nature of our world is in constant flux. In the face of uncertainty and rapid evolution, leaders must cultivate a mindset that embraces the fluidity of change. The ability to adapt, to pivot, and to stay attuned to the shifting currents of the business landscape becomes paramount.

Through the lens of this wisdom, organisations can navigate change with confidence and resilience. Rather than resisting change or clinging to the safety of the familiar, leaders are encouraged to view change as an opportunity–a gateway to exploration, growth, and Innovation. By embracing the fluidity of change, we can harness its transformative power, unlocking new possibilities and gaining a competitive edge.

It is within this fertile soil of exploration that groundbreaking ideas take root and flourish. By cultivating a culture that embraces curiosity, leaders inspire their teams to ask bold questions, challenge assumptions, and explore new avenues.

Moreover, a culture of experimentation allows organisations to learn, adapt, and iterate. It empowers teams to take calculated risks, to embrace failure as a stepping stone to success, and to embrace the spirit of continuous improvement. Just as an artist experiments with different brushstrokes to create a masterpiece, businesses and teams that foster a culture of curiosity and experimentation unlock the true potential of their collective creativity.

In the symphony of Innovation, Govindarajan's teachings emphasise the power of diversity and inclusion. He reminds leaders that diverse perspectives and inclusive practises fuel the fires of Innovation, propelling organisations towards unparalleled success. By embracing diversity in all its forms–gender, ethnicity, culture, and beyond–we tap into a wellspring of unique ideas, insights, and experiences.

When diverse voices are heard and respected, the tapestry of Innovation becomes richer and more vibrant. Different viewpoints challenge conventional thinking, shatter biases, and open doors to new possibilities. By embracing diversity and inclusion, leaders create an ecosystem where ideas collide, cross-pollinate, and evolve, ushering in a new era of Innovation and growth.

Govindarajan's strategic insights continue to inspire leaders, showing how to spark meaningful change across industries. By embracing his principles, we can drive Innovation and create opportunities that push organisations forward in powerful new directions.

May these learnings serve as guiding lights, illuminating our path towards a more inclusive, innovative, and prosperous tomorrow. For it is in this dance of unboxing and boxing, Strategy and ideas, that we unlock a future adorned with infinite possibilities.

# [ APPLYING THIS IN PRACTICE ]

**NURTURE A CULTURE:** Amidst the breadth of Govindarajan's teachings, a key takeaway emerges–a powerful commitment to the power of ideas. In the dance of strategic exploration, ideas are the lifeblood that breathes vitality into organisations. They hold the potential to disrupt industries, solve complex problems, and shape the course of human progress. By embracing this in the role of the Ideas Guy, leaders become catalysts, encouraging the generation and exchange of ideas within their teams.

To foster a culture of ideation, leaders must create an environment where curiosity thrives, where divergent thinking is celebrated, and where collaboration becomes the norm. They invite individuals from all corners of the organisation to contribute their unique perspectives, inviting them to step forward as active participants in the process of Innovation.

Drawing inspiration from the teachings of Vijay Govindarajan, leaders can implement practical strategies to cultivate the Ideas Guy culture. They can organise ideation sessions, where individuals from diverse backgrounds and disciplines converge to explore new concepts and approaches. These sessions foster an atmosphere of psychological safety, encouraging individuals to voice their thoughts without fear of judgement.

Furthermore, leaders can encourage the formation of cross-functional teams, where individuals with varied expertise collaborate on projects, bringing together diverse ideas and viewpoints. This interdisciplinary synergy sparks innovative thinking, as it allows for the cross-pollination of ideas from different domains.

In addition to these strategies, implement mechanisms for idea capture, providing channels for employees to share their thoughts, suggestions, and breakthroughs. This might include Digital platforms, suggestion boxes, or regular brainstorming sessions. By actively seeking and valuing input from every member of the organisation, leaders tap into an ocean of untapped potential.

To amplify the impact of the Ideas Guy culture, leaders must also foster an environment that nurtures experimentation and risk-taking. They should encourage their teams to prototype, test, and iterate on their ideas, recognising that failure is not a setback but a valuable opportunity for learning and growth. By embracing this mindset, organisations create a safe space for Innovation, empowering individuals to unleash their creative genius.

A powerful example of the Ideas Guy culture in action can be found in the story of Google's famous "20% time" policy. This initiative allowed employees to dedicate one-fifth of their work hours to pursuing their own passion projects. It resulted in groundbreaking Innovations such as Gmail and Google News, highlighting the tremendous potential of nurturing a culture that encourages ideation and collaboration. We will delve more deeply into this in Chapter 21.

As we weave together the teachings of Govindarajan and the essence of the Ideas Guy, organisations embark on a transformative journey. They become dynamic hubs of creativity, where the seeds of Innovation are sown, nurtured, and harvested. By embracing the power of ideas, organisations transcend the boundaries of what is possible, positioning themselves at the forefront of progress.

So, let us embark on this journey of strategic application, igniting the spirit of the Ideas Guy within our organisations. Let us create the fertile ground where ideas bloom, collaboration thrives, and Innovation becomes second nature. By embracing this transformative approach, we pave the way for a future that transcends our wildest dreams.

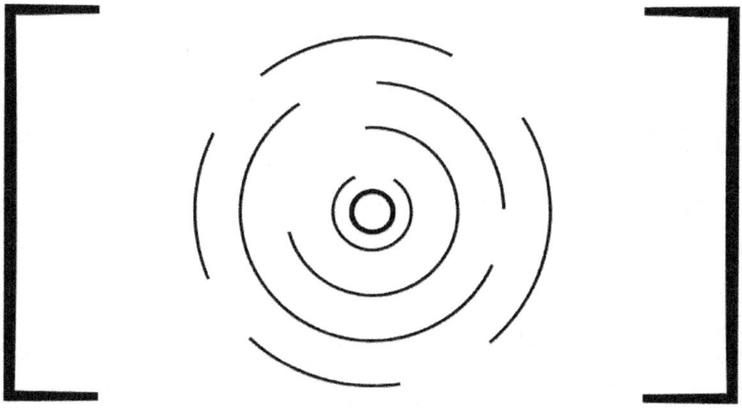

NURTURE A CULTURE

# [ PART VI ]

# THE GATHERING OF IDEAS

BE LESS CURIOUS ABOUT PEOPLE AND
MORE CURIOUS ABOUT IDEAS.
MARIE CURIE

We find ourselves standing on the precipice of understanding, at the crossroads where multiple paths of wisdom converge, paths that have been charted by visionaries, pioneers, innovators, educators, and storytellers alike. Paths forged by individuals who dared to dream, dared to question, dared to disrupt, dared to connect, and dared to be authentic.

In this moment of confluence, we bring together the wisdom from the likes of Steve Jobs, the maestro of Innovation; Ingvar Kamprad, the architect of simplicity; Elon Musk, the pioneer of the impossible; Anne Wojcicki, the visionary of genomic revolution; Tim Berners-Lee, the constructor of the world wide web; and Daniel Ek, the prophet of the music streaming era.

In the luminary assembly, we also salute Sam Altman, the investor who placed his bets on the future; Reid Hoffman, the orchestrator of professional networks; Maria Montessori, the advocate of child-centric learning; Sir Ken Robinson, the champion of creativity in Education; Sal Khan, the promoter of accessible learning; and Sugata Mitra, the believer in the inherent curiosity of children.

In this gathering, we also find Yvon Chouinard, the preserver of nature; Brené Brown, the explorer of vulnerability; Maya Angelou, the herald of human spirit; Phil Knight, the runner with a vision; Howard Schultz, the master brewer of community and connection; Jeff Bezos, the builder of an empire; Reed Hastings, the reinventor of entertainment consumption; and Vijay Govindarajan, the strategist of the three-box solution.

Twenty individuals, twenty trails of wisdom and exploration, twenty tales of vision, purpose and resilience. As we gather these ideas, we prepare to weave a narrative that encapsulates the essence of their wisdom. Each of them carries a sliver of understanding, a torch of enlightenment, which, when brought together, will guide us through the final stages of our exploration.

In the chapters to come, we will spotlight individuals who embody these five qualities in unison, those who have synthesised these lessons into a harmonious composition of effective entrepreneurship and impactful leadership. We embark on the final leg of our journey with Larry Page and Sergei Brin, the vanguards of information; Sheryl Sandberg, the exemplar of leadership; Joe Rogan, the conversational maestro; and Oprah Winfrey, the queen of media.

In their narratives, we will discover a symphony of IDEAS–Innovation, Digital, Education, Authenticity, and Strategy–elements that are not just solitary concepts but part of a larger, interconnected matrix. These are the currents that will guide us as we navigate the vast, sometimes tumultuous ocean of knowledge, success, and personal growth.

This gives us 24 chapters with 25 people (double whammy on Google!). They would make for an epic dinner party list. Aperitifs of grass-fed plans and organic intentions, followed by a hearty plate of inquisitiveness with a side of creativity, finished with a dessert of proposals and Strategy. We would be entertained late into the night with tales of endeavour and failure, folklore of lessons learned and anecdotes aplenty.

Each chapter, each narrative, has been a stepping stone leading us to this moment, to this synthesis of wisdom. Each lesson learned, each insight gained, has been a droplet contributing to this vast ocean. Now, as we prepare to dive further into the depths of understanding, we carry with us the lessons from each pioneer, each innovator, each educator, each storyteller.

As we hit this final section, the gathering is a blessed tempest of brilliance mixed with humanity. None of these following Ideas Guys are perfect; they have lived and learned, yet they follow some patterns.

Stay the course, fellow explorers. As we journey into the heart of this confluence, may we remain open, curious, and eager for the wisdom that is to unfold. And as we do so, let us never forget that we are all, in our own ways, pioneers charting our unique paths in the grand journey of life. Here's to the wisdom of the past, the understanding of the present, and the discoveries of the future. Here's to the gathering of IDEAS.

ALWAYS DELIVER MORE THAN EXPECTED.

**LARRY PAGE**

# [ CHAPTER 21 ]

# SYNERGY EQUATION

In the cosmos of human ingenuity, there lie stellar bodies, entities that have defied the laws of convention and ascended into the stratosphere of Innovation. Google, helmed by the dynamic duo, Sergei Brin and Larry Page, is a radiant celestial in this universe. This shows how powerful ideas become when matched with the persistent drive to bring them to life.

Our tale begins not with a bang but with a question: "What if we could organise the world's information and make it universally accessible and useful?"

This query was not just the birth of an idea, but a mission, an ambition that would set two bright minds on a course to change the world. Fuelled by their passion for **INNOVATION**, they embarked on a voyage into the world of ones and zeros.

Imagine, if you will, the early stages of this journey, Brin and Page in the labyrinthine depths of Stanford University's computer science building, their fingers dancing on keyboards, their minds teeming with equations, algorithms, codes–the initial lingua franca of Google.

Innovation was their compass, guiding their passage through this burgeoning landscape. Innovation is not merely a creative thought; it is a force of disruption, a charge against the status quo. It is about asking the right questions, challenging the existing, and imagining the impossible. This force propelled Brin and Page on their quest, a quest that wasn't merely about designing a search engine but sculpting a tool that would unlock the world's information.

The product of their innovative journey was an algorithm christened PageRank. Here was a map-maker, a compass in the tumultuous seas of data, drawing connections, charting relevance. This algorithm was their first ode to Innovation, their inaugural beacon in the **DIGITAL** wilderness.

However, this is just the prelude to our grand symphony. The crescendo of the IDEAS framework–Innovation, Digital, Education, Authenticity, Strategy–remains to be explored. The chords of this framework are interwoven, resonating together to create the symphony of Google's journey, a journey that echoes and guides the voyage of every Ideas Guy navigating the seas of entrepreneurship.

As our maestros, Brin and Page, struck their first notes of Innovation, the stage was being set for a remarkable transformation. At its core, Google was more than just an algorithm. It was an entity spearheading a revolution, a vanguard in the world's Digital evolution.

Google, with its transformative ethos, democratised the Digital realm. Through their search engine, they made the internet a public square where information flowed freely, accessible to anyone with a connection. They moved away from the conventional, commercial-centric model of the internet and prioritised the user.

It's easy to think of Innovation as the "spark" that ignited Google's journey. But in reality, it was more than just a spark. It was a steady flame, fuelled by persistent questioning and an undying curiosity. For Brin and Page, Innovation was not about sporadic bouts of creativity. Rather, it was a constant, ongoing process. It became a part of their daily rhythm, embedded in their corporate DNA.

Google's early days at Stanford's campus were all about innovative exploration. When Brin and Page first developed the PageRank algorithm, they dared to disrupt the status quo. It was a challenge to conventional search engines that simply counted the number of times a keyword appeared on a webpage. Their Innovation? Using backlinks to determine the importance of a page, an idea that was completely groundbreaking at the time.

Their relentless pursuit of the next didn't stop there. They continued to push the boundaries, to question, to innovate. Google Books, Google Earth, Gmail–all are testaments to Google's spirit. They came from the simple yet profound question: "What if?"

The magic of Google lies not just in its search engine prowess but also in its adventurous spirit, a spirit that dares to explore, to rethink, to venture into the unknown. This spirit finds its embodiment in Google X, an offshoot of Google that seeks to turn science fiction into reality. Like a maestro on a stage, it conducts a symphony of the future, composed not of musical notes, but of radical ideas and groundbreaking Innovations.

Google X, now simply known as X, is Google's moonshot factory, a place where audacious ideas are transformed into tangible projects. Founded in 2010, this semi-secret research lab is dedicated to inventing and launching technologies that aim to make the world a better place. Here, the seemingly impossible is brought to life, echoing the passion and vision of our maestros, Page and Brin.

From the Google Self-Driving Car Project, which seeks to transform mobility and reduce accidents, to Project Loon, which aimed to provide internet access to remote areas using high-altitude balloons, each project at X shows Google's unwavering commitment to Innovation. They dare to ask the legendary "What if?" and then venture forth to find the answer, pushing the boundaries of what's possible.

Think of X as the grand orchestra of the future. Each project, each moonshot, is a musician in this orchestra, playing its part to create a masterpiece of change. The aim is not to merely create products for immediate release but to tackle significant problems. The failures, the successes, the experiments–they all contribute to the harmony, shaping a melody that resonates with the future. So, for every Ideas Guy out there, Google X serves as an inspiration. It shows that no idea is too big, too bold, or too ambitious.

But Google is not just about Innovation and this doesn't exist in a vacuum; it's about Digital too. It embodies their mission to organise the world's information and make it universally accessible and useful. Whether it's improving machine learning algorithms or developing new ways to harness renewable energy, Google leverages Digital technology to transform the way we live and interact with the world

Every click, every query, every journey on Google was a democratic vote cast in the vast Digital universe. This sense of Digital democratisation did not stop at search. It found its expression in their ad platform, which offered a level playing field for businesses big and small. They went a step further by being a vanguard of user privacy, a trait that added to their Digital integrity.

In the Digital world, Google is more than a player; it's a titan, a trailblazer that consistently breaks boundaries. Google's journey has been a symphony of its own, a tale of transformation that has changed the face of the internet, and indeed, the world.

Imagine the expanse of the internet as an untamed wilderness, vast and filled with unlimited potential. Google arrived with the audacity to tame this wilderness, to carve out a path through the dense undergrowth of information. PageRank became the compass, guiding users through this landscape, transforming a wild forest into a navigable park. This was the beginning of their Digital journey.

Google Search democratised access to information, breaking down barriers, enabling people everywhere to learn, discover, and connect. And this was only the first step. The symphony was just beginning.

Google's suite of applications–Google Maps, Gmail, Google Drive, and the ubiquitous Google Chrome–each new application, each new service, was a step forward in their transformation. They didn't just provide tools; they redefined how we interact with the world.

Take Google Maps as an example. It's not just a navigation tool; it's a Digital representation of our physical world. It encapsulates Google's commitment to using technology to create tangible, real-world benefits. Maps became a symphony of data, algorithms, and user interaction, all coming together to transform how we traverse our world.

In the grand orchestra of Google, Artificial Intelligence (AI) and Machine Learning (ML) have emerged as soloists, taking centre stage in recent years. From optimising search results to powering the Google Assistant, AI and

ML have become integral parts of Google's symphony. They illustrate the transformative power of these technologies and demonstrate Google's commitment to staying at the cutting edge of the Digital frontier. And to be fair, we have just scratched the surface with where Google is going with this technology.

This growth mindset gave birth to the ambitious venture of Google Books, aiming to digitise every book ever published. And it's evident in the X lab, working on moonshot projects, pushing the limits of what's possible. It resonates in Google's constant updates and iterations to its services, each one fine-tuning the melody of their masterpiece.

Every note, every chord in Google's symphony is an embodiment of its commitment to Digital transformation. It's about reimagining what's possible, pushing boundaries, and constantly innovating. It's about using technology to make a real difference, to enhance lives, to shape a better future. Thus, it encourages every Ideas Guy to listen, learn, and contribute their own melody to this grand orchestra. It's an open invitation to join in, to shape the future, to be part of the symphony.

The next powerful chord is **EDUCATION**. Google, under Brin and Page, was not just a search engine; it was an educator, a vast, virtual library of Alexandria, a testament to their belief in the power of knowledge.

Google's venture into digitising libraries is one of the clearest examples of their commitment to Education. Google Books, an ambitious, audacious initiative, was a step towards a world where every page of every book was a click away. Education, in this age, was not confined to the four walls of a classroom. It was everywhere. It was in every search query, every click, every link.

It is the uplifting harmony that imbues the entire piece with purpose and direction. It is not merely a note, but a song of its own, sung by Google with the purpose of empowering individuals with knowledge and tools to shape their own futures.

At its core, Google believes that Education should be universally accessible, free from the constraints of location, economic status, or background. This belief translates into an array of Educational tools designed to democratise learning and make it universally accessible.

Take Google Classroom, not just an online platform for Education, but an online playground that breaks down the traditional walls of a classroom. It encourages collaboration and engagement among students, allows teachers to create, distribute, and grade assignments in a paperless way. It's a tool that exemplifies Google's approach to Education–using technology to transform the way we learn, making it more interactive, more engaging, and more accessible.

Then there is Google Docs, Sheets, and Slides–tools that have revolutionised the way we collaborate and learn. These tools provide a platform for cooperative learning, fostering creativity and critical thinking skills. They allow students from different corners of the world to work together in real time, to learn from each other, and to create something unique. This is the power of Google's approach to Education, the power of collaboration and Innovation.

But it doesn't stop there. Google's commitment to schools is also evident in initiatives such as CS First, a free computer science curriculum that makes coding easy to teach and fun to learn or the Google Certified Educator programme that champions teachers who want to bring the Digital revolution into their classrooms.

But Google's mantra is not just about tools and platforms. It's about fostering a culture of continuous learning and curiosity. It's about instilling the spirit of "What if?" and empowering individuals to seek answers, to learn, and to grow.

This is Google's grand composition for Education, a concerto that seeks to make learning an enjoyable, accessible, and fulfilling journey. Through its innovative tools and initiatives, Google inspires the Ideas Guy to never stop learning, to continuously seek knowledge, and to share this learning with others.

Just as Brin and Page took on the virgin Digital landscape with a hunger to learn and discover, so too does Google inspire this in all of us. The beat of the Education note continues, and the question to you, the Ideas Guy, is: What will you learn next, and how will you use this knowledge to change your world?

As we look further into the narrative, we arrive at the note of **AUTHENTICITY**, which has always been a guiding principle for Google.

Authenticity is not just about being honest; it's about standing true to your vision and values, even when the odds are stacked against you. When Google chose not to clutter its minimalist homepage with ads, when it made difficult choices to protect user privacy, when it ventured into unproven territories, it was Authenticity echoing.

It is not merely a characteristic but an underlying principle that defines their ethos and shapes their actions.

Imagine Brin and Page at the helm of their fledgling company, navigating through the complex world of technology, facing the myriad pressures and temptations that come with the territory. They could have easily compromised their principles for short-term gains, allowing their mission to be blurred by the noise of the market. But they didn't. They held steadfast to their original purpose.

Authenticity for Google means standing true to this mission, even when it's challenging. It means making decisions that align with their principles, even when they may not be the most profitable or popular.

Take, for instance, their commitment to user privacy. At a time when data is the new gold, Google has always placed a high premium on the privacy of its users. This has been a key principle for them from the very beginning, and they've striven to provide transparency, choice, and control when it comes to personal data. This unwavering commitment to privacy, even in the face of financial gain, is a testament to their Authenticity.

Furthermore, Google's Authenticity is embedded in its corporate culture. The famed "Don't be evil" mantra is not just a slogan but a call to action, a reminder of their responsibility to their users and the world at large. It's a commitment to a set of principles that prioritise the user and their experience. In an industry riddled with grey areas, Google took a stand, choosing not just to exist, but to exist authentically.

And it is this Authenticity that calls to the Ideas Guy. It invites you to be true to your purpose, to stand by your values, to act with integrity and transparency. It's a reminder that Authenticity is not just about being true to others but about being true to yourself.

In the grand narrative of Google, the voice of Authenticity resounds, calling us to a higher standard of action and responsibility. For the Ideas Guy, the challenge is to embrace this Authenticity, to act with integrity, to be guided by your values, and to make a positive impact in the world.

The overture, now layered with Innovation, Digital, Education, and Authenticity, was yearning for its final note, **STRATEGY.** The maestros, Page and Brin, well aware of the complex orchestra they conducted, strategised masterfully. Guided by their North Star–to organise the world's information and make it universally accessible and useful–they demonstrated their ability to orchestrate a Strategy that was not just about winning, but winning right.

With a melody as nuanced as Google's, Strategy became the baton that kept the music cohesive. The founders demonstrated this when they decided to extend their reach beyond the search engine, exploring uncharted territories and continuing to do the same. These ventures are not about diversifying for the sake of growth; they are strategic moves aligned with their mission.

And this was just the beginning. As Google grew, so did their strategic initiatives. They expanded their reach, entering new realms like online advertising with Google Ads, Digital content with Google Play, and hardware with the Google Pixel and Chromebook series, to name just a few. They foresaw the future of technology, investing in areas like artificial intelligence and quantum computing long before they were mainstream.

But Google's Strategy was not just about business growth. It was also about societal impact. They committed themselves to making technology useful for everyone. They developed Google for Education, providing tools and resources to educators and students worldwide. They invested in renewable energy, aiming to run their entire business on carbon-free energy by 2020. In 2007, they became carbon neutral for all operations and in 2017, became the first company of their size to match 100% of their global, annual electricity consumption with renewable energy. Over the past decade, Google purchased more renewable energy than any other company.

All these strategic decisions have been guided by a single, overarching mission. It's this commitment to their mission that has guided their Strategy, providing a direction for their initiatives, a purpose for their actions, and a context for their decisions.

And for the Ideas Guy, the story of Google's Strategy serves as a roadmap. It's a reminder that a clear and actionable methodology is crucial in turning ideas into realities. It encourages you to plan wisely, to act deliberately, and to remain focused on your mission. Whether you're embarking on a new project or navigating the complexities of your own journey, let Google's strategic approach inspire you, guide you, and remind you of the power of a well-crafted Strategy.

The story of Google, its birth, its journey, its transformation, is akin to a symphony. A symphony conducted by Brin and Page, guided by their IDEAS - Innovation, Digital, Education, Authenticity, and Strategy. Each of these elements is a note, a chord, a rhythm in Google's tune, contributing to the music that has and continues to transform our world.

Like a symphony, each of these elements does not exist in isolation; they're interwoven, creating a harmony that is distinct, resonating, and inspiring. This interplay, this synergy, is what makes Google's story extraordinary. It's a testament to the power of IDEAS and how, when they come together, they create music that changes the world.

This story is not just about Google. It's a narrative about the power of IDEAS and how they can transform the way we think, act, and innovate. As the Ideas Guy, you can take a leaf from Google's book. Consider how the elements resonate in your own context. Each of these elements holds the power to create a story, a melody that can inspire, challenge, and transform.

So, the next time you find yourself in the wilderness of information, the next time you dare to ask, "What if?", the next time you stand at the edge of a difficult decision, remember Google's opus. Remember the initiators, Brin and Page, remember their IDEAS. Let their music guide you, inspire you, and lead you to create your own soundtrack. Because, after all, every great song begins with a single note, a single IDEA.

In the end, what's the role of the Ideas Guy? It's to listen, to learn, and to lead. Listen to the symphony that's being played around you, learn from the maestros who've created world-changing melodies, and then lead with your own unique composition. Be the virtuoso of your own orchestra, strike your unique notes, and create a noise that's uniquely yours.

To embark on this journey, you don't need to be a genius or a prodigy. All you need is the courage to innovate, the commitment to transform, the will to educate and be educated, the resolve to be authentic, and the vision to strategise. You need IDEAS.

## [ APPLYING THIS IN PRACTICE ]

**FOSTER USER-CENTRICITY:** The essence of success then lies in comprehending and prioritising the needs of the user. Larry Page and Sergey Brin's captivating journey with Google has shown us the immense power of placing users at the heart of our Digital experiences. As the brilliant Donald Miller articulates in his Storybrand framework: the hero in the story is not the business; it's the customer. Stop making the story about you and your brilliant idea and make it about them and what they want and need.

Embark on a user-centric journey by honing the art of listening. Listen to your users attentively, seeking their voices, their stories, and their challenges. Delve deep into their needs, desires, and aspirations. Understand that every click, tap, or swipe offers a window into their desires, and each encounter is an opportunity to forge a genuine connection.

Embrace empathy as your guiding light. Step into the shoes of your users, walk the path they tread, and see the world through their eyes. It's not solely about developing features; it's about crafting experiences that resonate with the depths of their souls. Prioritise inclusivity and accessibility, ensuring that your wonders can be enjoyed by all, regardless of their abilities or backgrounds.

Unleash the power of data as your ally. Embrace analytics and user research to unveil the mysteries of the user's journey. Allow data to paint a vivid picture of their preferences, behaviours, and pain points. Let it guide your decisions, refine your creations, and shape your domain.

Remember, the user is not an abstract entity; they are real individuals with hopes, dreams, and a yearning for connection. Embrace the human side of technology, where ones and zeros come alive as conduits of joy, knowledge, and inspiration.

So, as you venture into your odyssey, make a solemn pledge: to be a fierce advocate for your users. Hear their voices reverberate in every line of code, in every design element, and in every interaction. Celebrate their triumphs as your own and learn from their struggles as your guide to growth.

In the heart of the Digital realm, where algorithms hum and screens gleam, the user is king. Embrace the wisdom of Page and Brin, and let user-centricity be the beacon that illuminates your path to greatness. For in this world of boundless possibilities, it's the human touch that weaves the magic, transforming the ordinary into the extraordinary.

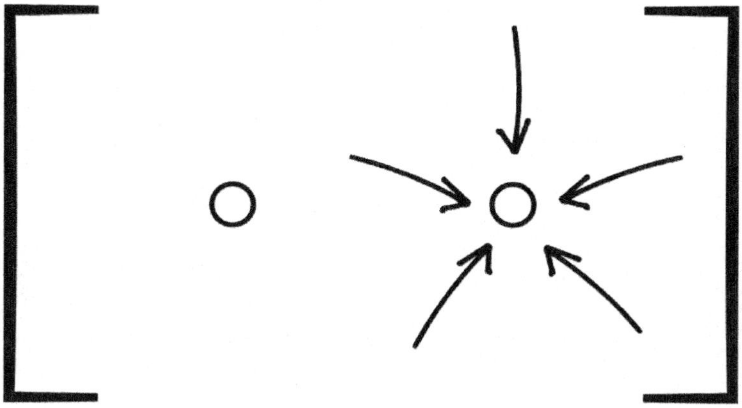

FOSTER USER-CENTRICITY

I REALLY BELIEVE THAT WHEN YOU GIVE PEOPLE AUTHENTIC IDENTITY, WHICH IS WHAT FACEBOOK DOES, AND YOU CAN BE YOUR REAL SELF AND CONNECT WITH REAL PEOPLE ONLINE, THINGS WILL CHANGE.

**SHERYL SANDBERG**

# [ CHAPTER 22 ]

# SHAPING THE FUTURE

The tale of Sheryl Sandberg is an intricate weave of ideas and audacity, braiding together ideas with calculated risks. Her dance with disruption is not a chaotic whirl, but a measured, methodical choreography that transforms uncertainty into opportunity. Sandberg, the tenacious heroine of this chapter, embodies a spirit of inventiveness that pulses through every strand of her career, weaving a tapestry of **INNOVATION** that is as intricate as it is impactful.

In the kingdom of Silicon Valley, a place defined by its relentless pursuit of the new, the different, the better, Sandberg stands out as an innovator par excellence. Not because she invented new technologies or founded tech giants, but because she reimagined the dynamics of leadership and corporate culture in a space traditionally dominated by men. Her Innovation was subtle, yet profound, changing not just the way businesses operate but also how they perceive and pursue success.

Consider her time at Google, where she was instrumental in developing the company's online advertising programmes. The novelty wasn't in the technology she built but in the approach she took. While most were engrossed in numbers and codes, Sandberg's vision extended beyond the algorithms. She looked at the people using the technology, understanding their needs, motivations, and behaviours. It was this user-centric Innovation that made Google's advertising programs some of the most successful in the world (just like we have seen in the last chapter; Sandberg was responsible for much of the execution of this vision).

When she moved to Facebook, her innovative spirit moved with her. Once again, she wasn't developing new technologies or coding revolutionary algorithms. Instead, she was redefining what leadership looked like in a tech company, transforming Facebook from a promising start-up into a global social media giant. It was her understanding of business Strategy and operational management, fused with an innate ability to nurture talent and foster a culture of openness and inclusivity, that drove Facebook's exponential growth.

The Lean In movement, Sandberg's call to arms for women in the workplace, is another testament to her innovative spirit. It wasn't merely a book or a campaign, it was an idea, a vision, a movement that aimed to alter the gender dynamics of the professional world. She identified a challenge – the underrepresentation of women in leadership positions – and addressed it not with silent acceptance, but with a groundbreaking Strategy to educate, encourage, and empower.

Innovation, in the world of Sheryl Sandberg, is not confined to products or technologies. It's about people, about processes, about challenging norms and redefining possibilities. It's about questioning the status quo and daring to dream bigger, better. It's about empowering people to be the best versions of themselves, to unlock potentials they didn't know they had.

It's not just about disrupting markets or creating wealth. It's about creating a ripple of change that can transform society, that can bridge gaps, shatter ceilings, and build bridges where there are walls. It's about creating a world where everyone, regardless of their gender, has an equal opportunity to succeed.

Innovation transcends being just another business strategy - it becomes a catalyst that reveals what's possible when bold thinking meets opportunity. It shows us how courage and creativity together can transform possibilities into reality.

It cannot be an end in itself, but a means to a greater, nobler end. Innovation is the seed of an idea, daring to sprout amidst challenges, daring to reach for the sun, daring to become a tree that shelters, nurtures, and sustains. It's the audacity of a single individual to stand up, lean in, and say, "We can do better." And then setting out to do just that. That's the true essence of Innovation, the real sound of disruption. That's the melody that Sandberg has been conducting, a melody that is far from finished.

Beneath the surface of the visible universe, a myriad of binary codes perform a complex ballet, creating a realm unseen yet profoundly impactful. This is the **DIGITAL** domain, a non-material cosmos where Innovation and information intermingle, igniting ideas and inspiring possibilities. Our protagonist, Sheryl Sandberg, is a master in this sphere, a Digital pioneer who wields technology not as a weapon, but as a tool for transformation.

Sandberg's engagement with this world is as graceful as it is effective. She navigates the expansive tapestry of binary with an agility both instinctual and learned, her movements sharpened by experience and fuelled by curiosity. Her footprints resonate through the virtual corridors of the Internet, echoing a rhythmic melody that speaks of change, possibility and progression.

At Facebook, a company intrinsically linked with the Digital world, Sandberg utilised the power of the platform to facilitate connections, initiate dialogues, and crucially, cultivate community. Yet, her understanding extended beyond the boundaries of Facebook. She recognised the potential of technology to democratise access to information, to dismantle barriers and erect bridges, to engender a sense of unity in a world divided by borders.

Under Sandberg's stewardship, Facebook evolved beyond its original guise as a social networking site. It transformed into a robust platform that encourages discourse, instigates action, and aids in the global distribution of information. Sandberg didn't merely follow the established path, she carved her own, shaping Facebook into an arena where voices are amplified, stories are disseminated, and change is catalysed.

From the standpoint of those holding equity in Facebook, Sheryl Sandberg's appointment was nothing short of a windfall. It was she who charted the course that transmuted Facebook from an appealing platform, with an expansive user base, yet lacklustre profitability, into one of the most financially successful enterprises ever to grace the globe.

Sandberg was also the mastermind behind the inception of Facebook's political affairs unit, an entity that now holds its ground as one of the most potent lobbying bodies worldwide. Under the stewardship of Sandberg, Facebook deployed its considerable resources to exert influence that reached beyond the corridors of political power.

The ripple of Facebook's influence extended to academic circles, thought tanks, and non-governmental organisations. It was Sandberg's strategic vision that ensured Facebook's interests were not merely tabled but effectively championed in any discourse concerning the destiny of the technology sector. Through this, she solidified Facebook's position not only as a Digital titan but as a formidable influencer in the wider socio-political landscape.

In these complex performances, these orchestras of silicon, Sandberg's Digital acumen shines bright. It's not just about comprehending the technology, but about leveraging its potential for progress, for change, for the greater good. It's about recognising the power of the Digital world to transform the physical one, to challenge the status quo, to mould the future.

To engage with the Digital, as Sandberg does, is to embrace the beat of the present, to anticipate the rhythm of the future. It's a dance that transcends the tangible, venturing into a realm where possibilities are boundless, where Innovation is the norm, not the exception. It's a jive that narrates progress, that echoes with potential, that resounds with the promise of a better tomorrow.

As we journey, we bear witness to her ability to harness technology for change, her capacity to envision a future where Digital is a facilitator, not an impediment. It's a waltz that remains unfinished, a disco still being played, a rumba yet to be fully told. And as the music continues, we eagerly anticipate the next steps Sandberg will bring to the dance floor, especially given her decision to leave Facebook in 2022 to focus on her philanthropic work.

**EDUCATION** is a potent catalyst for change, an ember that ignites the flame of progress. For Sandberg, Education is not a finite journey but an unending voyage of discovery and growth. Her Educational philosophy extends far beyond the traditional confines of classrooms and textbooks. It is a commitment to continual learning, a pledge to foster an environment that nurtures curiosity, encourages questions and cultivates wisdom.

In Sandberg's world, Education is not just about imparting knowledge; it's about kindling a spark that fuels the quest for understanding. It's about encouraging dialogue and discourse, about challenging established ideas and embarking on intellectual adventures. It's about fostering an environment that celebrates diversity of thought and champions the pursuit of knowledge.

Look at her own journey, a testament to the transformative power of Education. From Harvard to Silicon Valley, every step, every decision, every accomplishment was underpinned by an enduring dedication to learning. Her commitment, however, extends far beyond personal growth. Sandberg's dedication to fostering Educational opportunities is evident in her myriad initiatives aimed at empowering others through knowledge.

Consider the Lean In circles–a global community brought together by a shared commitment to learning. These circles aren't just about sharing experiences or offering support; they're platforms for Education. Each circle is a microcosm of a classroom, where participants learn from one another, challenge one another, and grow together. Sandberg's vision turned Lean In into a global classroom, underpinned by mutual respect, a thirst for knowledge, and a commitment to shared learning.

Beyond Lean In, Sandberg's dedication to Education is evident in her advocacy for Digital literacy. Recognising the pivotal role of technology in shaping the future, she's championed initiatives aimed at promoting Digital skills and awareness. It's not just about equipping individuals with technical knowledge; it's about fostering a broader understanding of the landscape and its potential to catalyse change.

Sandberg understands that Education cannot remain stagnant. It needs to evolve, to adapt, to remain relevant. She recognises that in the age of information, knowledge is power, and Education is the key to unlocking that power. It's a journey that's deeply personal yet universally impactful, a commitment that goes beyond the self, echoing into the lives of others, resonating in the broader society. It's a dance that never truly ends, a rhythm that beats with the promise of a brighter tomorrow, a song that resounds with the notes of change.

As we follow Sandberg's dance, we bear witness to her commitment to fostering a culture of learning, her dedication to nurturing knowledge, and her unwavering belief in the power of Education for real change. It's a rhythm that reverberates throughout her journey, that speaks of the transformative power of knowledge.

**AUTHENTICITY** is an elusive quality, difficult to define, yet immediately recognisable when we encounter it. For Sheryl Sandberg, being authentic is not a virtue to aspire to; it is a cornerstone of her leadership, a fundamental aspect of her character. It is not merely about being true to oneself; it's about aligning actions with beliefs, aligning deeds with words, and aligning decisions with principles. Authenticity, in its purest form, is about harmony–harmony between self and actions, thoughts and words, vision and reality.

In Sandberg's journey, this is not a static trait but a dynamic force. It's not about rigid adherence to a preconceived notion of self, but rather a commitment to continuous self-reflection and self-improvement. It's about recognising one's limitations, acknowledging one's mistakes, and having the courage to learn, grow, and adapt.

It was amidst the meteoric rise of Facebook, her role in shaping the platform's development, that life threw a cruel curveball at her. A sudden storm in the sunlit sky, the tragic passing of her beloved husband, Dave Goldberg. Struck by grief, grappling with a future she hadn't envisaged, Sandberg faced the toughest challenge life could offer.

In the wake of profound loss, she did something remarkable, something authentic. With raw vulnerability and deep introspection, she penned "Option B: Facing Adversity, Building Resilience, and Finding Joy". Sandberg didn't just write a book, she offered a torchlight for others navigating the dark labyrinth of grief, loss, and adversity.

In "Option B", Sandberg chronicled her tumultuous journey through the murky depths of mourning, sharing poignant, personal narratives that revealed a resilience borne of pain. With co-author Adam Grant, a psychologist, the book transformed personal experience into a universal map for resilience, a guide to finding joy even when life doesn't go as planned.

Her book is a testament to the strength of the human spirit and offers a powerful reminder: We can't change the obstacles life throws our way, but we can choose how we respond. We can choose to find joy, to build resilience, and in doing so, we create our own "Option B".

Her Authenticity shone through these raw and honest revelations, reaffirming her as not just a corporate leader, but as a woman of depth and compassion. Sandberg's personal story was a stark reminder that life isn't a straight line, but a journey full of twists and turns. She boldly embraced her trials and channelled them into a beacon of hope for others, reinforcing her commitment to remain authentic, to remain human, amidst the tempest of personal loss.

Sandberg's Authenticity is not a corporate Strategy. It's not a marketing tool. It's a deeply ingrained part of her persona, visible in her personal life and her professional choices. It's a testament to her belief that in acknowledging our human frailties, in being honest about our shortcomings and challenges, we can find strength and resilience.

Reflect on Sandberg's public admissions of vulnerability, her candidness about her struggles, her openness about her journey. There's a sincere honesty that transcends the corporate veneer, reaching out to people on a fundamentally human level. When she speaks, it's not just a business leader sharing insights; it's a fellow traveller on life's journey sharing experiences, offering solace, and extending a hand of friendship.

This then extends beyond her personal narrative to permeate her professional outlook. Look at Facebook's corporate culture under her stewardship, characterised by openness, transparency, and accountability. She champions a culture where difficult questions are not just tolerated but encouraged, where constructive criticism is valued over blind compliance, where integrity is prized over appeasement.

Consider, too, her book, *Lean In*. It's not just a call to action, but an honest reflection on the realities of being a woman in the business world. She doesn't shy away from uncomfortable truths, doesn't sugarcoat challenges, doesn't offer easy solutions. Instead, she presents a raw account of her experiences, challenges preconceived notions, and calls for a concerted effort to address systemic issues. It's a testament to her Authenticity, her courage to speak her truth, her commitment to sparking meaningful conversations.

In Sandberg's world, Authenticity is more than a virtue; it's a touchstone for ethical leadership. It's a commitment to be true to oneself, a pledge to uphold one's beliefs, a promise to align actions with values. It's about creating an environment where honesty is celebrated, where decency is the norm, and where integrity is the guiding principle.

So, we bear witness to a leader who dares to bare her soul, who dares to challenge the status quo, who dares to be her authentic self. It's a tribute to the strength of character, a melody that resonates with truth and sincerity.

And it is in this vein that we see Sandberg's commitment to **STRATEGY**. Strategising, in its essence, isn't merely a process of planning; it's the art of visualising the path ahead, identifying potential obstacles, and formulating the most effective route to reach the desired destination. In the hands of Sheryl Sandberg, it is a craft honed through years of experience, shaped by thoughtful deliberation, and wielded with finesse and precision.

When Sandberg took up the mantle as the Chief Operating Officer at Facebook, the platform was brimming with potential, yet riddled with uncertainty. It was a wild frontier, untamed and unpredictable. It needed a strategic vision, a roadmap to guide its journey. And that's precisely what Sandberg provided.

From her vantage point, Sandberg could see what many couldn't. She envisaged a global community, interconnected through the Digital medium, sharing their lives, forging relationships, creating a global dialogue. She saw a platform that could become a vital part of people's lives, a tool to facilitate communication, foster relationships, and bridge cultural gaps. And with this vision, she began to strategise.

Sandberg's Strategy didn't merely focus on expanding Facebook's user base or boosting revenues. Of course, these were crucial aspects of her plan. Still, her Strategy went deeper, into the realm of the platform's fundamental purpose - to connect people. Every move she made, every decision she took, every initiative she undertook was oriented towards this central objective.

Observe how she prioritised user experience over short-term profits, opted for sustainable growth over fleeting success, advocated for responsible use of data over unregulated expansion. This wasn't Strategy birthed out of opportunistic exploitation; it was Strategy born out of principled leadership.

This extended beyond the realm of business, seeping into the world of social impact. She used her position at Facebook to champion causes she believed in, leveraging the platform's reach to amplify her voice. From advocating for women's leadership to promoting resilience in the face of adversity, her strategic moves were driven by a desire to make a positive difference.

Moreover, Lean In was a strategic move in itself. It was a calculated endeavour to ignite a global conversation about gender equality, to challenge societal norms, to inspire women to assert themselves in the professional sphere. It was Strategy with a purpose, Strategy with a vision, Strategy with an impact.

As we step back and appreciate Sandberg's journey, we observe a master strategist at work. Her vision, her acumen, her resolve are reflected in every decision, every move, every step of her strategic path. And as we anticipate the next phase of her journey, we can't help but feel a sense of eager anticipation, for we know that whatever Strategy she devises, it will be thoughtfully conceived, meticulously executed, and aimed towards a purpose larger than herself. This, then, is the art of Sandberg's plan–a testament to her visionary leadership and her relentless pursuit of a better, more connected world.

In the world stage of business, Sheryl Sandberg stands as another beacon of the power of the IDEAS framework and how what can be accomplished when orchestrated with vision and precision.

Sandberg's story carries a profound lesson for every aspiring Ideas Guy Innovation isn't simply about creating a unique product, but about approaching problems with a new perspective. Her transformation of Facebook's advertising Strategy exemplifies the power of Digital transformation, while her investment in educating employees and promoting female leadership highlights the value of Education as a tool for organisational growth.

Her Authenticity, expressed in her personal and professional life, in her book and her public endeavours, shines a light on the power of genuine human connection in a digitised world. And finally, her strategic acumen, her ability to envision, execute, and adapt strategies, has proven instrumental in shaping Facebook into the global force it is today.

Sheryl Sandberg embodies the essence of the Ideas Guy, but her story is more than a business case study. It's a human story. A narrative of resilience in the face of personal tragedy, of relentless pursuit of purpose, of a woman who dared to challenge norms and forge her own path.

For every Ideas Guy out there, her journey is an invitation to embrace these IDEAS, to challenge conventions, to innovate, to be authentic, and most importantly, to never stop learning. The music of IDEAS is playing, ready for all those who dare to listen, to learn, and to lead.

# [ APPLYING THIS IN PRACTICE ]

**CULTIVATE RESILIENT LEADERSHIP:** it is not simply about facing challenges; it's about the transformative power that emerges from embracing the journey with unwavering determination and Authenticity. As we navigate the dynamic Digital landscape, let us embrace these principles of resilience, empowering us to make a positive impact on the world.

At the core of resilient leadership lies a growth mindset–the unwavering belief in the capacity for growth, learning, and development. Sandberg's tale reminds us that every setback is an opportunity to learn, adapt, and grow. In the face of the unpredictable, remain steadfast in your commitment to growth and self-improvement. Embrace the challenges that come your way, for they are not hurdles to deter you but stepping stones to elevate you. The Digital realm may be ever-changing, but with a growth mindset, you can navigate its intricacies with resilience and adaptability.

Resilient leadership doesn't mean being invincible; it means embracing vulnerability with Authenticity. Her candidness about her own struggles creates a profound connection with her team and followers. In your endeavours, be open about the journey, the obstacles, and the emotions that accompany them. By fostering a culture of vulnerability, you encourage others to share their experiences and create a space where empathy and support flourish.

Just as resilience is not a solitary journey, neither is leadership. Cultivate a supportive ecosystem that empowers others to flourish and thrive. Amplify the voices around you, lift others up, and ignite their potential. Celebrate the accomplishments of others, for their success becomes your success. Be a mentor, a collaborator, and an advocate for those within your team and community.

Resilience is not about forging ahead without consideration for others; it's about leading with empathy and compassion. Take the time to connect with your team, understand their needs and challenges, and offer support and encouragement. Lead with empathy and understanding, and foster a culture where everyone feels seen, heard, and valued. As a resilient leader, your ability to show compassion and empathy creates a harmonious work environment where trust and collaboration thrive.

Champion diversity in your team and community, and create an environment where everyone feels welcomed and empowered to contribute. Embrace the richness that inclusivity brings to your projects, for it ignites Innovation and fosters creativity.

Remember that transformative impact is not solely defined by the destination but by the growth and progress you achieve on the journey. Allow yourself to learn and grow from both successes and failures, for each experience contributes to your evolution as a resilient leader.

Through resilience, we transcend challenges and transform adversity into strength. Let us navigate the world we face with resolve, cherishing every step of the journey and making a lasting impact that resonates far beyond our ventures. The world awaits the transformative leadership that emerges from cultivating resilience. Let us be the pioneers of change, the architects of a brighter future.

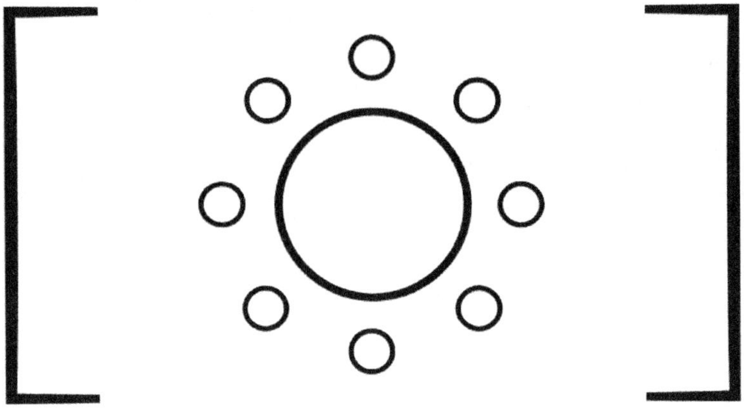

# CULTIVATE RESILIENT LEADERSHIP

THE KEY TO HAPPINESS DOESN'T LAY IN NUMBERS IN A BANK ACCOUNT BUT IN THE WAY WE MAKE OTHERS FEEL AND THE WAY THEY MAKE US FEEL.

JOE ROGAN

# [ CHAPTER 23 ]

# DISRUPTIVE DIALOGUE

To talk about disruptive dialogue means conversations that shake the status quo, ruffle feathers, and provoke thought. Enter the arena, Joe Rogan, a figure whose innovative approach to dialogue has set him apart from the crowd. His **INNOVATION** isn't a product, a gadget, or a novel algorithm. It's an approach, a mindset, and a dare to be different.

Picture a wall, a towering structure of solid conventions, traditional formats, and familiar styles. Now envision Rogan, who approached this daunting edifice not with a sledgehammer of destruction, but with the chisel of Innovation. His podcast, The Joe Rogan Experience, wasn't designed to tear down the wall, but to carve a unique, intriguing doorway through it. A doorway that led to new ways of doing conversation, a space where dialogues weren't hemmed in by time constraints or scripts.

A traditional talk show might allot guests a few minutes, maybe half an hour at most, to discuss their life's work, their experiences, and their insights. Rogan looked at this convention and asked, "What if?" What if he gave his guests not minutes, but hours? What if the conversation wasn't guided by a set list of questions, but by the natural ebb and flow of curiosity and exploration? What if a podcast wasn't just a fleeting exchange, but a deep dive into the minds of some of the most interesting individuals on the planet?

So, he forged ahead, testing the waters of long-form dialogue. This wasn't Innovation within the comforts of a tried-and-tested formula; it was sailing into uncharted waters with nothing but a compass of curiosity. The Joe Rogan Experience is a testament to this Innovation - a platform where dialogues aren't rushed but savoured, where guests aren't mere talking points but the focal point of the conversation.

Innovation, as demonstrated by Rogan, doesn't always mean reinventing the wheel. Sometimes, it's about taking a different route, about asking, "What if we didn't follow the road most travelled?" Sometimes, Innovation is not about what you do differently, but about how you think differently. It's about daring to challenge the norms, to question the tried-and-true, to explore the possibilities that lie beyond the familiar path.

For Rogan, this exploration has manifested in a variety of forms. From the discussions about mixed martial arts and psychedelics, to conversations with comedians and astronauts, his approach to dialogue embraces diversity, complexity, and depth. It's a space where a neuroscientist can unpack the intricacies of the brain, a philosopher can muse about the mysteries of existence, or a politician can outline their vision for the future. All in the same week.

This is the innovative spirit of the Ideas Guy - the willingness to depart from the traditional, to take a chance on something different. Rogan's Innovation didn't just disrupt the talk show format; it broadened the horizons of what a podcast could be. It invited listeners to engage, to think, to question, and to join in a journey of exploration. It turned dialogue from a one-way street into an open highway.

For those striving to be an Ideas Guy, Rogan's approach to dialogue offers a fascinating lesson. Innovation isn't a destination, it's a journey. It's not about finding the right answer, but about asking the right question. It's about looking at the walls that confine us and asking, "What if there's a different way?" It's about the audacity to try, the courage to experiment, and the resolve to keep exploring. For when you dare to innovate, you don't just create something new, you open a doorway to possibilities that were once unimagined. That's the disruption that Joe Rogan, in his own unique way, has brought to the world of dialogue.

In the depths of this sea, amidst the schools of viral videos, shoals of tweets, and flocks of memes, one can spot the steady current of the Joe Rogan Experience, carving out its own unique path.

Rogan's podcast is a lesson in embracing the **DIGITAL**, leveraging the virtual world not as an echo chamber, but as a meeting point for diverse perspectives. And in doing so, he's done more than just build a popular podcast; he's built a community, a network of listeners keenly tuned into the disruption of dialogue he's championed. He made a bold decision in his deal with Spotify but one which allowed him to maintain his autonomy.

His show was a colossus, a behemoth, with a YouTube following like a ravenous choir. Spotify saw this and boom: licensing agreement, as a VIP pass to the inner chambers of audio stardom. The whisper is that the payment was north of $200 million. Three and a half years, a monumental alliance is inked. But it meant Spotify had exclusivity, no longer free to roam wherever it landed.

But, with the vast reach of the internet, Rogan has created a platform that can extend beyond geographical, political, and cultural boundaries. It's a place where a listener in London can tune into a discussion on the nuances of American politics or an audience member in Sydney can get a crash course on quantum physics from a leading expert. This reach, the ability to bridge divides and foster global conversations, is a testament to the power of online channels when used with intention and respect for diversity of thought.

Joe Rogan hasn't simply jumped on the Digital bandwagon, he's commandeered the driver's seat. As we sift through the panorama of the 21st century, The Joe Rogan Experience stands out as a harbinger, showcasing how Digital platforms can be used to transcend traditional media, redefine engagement, and pioneer novel formats of dialogue. He owns the long-form conversation and the statistics confirm his position.

Remember, we're talking about a platform that's consistently among the top podcasts on various charts worldwide, an arena that has become synonymous with long-form, open, and in-depth conversations. These achievements didn't happen overnight. They're the result of a consistent presence, a commitment to quality content, and a knack for engaging listeners in an era of fleeting attention spans.

Digital platforms, for all their potential, can be a double-edged sword. On one hand, they provide an unparalleled opportunity for global reach. On the other, they can make us susceptible to the pressures of viral content, clickbait headlines, and the allure of quantity over quality. Rogan's tactics provide a refreshing counterpoint. His podcast underlines the fact that in the rush for viral content, we must not lose sight of the value of depth, relevance, and credibility.

Rogan reminds us that dialogue isn't just about speaking; it's about being heard. His podcast doesn't just populate the airwaves; it engages with it. It's not just about contributing to the online noise, but about adding value to the dialogue.

To be an Ideas Guy in the Digital age, to truly make a difference, one must not just understand the power of the Digital, but know how to wield it effectively. It's not enough to be part of the vista; one must also shape it, guide it, and, when needed, disrupt it. This is a lesson we can all learn from Rogan's path.

He has demonstrated that Digital platforms can be more than just a stage; they can be a tool for change, a catalyst for dialogue, and a conduit for innovative ideas. We would do well to remember that being online isn't just about being seen, it's about making a meaningful impact.

Joe Rogan stands on the shores of the vast sea of knowledge, ever ready to dive in, hungry for new insights and revelations. His podcast is a ship that sails these seas, inviting us all on an extraordinary voyage of discovery. His compass? Endless curiosity. His destination? The yet unknown. And his cargo? A treasure trove of wisdom and insight, shared by the remarkable guests he brings on board.

Imagine the scene. There's Neil deGrasse Tyson, the charismatic astrophysicist, engaging us with his passion for the cosmos, rendering the intricate science of astrophysics accessible to everyone. A little further on the trek, we encounter Dan Carlin, the renegade historian, sharing gripping tales from the annals of world history, making us view the past in a whole new light. Consider when Elon Musk, a titan of technology, Innovation, and space exploration, graced the podcast. In a conversation that covered everything from artificial intelligence to the future of human civilisation on Mars, Rogan served as an able guide, extracting insights and provoking thoughts in ways that were both accessible and engaging. The audience was not merely spectators but active participants in a vibrant pilgrimage of shared discovery and learning.

In another memorable episode, Rogan converses with theoretical physicist Brian Greene. The exchange veers into the realm of quantum physics, string theory, and the very nature of reality itself. Rogan, the curious explorer, navigates these profound topics with aplomb, embodying the role of the eternal student, ever-eager to learn and grow.

Then there's Dr. Rhonda Patrick, a frequent guest on the show, whose discussions with Rogan revolve around health, nutrition, and wellness. From the intricate dynamics of the human body to the beneficial effects of certain foods, these conversations turn complex scientific knowledge into digestible, actionable insights.

The dialogue with Jordan Peterson, the controversial psychologist, is a testament to this. They delve into the very nature of truth, an intellectual dance that leaves one considering the very fabric of reality. Or the conversation with sleep scientist Matthew Walker, which gives us a fresh appreciation for the importance of a good night's rest, making us reevaluate our sleep patterns.

The dynamic with Rogan is always evolving. He's a traveller on the voyage of discovery, a dedicated seeker of truth. He isn't afraid to pose difficult questions or confront his own limitations, and it's precisely this integrity that makes his audience feel included in the process of learning. Rogan's thirst for knowledge is insatiable, and it's this unending curiosity that transforms each podcast episode into an immersive learning experience.

In Rogan's world, **EDUCATION** isn't bound by the traditional classroom or textbook framework. It thrives in the open, in the wild exchange of ideas, in a space that encourages questioning and pushes the boundaries of understanding. The essence of Rogan's approach to Education can be distilled into a simple yet powerful idea: to learn is to evolve, to grow, and to understand the world in all its complexity. In each dialogue, we delve deep, not just into the realm of the guest's expertise, but also into the workings of their minds, understanding their perspectives, sharing their passion, and learning from their wisdom. Every episode is a masterclass in its own right, a rich source of knowledge shared over casual, engaging conversations.

Through his podcast, Rogan underlines the significance of lifelong learning, of remaining perpetually open and curious. His podcast strikes a resonant chord for Education. This melody resonates with his audience and encourages us all to keep learning, to keep questioning, and to remain open to the marvels of the world around us. Rogan emerges as an unlikely yet impactful educator for our times.

Education isn't a linear journey with a set destination; it's more of an expansive landscape, a fertile field where seeds of curiosity are sown and cultivated. It's not about regurgitating facts nor cramming the night before an exam. No, it's about a relentless pursuit of understanding, a ceaseless quest for the why, the how, and the what if. It's about the questions that don't have easy answers, the topics that make us uncomfortable, and the conversations that challenge our deeply ingrained beliefs.

And the guests–experts, outliers, thinkers, and even provocateurs–serve as informal professors in this global classroom Rogan has created. Their varied backgrounds, from scientists to artists, from historians to athletes, enrich the Educational experience, offering a kaleidoscopic view of human knowledge and potential. Each guest brings their own unique syllabus, inviting us to explore unfamiliar territories, to rethink our assumptions, and to expand the horizons of our own understanding.

What's particularly captivating is Rogan's role as both student and teacher in these dialogues. He listens, prods, and often pushes back, embodying the kind of active, engaged learning that traditional Education often lacks. And just like that, without the rigid structures or ivory towers, we're all transformed into eager students in the most eclectic, wide-ranging university one could imagine. This isn't just Education; it's Education reimagined, redefined, and reborn in the crucible of curiosity.

In the modern media landscape, **AUTHENTICITY** is a scarce thread, often overshadowed by the glitz of performance or the gloss of production. Yet, it's this thread that makes the difference, creating a distinctive resonance that reverberates with the audience, making them feel seen, heard, and connected. Rogan, through his various endeavours, has consistently embodied this Authenticity, weaving it into the very fabric of his work, his podcast, and his identity.

Take the first step on Rogan's path, and we find ourselves in the mixed martial arts (MMA) arena. Rogan, an ardent fan and practitioner of martial arts since age 13, gained a black belt within two years and entered the world of MMA commentary way back in 2002, when he started on the UFC. He offered insights not from an ivory tower of detached analysis but from the gritty reality of personal experience and passion. His Authenticity shone through his understanding and respect for the fighters, his palpable enthusiasm for the sport, and his determination to articulate the complexities of each match with the same energy and excitement he felt. And over twenty years later, he is still the voice of UFC.

His journey was not prescribed nor conventional. Picture Rogan as a young man, stepping onto the stage of a comedy club, microphone in hand, the spotlight glaring down. His beginnings in stand-up comedy were not marked by instant success or fanfare. Rather, it was an odyssey punctuated by small victories, setbacks, and continuous learning. The raw, unfiltered nature of stand-up comedy necessitated Authenticity, demanding that Rogan bare his soul, explore his perspectives, and deliver it all with a relatable, human touch. This experience, you see, shaped Rogan's approach to his work and life, grounding it in a bedrock of integrity.

Through the podcast, as we have seen, Rogan's realness takes centre stage, fostering an environment where guests feel safe to be their genuine selves. The conversations are free-flowing, akin to sitting by the fire and sharing stories with an old friend. Rogan engages with his guests on a profound level, unafraid to express his curiosity, admit his ignorance, and explore the depths of a topic. His Authenticity radiates through his willingness to let the conversation take its natural course, unscripted and unforced. When he asks questions, it feels as though he's genuinely interested. Because he is.

In one particularly striking episode, Rogan invited actor and comedian Kevin Hart onto the show. The conversation was not just about Hart's career but also about his life philosophy, his approach to success and failure, and his perspective on personal growth. Rogan's Authenticity in these exchanges cultivated an atmosphere of trust and openness, allowing Hart to share personal anecdotes and insights that would typically remain behind the curtain of celebrity.

Joe Rogan's Authenticity is an ongoing performance, a commitment to remain true to his beliefs and interests, regardless of the stage he finds himself on. He demonstrates that one's authentic self is the most compelling character one can play, and the most engaging story one can tell. In a world saturated with carefully curated personas and narratives,

Rogan stands apart, reminding us all of the power and connection that stems from simply being oneself.

For **STRATEGY**, Joe Rogan exemplifies a keen sense of adaptability and foresight like few others. Throughout his career, he has demonstrated a remarkable ability to navigate the ever-changing landscape of media and entertainment, staying true to his vision while exploring new opportunities.

Rogan's strategic prowess is evident in his decision to embrace the podcasting medium and capitalise on its potential. When he started JRE in 2009, podcasting was still a relatively niche market. However, he recognised the power of long-form conversations and the unique opportunities this format provided for in-depth discussions.

By committing to unscripted and unfiltered conversations with a diverse array of guests, embracing the concept of "Disruptive Dialogue," he challenged the norms and turned his podcast into a platform where meaningful conversations could flourish.

As his podcast grew in popularity, Rogan continued to innovate and strategise. He expanded his reach by making strategic partnerships, eventually landing an exclusive licensing deal with Spotify. To be exclusive on their platform was a masterstroke. This move was a testament to his forward-thinking approach, recognising the evolving landscape of media consumption and the potential of streaming platforms.

The Spotify deal was a game-changer, solidifying Rogan's position as one of the most influential figures in podcasting and securing a massive audience. Yet, despite the exclusivity of the deal, Rogan remained true to his raw, real self, retaining creative control over the content and continuing to provide an unfiltered platform for open discourse.

His business ventures extend beyond the podcast realm as well. Rogan has dipped his toes into various entrepreneurial endeavours, ranging from stand-up comedy tours to ventures in mixed martial arts (MMA). More recently, he has invested too, including Onnit, a health and wellness company, and AlphaBrain, a nootropic supplement business. These ventures demonstrate his versatility and willingness to explore new opportunities aligned with his interests. And the launch of his own club,

The Comedy Mothership, is further evidence of his keenness to think strategically.

Rogan's approach to Strategy is not solely about maximising profits or expanding his empire; it's about crafting a journey that remains true to his vision while embracing the possibilities of the Digital age. He has adapted to the changing times, harnessing technology to connect with millions of listeners worldwide. Moreover, he has remained open to exploring new avenues that align with his authentic self and passions.

He has disrupted the traditional media landscape by providing a platform for diverse voices and fostering meaningful conversations. The success of his podcast and business ventures stems from his unwavering commitment to staying true to his values, seeking knowledge through engaging conversations.

Joe Rogan's road as an Ideas Guy is a testament to adapting and growing while maintaining his authentic voice. Rogan's disruptive dialogue has opened doors for countless conversations, challenged norms, and inspired millions.

Through his disruptive dialogue, Rogan has played a vital role in giving a voice to those whose stories might have remained unheard. He fearlessly tackles complex issues, diving deep into topics that others might shy away from. This courageous approach to conversation has inspired millions of listeners to think critically, challenge their preconceptions, and engage with the world more thoughtfully. He has been an advocate for Protect our Parks, a volunteer non-profit organisation dedicated to keeping public park land open to the public, as well as The Innocence Project, who work to free the innocent, prevent wrongful convictions, and create fair, compassionate, and equitable systems of justice for everyone. His platform has been used to champion others, and it has been a Strategy that doesn't just make business-sense but ethical and moral sense, too.

Rogan's impact has been monumental. Leveraging the power of technology, his podcast has transcended geographical boundaries, reaching audiences from all corners of the globe. This Digital transformation has allowed him to create a vibrant community of like-minded individuals, but he has remained unapologetically authentic. He has never compromised his unique voice, delivering content that is true to his vision and resonates deeply with his audience, earning him the unwavering loyalty of listeners and the admiration of his guests.

Rogan shows us that being true to oneself is not only empowering but also essential for creating genuine connections and meaningful impact. By staying authentic, Rogan has built a community that celebrates individuality and embraces diverse perspectives.

As we reflect on Joe Rogan's experience as an Ideas Guy, we recognise the profound impact of his style. His journey encourages us to embrace change while remaining grounded in our true selves. By daring to disrupt and staying true to our values, we too can shape the future and leave a lasting impact on the world.

Joe Rogan stands as a symbol of possibility, urging us to harness the power of technology, embrace Authenticity, and break free from the confines of convention. Let us be disruptors in our own right and dare to embark on the ride to the new. Through our actions and voices, let us contribute to a world where meaningful conversations and authentic connections thrive.

## [ APPLYING THIS IN PRACTICE ]

**ASK GREAT QUESTIONS:** In Rogan, we discover the profound impact of genuine enquiry and the art of uncovering truth.

At the core of Joe Rogan's magnetic presence is his insatiable curiosity. He approaches each conversation with a genuine desire to learn, to understand, and to connect. We can learn from Joe Rogan's example and embrace the art of asking great questions. By engaging in genuine enquiry, we not only gain knowledge but also forge authentic connections with our people.

The essence of Joe Rogan's podcast lies in the power of open dialogue. In an era where scripted interviews and rehearsed exchanges abound, his willingness to explore uncharted territories and candidly discuss diverse topics is refreshing. We can follow his lead and cultivate an environment of openness, where great questions lead to unfiltered conversations that inspire and transform.

In the pursuit of IDEAS, we can learn from Joe Rogan's art of uncovering truth. He fearlessly delves into the depths of his guests' perspectives, unearthing their true selves and revealing the essence of their stories. As Ideas Guys, we can embrace the art of asking great questions that lead to profound insights and captivating storytelling. By uncovering truth, we create content that resonates deeply and leaves a lasting impact.

Where virtual interactions are abundant, the art of asking great questions becomes a powerful tool for fostering genuine connections with our audience. By seeking to understand and connect with others through curiosity, we create a sense of community and belonging that transcends the Digital space.

Carry the art of asking great questions with us. Embrace the power of curiosity, engage in open dialogue, uncover truths through genuine enquiry, and use great questions to forge heartfelt connections. By doing so, we can cultivate a presence that not only informs but also inspires and transforms.

ASK GREAT QUESTIONS

DO THE ONE THING YOU THINK YOU CANNOT DO. FAIL AT IT. TRY AGAIN. DO BETTER THE SECOND TIME. THE ONLY PEOPLE WHO NEVER TUMBLE ARE THOSE WHO NEVER MOUNT THE HIGH WIRE. THIS IS YOUR MOMENT. OWN IT.

OPRAH WINFREY

# [ CHAPTER 24 ]

# EMBRACING IDEAS

In media and entertainment, there exists an icon whose name resonates with an unmistakable aura of power: Oprah Winfrey. Her story is one of extraordinary transformation, inspiring millions to embrace life's journey with passion. From humble beginnings in rural Mississippi to becoming a media mogul and philanthropist, Oprah's indomitable spirit has left an indelible mark on the world.

Born amidst modest circumstances, Oprah faced challenges and adversity in her early years. She was born into poverty to a single teenage mother and later raised in inner-city Milwaukee. She has stated that she was sexually assaulted during her childhood and early teenage years and became pregnant at 14. Her son was born prematurely and died in infancy. Despite horrendous beginnings, the fire within her burned bright, fueling an insatiable curiosity and an unyielding thirst for knowledge. Her relentless pursuit of learning and self-improvement became the cornerstone of her remarkable journey.

Venturing into the world of media, Oprah's ability to connect with people of all walks of life set her apart. Her talk show, "The Oprah Winfrey Show," became a sanctuary of candid conversations, tackling a myriad of topics with sensitivity and empathy. Each episode was a window into the human experience, and Oprah's genuine affinity with her guests and audience touched the hearts of many.

Beyond the trappings of wealth of her media success, Oprah's commitment to lifelong learning shone brightly through her book club and various Educational initiatives. She wielded her platform to promote literature, critical thinking, and personal growth, empowering countless individuals to embrace the transformative power of knowledge.

Amidst the ever-changing tides, Oprah demonstrated vision and business acumen, leading her to establish the multimedia empire known as OWN (Oprah Winfrey Network). Her ability to navigate challenges and make strategic decisions aligned with her values created a platform that celebrates diverse voices and fosters personal growth.

In the face of personal struggles and setbacks, Oprah remained resilient, channelling her experiences into opportunities for growth and transformation. Her vulnerability in sharing her own life journey resonated deeply with many, creating a sacred space for healing and empowerment among her audience.

Beyond the glittering lights, Oprah's dedication to philanthropy and social impact has become a hallmark of her character. Through the Oprah Winfrey Foundation, she has supported numerous Educational and empowerment initiatives, illuminating the path for countless individuals, particularly young girls and women.

Oprah's life story stands as an eternal source of inspiration, reminding us that embracing life's trials and triumphs with purpose can lead to extraordinary achievements and profound connections. Her influence on popular culture and society at large is immeasurable, as she continues to be a guiding beacon for those seeking personal growth and a deeper understanding of the world.

As we delve into Oprah's opus of embracing the essence of life, we are invited to reflect on our own paths of self-discovery and empowerment. Her story is a symphony of resilience, integrity, and impact, orchestrating an unforgettable legacy that echoes through generations, inspiring us all to embrace the beauty of our own explorations and discover the transformative power within us.

Oprah Winfrey stands as a shining example of **INNOVATION**, igniting a transformational journey that has transcended the boundaries of what might be expected of her. From her early days as a radio host to becoming a multimedia mogul, Oprah's innovative spirit has continuously redefined the landscape of media, inspiring millions to embrace their own potential and forge their unique paths to greatness.

At the heart of Oprah's Innovation lies an insatiable curiosity and an unyielding desire to explore the human experience. Her mission began in radio, where she displayed an innate talent for connecting with her audience, guiding them through an array of emotions and life's complexities. She began her radio work whilst still in high school and won the International Radio and Television Society Foundation Gold Medal Award in 1996. Her innovative approach to radio broadcasting was a precursor to the groundbreaking success that awaited her in television.

In the early 1980s, "The Oprah Winfrey Show" took the world by storm, heralding a new era of talk shows that transcended traditional celebrity interviews. Oprah's unique brand of vulnerability became the cornerstone of her Innovation. She wasn't just a talk show host; she was a compassionate confidante, an empathetic listener, and an unapologetic advocate for open dialogue. Her innovative approach to storytelling led her to delve into issues rarely discussed on television, from personal struggles to social injustices, fostering a sense of connection and understanding among her viewers.

As she weaved the tapestry of her talk show, Oprah's spirit of Innovation extended beyond the screen. Her book club became a literary revolution, igniting a passion for reading and intellectual exploration among her audience. Through her Book Club, she leveraged her platform to elevate literary voices and introduce a myriad of literary treasures to the masses.

Oprah embraced new media with open arms. She utilised social media platforms to connect with her audience on a deeper level, transcending geographical barriers and fostering a global community. Her online presence allowed her to continue her legacy of inspiring others, as she fearlessly ventured into unexplored realms, using new technology to amplify her message of hope and transformation.

Throughout her journey, Oprah's ingenuity was not confined to the world of media. She embodied the essence of Innovation in her approach to life, embracing challenges as opportunities for growth and personal evolution.

Her genuine kinship with her audience were the driving forces behind her success, as she fearlessly navigated stormy seas and expanded the boundaries of what was possible.

Innovation, for Oprah, wasn't just about inventing new technologies or products; it was about pushing the boundaries of human connection, sparking conversations that mattered, and creating spaces for transformative experiences. Her innovative spirit inspired others to embrace their unique voices and to boldly embark on their own journeys of discovery and self-fulfilment.

Throughout the chapters of Oprah's life, we witness the symphony of Innovation playing its mesmerising tune, orchestrating a legacy that has touched hearts and souls across the globe. Oprah's journey reminds us that it is not limited to a specific field or industry; it is a mindset, a way of approaching life with an open heart and an unwavering commitment to growth.

Her pioneering spirit has shown us that Innovation is not just about finding answers; it is about asking the right questions, seeking deeper understanding, and continuously evolving.

In the **DIGITAL** landscape, Oprah Winfrey's journey has been one of embracing the power of technology and Digital platforms to amplify her voice and extend her impact to every corner of the globe. From the early days of her talk show to the dawn of the internet age, Oprah's Digital prowess has been a testament to her pioneering spirit and her unyielding commitment to staying relevant in an ever-evolving world.

As this online revolution swept across the media landscape, Oprah recognised the immense potential it held to connect with audiences on a deeper level. Her website became a sanctuary, offering a rich array of content, from behind-the-scenes glimpses of her show to empowering interviews and thought-provoking articles. Oprah's Digital platform served as an extension of her on-screen presence, providing a space for her audience to engage with her message of inspiration and personal growth.

As social media emerged as a powerful force, Oprah embraced it with open arms. Her presence extended to various platforms, where she engaged with her audience in real-time, fostering a sense of community and connection.

Through Twitter, Facebook, and Instagram, she shared wisdom, reflections, and moments of vulnerability, inviting her audience into her world and inviting them to be part of her journey.

Oprah's brand wasn't just about broadcasting her message; it was about harnessing the power of technology to amplify voices that had long been silenced. Through her platform, she elevated marginalised voices and provided a platform for diverse perspectives and stories. From shining a spotlight on issues of social justice to promoting the work of emerging artists and authors, Oprah used her influence to champion causes and amplify voices that often went unheard.

With the OWN network, she ventured into the world of streaming, providing audiences with on-demand access to an array of empowering content. The platform allowed viewers to consume content at their convenience, breaking free from traditional television schedules and further expanding Oprah's reach to a global audience.

In her partnership with Apple to create "Oprah's Book Club", this collaboration utilised the power of technology to engage and meet with readers around the world. The book club brought together a community of book lovers, encouraging dialogue, and fostering a love for reading and learning.

As the landscape continued to evolve, Oprah's innovative spirit kept pace. Her book club expanded to include interviews with authors and discussions that reached audiences beyond the written word. Through her platform, she offered a unique and interactive experience, bridging the gap between author and reader.

Oprah's journey in the Digital world shows her adaptability and her willingness to embrace change. As technology evolved, she leveraged its power to continue her mission of empowering and inspiring others. It was never about the medium itself; it was about the message she sought to share and the connections she sought to forge.

Oprah has continued to push the boundaries, embracing new platforms and technologies to remain at the forefront of media and storytelling. She has created a global community, united by a shared sense of purpose and a collective desire for personal growth and transformation. Oprah shows us that technology is a canvas for empowerment, a platform for impact, and a gateway to connection.

Oprah's pursuit of **EDUCATION** goes beyond the traditional classroom; it is a lifelong journey of self-discovery and an unwavering belief in the power of learning to transform lives.

Oprah's dedication to this is evident in the establishment of the Oprah Winfrey Foundation, which focuses on providing Educational opportunities and support to underserved communities. Through scholarships and grants, the foundation has enabled countless students to access quality Education, breaking down barriers and opening doors to a brighter future.

Beyond financial support, Oprah's commitment is deeply rooted in her passion for reading and learning. She has used her influential platform to promote literacy and the love of reading. As we have mentioned, her Book Club became a literary phenomenon, encouraging millions of people to pick up books and engage in meaningful conversations about literature.

Oprah's dedication also extends to empowering young girls and women. The Leadership Academy for Girls in South Africa, founded by Oprah in 2007, is another remarkable example of her dedication. The academy provides a nurturing and empowering environment for girls from disadvantaged backgrounds to receive a quality Education. Beyond academic learning, the academy focuses on developing leadership skills, self-confidence, and a sense of purpose in each student. Graduates of the academy have gone on to become leaders in their communities and are making a positive impact in various fields.

Gugulethu Thwala, affectionately known as Gugu, is a shining example of one of these graduates. Hailing from the vibrant land of KwaZulu-Natal, South Africa, Gugu's journey exemplifies the profound impact of a dedicated pursuit of knowledge and the indomitable spirit of resilience. Gugu's life changed irrevocably when she entered the gates of the Leadership Academy in 2007. In a world where opportunities were scarce, the academy provided her with hope and possibility. Here, she discovered a nurturing environment that encouraged her to dream boldly and recognise her boundless potential.

Academic excellence, leadership development, and character building formed the pillars of the academy's ethos, and it was within this nurturing framework that Gugu blossomed. The academy's devoted educators and mentors nurtured her natural talents and helped her unlock the hidden depths of her potential.

While her academic prowess flourished, it was not the sole measure of her growth. Gugu thrived within the cocoon of the Leadership Academy, honing her public speaking skills, cultivating her critical thinking abilities, and embracing a strong sense of social responsibility.

With 2011 marking her graduation, Gugu's journey toward becoming a doctor began to unfold. Equipped with a full scholarship to the University of Pennsylvania, USA, she embarked on a path of excellence, majoring in neuroscience and minoring in global health. During her time in the United States, her passion for scientific research took flight, and her desire to make a meaningful impact in her homeland grew stronger.

Gugu's return to South Africa after completing her undergraduate studies marked a new chapter in her journey. Driven by a sense of duty to her community, she embraced the challenge of researching the impact of HIV and tuberculosis on the brain at the Africa Health Research Institute. Through her dedication to improving healthcare outcomes, she has become an advocate for change and a beacon of hope for her fellow citizens.

Her remarkable accomplishments did not go unnoticed. In 2018, Oprah extended an invitation to Gugu to be a guest on "The Oprah Winfrey Show." On that momentous stage, Gugu shared her awe-inspiring story, highlighting the profound influence of Education in transforming her life.

Gugu's narrative exemplifies the enduring legacy of Oprah's Academy. Beyond academic achievement, the academy instils a sense of self-assurance, compassion, and resilience in its graduates, shaping them into empowered, driven, and purposeful leaders.

As Gugu continues to blaze her trail, she remains a shining example of the lasting impact of transformative Education. Her journey echoes the values instilled by Oprah's visionary academy, reflecting the immense power of knowledge and the strength to rise above challenges.

One of the remarkable aspects of Oprah's approach to Education is her focus on personal development and self-discovery. She believes that Education is not just about acquiring knowledge but also about understanding oneself and finding one's purpose. Oprah's journey of self-exploration, as showcased in her widely acclaimed television show "Super Soul Sunday," has inspired millions to embark on their own path of self-discovery and spiritual growth. Oprah's approach is holistic, encompassing not just academic knowledge but also emotional intelligence, grit, and the pursuit of purpose. Her journey is a reminder that Education is a lifelong pursuit, a journey of self-discovery, and a path to empowerment and fulfilment.

As an advocate for Education, Oprah has partnered with various Educational organisations and institutions to promote access to quality learning opportunities. She has supported initiatives that provide Educational resources to children in need and promote innovative teaching methods.

Throughout her career, she has used the art of storytelling to share the experiences, challenges, and triumphs of individuals from all walks of life. These stories have not only entertained but have also educated and fostered empathy, breaking down barriers and bringing people closer together.

At the core of Oprah Winfrey's magnetic presence lies a commitment to **AUTHENTICITY**–a profound honesty that has endeared her to millions around the world. As a trailblazer in media, she has consistently remained true to her roots, and her credibility radiates through her every endeavour.

Oprah has an unrivalled willingness to confront racial issues head-on. In her transformative talk show, she fearlessly delved into discussions on race, challenging societal norms, and prejudices. Her unyielding dedication to fostering open conversations about racial disparities and social justice became a powerful force for change.

In 1987, Oprah hosted a groundbreaking episode that left an indelible mark on television history. Titled "The Show About Being Black," the episode saw her inviting an all-African American audience to candidly share their experiences, perspectives, and challenges. It was a powerful moment that illuminated the diverse realities faced by Black Americans, prompting a national conversation on race relations.

Moreover, Oprah's Authenticity is evident in her advocacy for justice. Throughout her career, she has used her influence and resources to support organisations and initiatives addressing racial inequality. From funding Educational programmes for underprivileged communities to amplifying the voices of activists and thought leaders, her authentic commitment to change shines through.

In addition to her racial advocacy, Oprah's Authenticity is interwoven with her humility and vulnerability. She has never shied away from sharing her personal struggles and triumphs, empowering others to embrace their imperfections and find strength in vulnerability. Whether she spoke candidly about her difficult upbringing or her battles with weight and body image, her honesty created a profound connection with her audience.

Her iconic "Live Your Best Life" segments, which featured intimate interviews with celebrities and everyday individuals, further exemplified her genuineness. By creating a safe space for vulnerability and introspection, Oprah invited her guests and viewers to explore their inner selves authentically and uncover the essence of their humanity. Her sincerity and genuine compassion for uplifting others are evident in her tireless efforts to empower the next generation.

Throughout her extraordinary journey, Oprah has remained steadfast in her commitment to being real. By embracing her own vulnerability, championing racial conversations, and uplifting marginalised voices, she has set a powerful example for individuals worldwide. Her authentic approach to life, love, and purpose continues to inspire and catalyse positive change in the lives of millions.

Oprah Winfrey's journey is a beacon of hope for those seeking to embrace their Authenticity and carve their paths in a world that often demands conformity. By staying true to her values, amplifying unheard voices, and advocating for racial justice, she has shaped a legacy that transcends entertainment and resonates as a profound force for social change. In embracing Authenticity, Oprah has empowered countless individuals to find their voices, embrace their uniqueness, and leave their indelible mark on the world with profound IDEAS.

Oprah Winfrey's brilliance in **STRATEGY** lies in her multifaceted approach to impact and influence. From the inception of her media empire to her profound philanthropic ventures, she has exemplified a strategic mindset that transcends boundaries and has built a lasting legacy.

One of Oprah's key strategic moves was her decision to create a multimedia platform that extended beyond television. With the establishment of O, The Oprah Magazine, she expanded her reach to the print world, providing readers with a curated mix of inspirational stories, lifestyle advice, and thought-provoking content. This strategic move not only deepened her connection with her audience but also diversified her brand's footprint.

Recognising the transformative power of the internet, she launched Oprah.com, a Digital platform that offered a wealth of resources, from self-improvement tools to inspirational stories. Embracing this space allowed her to engage with a global audience and extend her influence far beyond the borders of television.

Moreover, Oprah's strategic brilliance is evident in her visionary approach to partnerships and collaborations. Her 25-year partnership with Weight Watchers, where she not only invested in the company but also became its spokesperson, showcased her ability to align herself with brands that align with her values and amplify her commitment to wellness and self-improvement.

Oprah has a Strategy for giving back that has led her to support initiatives and organisations addressing social justice, mental health, and environmental issues. Her strategic giving reflects a deep understanding of the root causes of societal challenges and a commitment to creating lasting change.

As the co-creator and producer of "Greenleaf," a critically acclaimed television drama series, she has ventured into narrative storytelling, showcasing her ability to champion diverse and compelling narratives. Additionally, her decision to collaborate with Apple for her own talk show, "The Oprah Conversation," illustrates her forward-thinking approach to technology and media distribution. By embracing streaming platforms, she continues to reach new audiences while staying true to her commitment to authentic and impactful conversations.

Throughout her journey, Oprah Winfrey has embraced a strategic mindset that goes beyond traditional boundaries. Her innovative approach to media, philanthropy, and partnerships has resulted in an enduring legacy of empowerment and inspiration.

In embracing IDEAS, Oprah has crafted a remarkable journey of transformation and influence. Her dedication to creating positive change in the world has not only inspired millions but has also opened doors for countless individuals to embark on their own journeys of personal and societal growth.

As we dig into the depths of Oprah Winfrey's life and impact, we witness the embodiment of the Ideas Guy framework. Her innovative spirit, Digital prowess, commitment to Education, Authenticity in every interaction, and strategic brilliance are woven into the very fabric of her being.

Throughout her decades-long career, Oprah has shattered barriers, challenged norms, and empowered individuals to embrace their authentic selves. She has harnessed the power of media to foster empathy, compassion, and understanding, cultivating a global community bound together by shared experiences and aspirations.

# [ APPLYING THIS IN PRACTICE ]

**CONNECT APPROPRIATELY**: Oprah has left an indelible mark on the world, not only through her iconic talk show but also through her genuine and profound connections with people. As we explore the Oprah Winfrey approach, we uncover the power of connecting appropriately–the heart of her extraordinary influence.

Throughout her illustrious career, she has engaged in heartfelt conversations that transcend the surface, delving into the essence of the human experience. Oprah's approach to connection is not about seeking attention or simply going for popularity; it's about building meaningful relationships that touch lives and make a difference. This authentic bond she creates with her audience is what sets her apart and makes her a beloved figure to millions worldwide.

In the age where social media and online platforms dominate, Oprah's approach to connecting appropriately remains as relevant as ever. Many content creators and influencers focus on acquiring large followings and garnering likes and shares, but they often miss the essence of what truly matters: connecting with others in a way that is meaningful and appropriate. Oprah's example reminds us to go beyond vanity metrics and embrace a more profound approach. It's not about how many followers you have, but how deeply you can touch the lives of those who choose to connect with you.

To apply the Oprah Winfrey approach in practise, we must prioritise active listening and empathy. Connecting appropriately means being present in the moment, truly hearing what your people are saying, and responding with genuine care. It's about creating a safe and supportive space where individuals can share their thoughts, experiences, and emotions without fear of judgement. This kind of dialogue fosters a sense of community and belonging, where people feel valued and understood.

Her commitment to genuine engagement, active listening, and uplifting others has inspired millions and left an enduring legacy. As we go forward, let us carry the spirit of Oprah's approach with us. By prioritising appropriate connections, using our platforms to uplift others, and promoting positive change, we can create a presence that leaves a lasting impact and fosters a more compassionate and connected world. Remember, it's not just about the numbers; it's about the hearts you touch and the lives you inspire through the power of connecting appropriately.

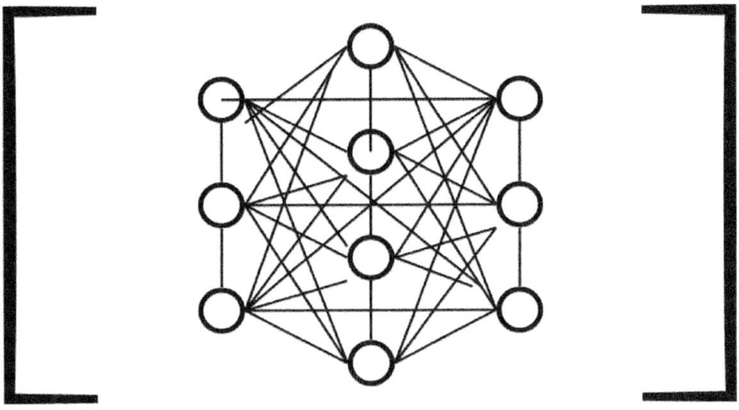

CONNECT APPROPRIATELY

[ EPILOGUE ]

# THE WORLD WAITS

This is where the book ends, right? Where the narrative slows, the curtain closes, the house lights come on, and we rise from our seats, taking a final glance at the stage. But is it really the end?

The book, yes, has run its course. The pages have been turned, the chapters read, the words absorbed. But your journey? It's just beginning.

Remember, as we journeyed through this book, we wandered through the realms of Innovation, Digital, Education, Authenticity, and Strategy. Each one a vast landscape brimming with possibilities. We've met pioneers, change-makers, and visionaries–those who've dared to challenge, to question, to transform.

And throughout this expedition, there was one thread that held everything together, the notion of the Ideas Guy. An elusive figure, almost mythical in its grandeur. The one who dares to think differently, who dares to turn the tide, who dares to change the world. But this Ideas Guy, it's not a title for a chosen few. It's not reserved for the prodigies, the geniuses, the outliers. It's you.

Yes, you.

The one holding this book, reading these words, dreaming of change. The one with ideas that bubble beneath the surface, waiting for the right moment to burst forth. The one who's just finished a journey through a book and is ready to embark on a new one–a personal journey of transformation.

You see, the Ideas Guy is not a mythical figure from a far-off land. It's not a character from a fable or a tale. It's you, with your thoughts, your dreams, your potential. It's you, with your unique viewpoint, your distinct voice, your irreplaceable contribution.

As you rise from the metaphorical seats of this book's audience, remember that the stage is now yours. You're not merely a spectator, but a performer. You're the protagonist of your own narrative, the maestro of your own symphony, the artist of your own masterpiece.

So, rise.

Rise from the constraints of self-doubt and the inertia of the status quo. Rise above the noise of naysayers and the murmur of mediocrity. Rise with the power of your ideas, the boldness of your dreams, the courage of your convictions.

This world, our world, waits. It waits with bated breath for your voice to join the chorus of change-makers. It waits for your story to unfold, for your ideas to take flight, for your dreams to transform into reality.

Don't let this be the end. Don't let the turning of the last page or the closing of the cover be the final act. Instead, let it be the prologue to your story, the overture to your symphony, the first stroke on your canvas.

Take this momentum, this ignition of inspiration, this spark of potential, and use it to fuel your journey. Let it be the wind beneath your wings, the beacon guiding your path, the force propelling you forward.

Carry the echoes of the voices we've heard throughout this book, the lessons we've learned, the perspectives we've gained. But most importantly, carry your own voice, your own lessons, your own perspectives. Because they are what truly make you the Ideas Guy.

As you step forth into your journey, remember that every great idea, every monumental change, every significant invention started with a single step.

A step taken in the face of uncertainty, a step propelled by belief, a step emboldened by courage.

That's your next step. A step into the unknown, illuminated by the brilliance of your ideas.

The world is waiting. Your journey is waiting.

So, let's step forth.

You've got IDEAS–mighty fine ones.

Now, it's your turn to make it happen.

And remember, you're the Ideas Guy, and there's no one quite like you.

So, go ahead. Make your mark. Sing your song.

And let the world revel in the melody of your revolution.

This is not the end. It's the beginning of your story.

Your journey awaits, Ideas Guy.

Let's turn the page.

Tig, you're it.

# [ REFERENCES ]


Angelou, Maya, *And Still I Rise* (2020)

Angelou, Maya, *I Know Why The Caged Bird Sings* (1984)

Angelou, Maya, *Rainbow in the Cloud: The Wit and Wisdom of Maya Angelou* (2016)

Behar, Howard & Goldstein, Janet, *It's Not About the Coffee: Lessons on Putting People First from a Life at Starbucks* (2009)

Berners-Lee, Tim, *Weaving the Web: The Original Design and Ultimate Destiny of the World Wide Web* (2000)

Blumenthal, Karen, *Steve Jobs The Man Who Thought Different Paperback* (2012)

Brandt, Richard, *The Google Guys: Inside the Brilliant Minds of Google Founders* (2011)

Brown, Brené, *Braving the Wilderness: The quest for true belonging and the courage to stand alone* (2017)

Brown, Brené, *Daring Greatly: How the Courage to Be Vulnerable Transforms the Way We Live, Love, Parent, and Lead* (2015)

Brown, Brené, *The Gifts of Imperfection: 10th Anniversary Edition: Features a New Foreword and Brand-New Tools* (2022)

Brown, Brené, *Dare to Lead: Brave Work. Tough Conversations. Whole Hearts* (2018)

Bryar, Colin & Carr, Bill, *Working Backwards: Insights, Stories, and Secrets from Inside Amazon* (2022)

Carlsson, Sven & Leijonhufvud, Jonas, *The Spotify Play: How CEO and Founder Daniel Ek Beat Apple, Google, and Amazon in the Race for Audio Dominance Paperback* (2021)

Casnocha, Ben & Hoffman, Reid, *The Start-up of You: Adapt to the Future, Invest in Yourself, and Transform Your Career* (2013)

Chouinard, Yvon, *Let My People Go Surfing: The Education of a Reluctant Businessman—Including 10 More Years of Business Unusual: The Education of a Reluctant Businessman - Including 10 More Years of Business as Usual* (2016)

Dormehl, Luke, *The Apple Revolution: Steve Jobs, the Counterculture and How the Crazy Ones Took over the World* (2013)

Fisk, Peter, *Business Recoded - Have the Courage to Create a Better Future for you and your Business: Have the Courage to Create a Better Future for Yourself and Your Business* (2020)

Garson, Helen, *Oprah Winfrey: A Biography* (2012)

Govindarajan, Vijay & Trimble, Chris, *Beyond the Idea: Simple, powerful rules for successful innovation* (2013)

Govindarajan, Vijay & Trimble, Chris, *Reverse Innovation: Create Far From Home, Win Everywhere* (2020)

Govindarajan, Vijay, *The Three-Box Solution Playbook: Tools and Tactics for Creating Your Company's Strategy* (2020)

Hoffman, Reid & Yeh, Chris, *Blitzscaling: The Lightning-Fast Path to Building Massively Valuable Companies* (2021)

Isaacson, Walter, *Elon Musk by Walter Isaacson* (2024)

Isaacson, Walter, *Steve Jobs by Walter Isaacson* (2011)

Jeppsson, Staffan, *Legendary Letters - Ingvar Kamprad´s Visionary Leadership at IKEA Paperback* (2021)

Khan, Salman, *The One World Schoolhouse: Education Reimagined* (2013)

Khan, Salman, *Brave New Words: How AI Will Revolutionize Education (and Why That's a Good Thing)* (2024)

Knight, Phil, *Shoe Dog: A Memoir by the Creator of NIKE* (2018)

Levy, Lawrence, *To Pixar and Beyond: My Unlikely Journey with Steve Jobs to Make Entertainment History* (2017)

Marsden, James, J*oe Rogan: The Complete Biography: Biographies of Famous People [Volume 1]* (2022)

McKenzie, Hamish, *Insane Mode: How Elon Musk's Tesla Sparked an Electric Revolution to End the Age of Oil* (2019)

Mcvay, April, *Steve Jobs Biography: The Life of a Visionary* (2023)

Meyer, Erin & Hastings, Reid, *No Rules Rules: Netflix and the Culture of Reinvention* (2024)

Mitra, Sugata, *The Future of Learning* (2016)

Mitra, Sugata, *The Hole in the Wall: Beginnings of a New Education* (2021)

Montessori, Maria, *The Absorbent Mind* (2009)

Montessori, Maria, *The Secret of Childhood* (1982)

Randolph, Marc, *That Will Never Work: The Birth of Netflix* (2021)

Ridge, Mitchell, *Sam Altman: A Biography of the Successful Entrepreneur and Innovator* (2023)

Robinson, Ken, *Finding Your Element: How to Discover Your Talents and Passions and Transform Your Life* (2014)

Robinson, Ken, *The Element: How Finding Your Passion Changes Everything* (2010)

Robinson, Ken, *Out of Our Minds: The Power of Being Creative* (2021)

Robinson, Ken & Robinson, Kate, *Imagine If…: Creating a Future for Us All* (2022)

Sandberg, Sheryl, *Lean In: Women, Work, and the Will to Lead* (2015)

Sandberg, Sheryl & Grant, Adam, *Option B: Facing Adversity, Building Resilience, and Finding Joy* (2017)

Sawyer, Rosario, *IKEA: The Flat-Pack Revolution - How Ingvar Kamprad Changed the World of Furniture* (2021)

Schultz, Howard, *Pour Your Heart Into It: How Starbucks Built a Company One Cup at a Time* (1999)

Schultz, Howard, *Onward: How Starbucks Fought for Its Life Without Losing Its Soul* (2012)

Standing, E.M., *Maria Montessori: Her Life and Work* (1998)

Stanley, Vincent, *The Future of the Responsible Company: What We've Learned from Patagonia's First 50 Years* (2023)

Stone, Brad, *The Everything Store: Jeff Bezos and the Age of Amazon* (2014)

Stone, Brad, *Amazon Unbound: Jeff Bezos and the Invention of a Global Empire* (2022)

Stuart, Sean, *The Curious Ape: The 25 Most Powerful Ideas from the Joe Rogan podcast* (2020)

Winfrey, Oprah, *What I Know for Sure* (2014)

Winfrey, Oprah, *The Path Made Clear: Discovering Your Life's Direction and Purpose* (2019)

Zook, Chris & Allen, James, *The Founder's Mentality: How to Overcome the Predictable Crises of Growth* (2016)

# [ ACKNOWLEDGEMENTS ]

Auntie Jacqui for the first proofreading. Your patience, encouragement and attention to detail helped me with my first drafts.

Mike Walker for lots of the creative design. You see things others don't and how you have helped me craft my IDEAS into design with the cards and other stuff too is remarkable.

Stefan Powell for being my coach. You helped me see and frame IDEAS and have brought out my very best self.

Steve Hope and Dan Fitzpatrick for being my partners in crime for the Edufuturists podcast. It's been a blast.

Wendy and Mick Whitaker, Mum and Dad for helping me follow my dreams. Always.

Ali Groves for the counselling and encouragement to seek out help for my ADHD. I have always known, as have so many others, but you made me feel like it was ok to get help.

Al Kingsley, the nicest guy in EdTech for giving me my first ever paid self-employed gig. You will never know how much that meant to me, my friend.

# [ ABOUT THE AUTHOR ]

Ben is a freelance consultant working with a number of clients on both digital and cultural transformation. Prior to this, Ben worked in education for 15 years as an Assistant Principal and Curriculum Manager, focusing on Apprenticeships, Digital Transformation, and formerly in his subject specialisms of Religious Studies and Sociology. He is co-host of the popular Edufuturists podcast where he explores the future of education by interviewing thinkers from around the world, most notably around the implications of A.I. in Education. Ben has travelled around the world talking about effective tech integration that has an impact on learning and culture.

Ben is chair of governors at a primary school but most importantly he is husband to Amanda, and dad to Niamh (14) and Martha (10).

# [ CODE BREAKER ]
# LEADERSHIP SERIES

# [ CODE BREAKER ]
# KID COLLECTION

Printed in Great Britain
by Amazon

56617710R00185